# Emotional Vampires  at Work

*Dealing with Bosses and
Coworkers Who Drain You Dry*

## Albert J. Bernstein, PhD

Mc
Graw
Hill
Education

New York   Chicago   San Francisco   Lisbon   London
Madrid   Mexico City   Milan   New Delhi   San Juan
Seoul   Singapore   Sydney   Toronto

1 2 3 4 5 6 7 8 9 0    DOC/DOC    1 9 8 7 6 5 4 3

ISBN      978-0-07-179093-2
MHID           0-07-179093-4

e-ISBN    978-0-07-179094-9
e-MHID         0-07-179094-2


**Library of Congress Cataloging-in-Publication Data**

Bernstein, Albert J.
    Emotional vampires at work : dealing with bosses and coworkers who drain you dry / by Albert Bernstein.
       pages cm
    ISBN 978-0-07-179093-2 (alk. paper) — ISBN 0-07-179093-4 (alk. paper)    1. Verbal self-defense.    2. Interpersonal conflict.    3. Interpersonal communication.    I. Title.
    BF637.V473.B47 2013
    650.1'3—dc23                                                    2013002310


Illustrations by Annabelle Metayer.


McGraw-Hill Education books are available at special quantity discounts to use as premiums and sales promotions or for use in corporate training programs. To contact a representative, please e-mail us at bulksales@mcgraw-hill.com.


This book is printed on acid-free paper.

*To Josh*

# Contents

# Preface

IN THE 13 YEARS since the original *Emotional Vampires* was published, I have received many e-mails and reader reviews thanking me for writing a book that explains so many difficult relationships both at home and at work. There have also been two consistent and contradictory requests: that I give more information about vampires at work and that I give more information about vampires in readers' personal lives.

My publisher, McGraw-Hill, took these requests to heart. In its wisdom, it offered me the opportunity to revisit each topic separately, with the benefit of 13 more years of practice and research. I was happy to oblige.

First, I revised and updated the original version of *Emotional Vampires* to deal exclusively with personal relationships.

Now, I am happy to offer you a book that deals exclusively with emotional vampires at work.

I don't have to tell you that work is different now from what it was at the turn of the last century. Businesses, nonprofits, governments, and the military have all changed considerably. Emotional vampires have not. In the confusion and uncertainty of the past few years, they have become more powerful and even more dangerous—unless you recognize them for what they are and know how to deal with them effectively. It is my hope that this book will teach you what you need to know to protect yourself.

In my 40 years as a psychologist and business consultant, I have always believed that if people really understand how human minds operate— whether those minds are their own or those of other people—they can use that knowledge to get more of what they want from their jobs and their lives.

My job is to explain psychological concepts clearly enough for people to use them on a daily basis. This book is my latest attempt. In it, I have tried to describe the most difficult and draining people you will encounter at work and to tell you exactly what to do to gain some control over your interactions with these emotional vampires.

The material I present is serious, but that doesn't mean I have to present it in a deadly serious manner. I do hope you'll find a laugh here and there. Based on so many years of sitting face-to-face with human misery, I know that humor has tremendous power to heal. Without it, we are all doomed.

Here is *Emotional Vampires at Work*. I hope you find something in it to help you.

AL BERNSTEIN
Portland, Oregon

# Acknowledgments

WITHOUT THE FOLLOWING people's help and support, this book could never have materialized:

Mindy Ranik, who came up with the title and about 10,000 miles worth of support during the writing of all the vampire books.

My esteemed colleagues, Bill Casey and Wendi Peck, who have graciously provided many insights, and even more graciously allowed me to steal some of their best ideas.

Dr. Rick Kirschner, whose perceptive comments have helped me create a better and clearer book.

Luahna Ude and Bob Poole, clinicians of rare wisdom and rarer wit, who have always been there to help me figure out the most difficult vampires.

My agent, Janet Rosen of Sheree Bykofsky Associates, who is always there with an idea when I need one.

My editor, Casey Ebro, who has shepherded me through the process of writing and production.

My friends Peter Bessas, Sundari SitaRam, Donna Sherwood, and Janine Robbins, who have helped and supported me through various aspects of this project.

Most of all, I want to thank my family—Luahna, Jessica, Josh, and Clara—for putting up with me while writing, a feat requiring as much courage and forbearance as visiting Carfax Abbey at midnight.

# Emotional Vampires

## Who Are They?

V AMPIRES STALK YOU even as we speak. They're in the next cube, down the hall, or upstairs, in the corner office. It's not your blood they drain; it's your emotional energy. We're not talking about everyday annoyances here: the surly, clueless, and unmotivated folks you learned about in the Handling Difficult People workshop. These are authentic creatures of darkness. They have the power not only to aggravate you but also to cloud minds with false promises and to hypnotize everyone into believing they are the best person for the job, whatever that job might be. They draw people in, then drain them, leaving everyone burned out and exhausted, yet lying awake at night wondering: *Is it them, or is it me?*

It's them, *emotional vampires.*

The organizational world is full of emotional vampires, even at the very top. Their ability to change shape and cloud minds allows them to thrive in cultures where what something looks like is more important than what it is. In fact, as we shall see, it was emotional vampires who created these cultures.

No matter where you work, you cannot escape them. How you handle the emotional vampires in your organization will have a profound effect on the course of your career and the quality of your life.

So, who are these predatory, mind-clouding, shape-shifting creatures of darkness who wield such power in businesses, nonprofits, the military, and politics? Actually, they are people with a particular kind of psychological disability.

At the turn of the twenty-first century, I first used the term *emotional vampires* to describe people with personality disorders. The melodramatic metaphor is merely clinical psychology dressed up in a Halloween costume, but it *does* fit. Vampires are dangerous predators who are evaporated by sunlight, but aside from that, they are much more exciting and attractive than other people. These days, everybody wants to be a vampire, date a vampire, or at least read books and watch movies about them. The same is true of people with personality disorders. They may be immature and dangerous, but we fall in love with them, elect them to office, hire them to run major corporations, and watch them on reality TV.

People with personality disorders, like vampires, are, first and foremost, *different*. They seem so much better than regular people, but often they act much worse. Vampires certainly do things that hurt other people, but that's not what makes them so dangerous and draining. It is our own expectations that, over time, cause the most harm. If we assume that they think and act in the same way we do, we will usually underestimate the risk, thinking that surely this time they will listen to reason. They won't, and they will get us every time. Knowledge is the only protection. To keep from being drained, we must know that emotional vampires are different, and understand exactly what those differences are.

In graduate school, I learned this simple distinction: When people are driving themselves crazy, they have neuroses or psychoses. When they drive other people crazy, they have personality disorders.

What a personality disorder is and what it should be called are a matter of some political dispute within the psychiatric community. A new diagnostic manual, *DSM 5*, is in the works and may well be out shortly. The new manual collapses 10 more familiar personalities into 5 larger categories. Over the years the names of personality disorders have changed several times for political reasons, but the ways of thinking and acting that the diagnostic labels describe have remained consistent. The nomenclature I'm using here is from the manual in current use at the time of writing, the *DSM IV*\*, published in 1994 by the American Psychiatric Association. According to that manual, this is what a personality disorder is:

> An enduring pattern of inner experience and behavior that deviates markedly from the expectations of the individual's culture. The pattern is manifested in two or more of the following areas:

---

\*American Psychiatric Association: *Diagnostic and Statistical Manual of Mental Disorders,* 4th ed. Washington, DC: American Psychiatric Association, 1994.

1. Ways of perceiving and interpreting self, other people, and events.
2. Range, intensity, liability, and appropriateness of emotional response.
3. Interpersonal functioning.
4. Impulse control.

This description makes it clear why people with personality disorders might be difficult, but it does not explain why these same people are so devilishly attractive and how they can often be quite successful in the organizations in which they work. To understand that, we have to look a bit more closely at the symptoms and where they come from.

*Liability*, which means rapidly moving from one emotional state to another, poor impulse control, and distortions of perception, like seeing yourself as the center of the universe, are characteristic not only of people with personality disorders but also of normal infants. Here then is the first thing we need to understand: emotional vampires, these children of the night, are indeed children. They have not matured enough to feel empathy. Like infants, they believe other people are not people like them, but instead are objects created to fill their needs.

Infants are pretty good at getting their needs met, but infantile adults are even better. One minute, they can be as charming and ingratiating as children; the next, they can be just as heedless of other people's feelings and just as intolerant of anything that stands between them and what they want.

People with personality disorders can be successful in all sorts of endeavors because they are willing to do whatever it takes to get what they want. Compared to normal people, they are less hampered by shame, embarrassment, or worry about the effects that their actions may have on others. Their main, and often only, concern is their own bottom line.

Emotional vampires may be immature and psychologically impaired, but they are not dysfunctional people who never get anywhere. Often, because of their almost supernatural ability to look good, they are first on the list to be hired or promoted. Your boss and the president of your organization might even be emotional vampires.

Not only will you have to deal with them directly, but you will also discover that when emotional vampires are in positions of authority, the cultures of the departments and organizations they control take on aspects of their personalities. You cannot escape them. To protect yourself, you will have to recognize them and understand how they think.

The present diagnostic manual describes patterns of thoughts and behavior for 10 different personality disorders, of which we will consider the 5 most likely to cause you trouble at work: *Antisocial, Histrionic, Narcissistic, Obsessive-Compulsive,* and *Paranoid.*

A few more words about nomenclature might be useful here. Everything human is distributed along a continuum, including the traits that make up personality disorders. Everybody has some symptoms, but most people do not have enough to warrant a diagnosis. Even normal people have a few little quirks. The people I refer to as emotional vampires qualify for a specific diagnosis or come close. The checklists will help you to identify them. You may also find some that score high in more than one area. If so, watch out!

At the far end of the personality disorder spectrum are people who are popularly referred to as *psychopaths,* a term that is imprecise and sometimes overused. Psychopaths are the worst of the worst. Most often they are extreme Antisocials, but they can also be Narcissistic or Paranoid. I hope you won't find any of them at your workplace. If you do encounter people with perfect scores on any of the checklists, my best advice is that you stay as far away as possible. They can be extremely dangerous to your health, wealth, and sanity.

Emotional vampires are people you probably *will* find at work. They are not psychopaths, but still they are dangerous enough to cause plenty of trouble if you don't recognize them as playing by a different set of rules than you do.

The most useful way to understand people with personality disorders is to recognize the hunger that motivates them. Each of the types we will discuss is driven by a particular immature and impossible need that, to them, is the most important thing in the world. Their singular drive is the secret of their success—and of their failure. There may be some consolation in knowing that though emotional vampires may be successful in some areas, they are generally not very happy. There is never enough of what they need to satisfy them. In the end, they often self-destruct, but the process can cause a tremendous amount of collateral damage.

Emotional vampires themselves are not necessarily aware of the irrational needs that animate them. Like young children, they don't do much self-examination; they just go after what they want. This is the area of vulnerability you must exploit. If you know the need, you know the vampire. If you know what to expect, then you can defend yourself.

Knowing the vampires is necessary, but it's not sufficient for protection. You must also know yourself. As we will see throughout this book, your own personality style will offer its own particular strengths and weaknesses in dealing with the various vampire types. In Chapter 3, you will have an opportunity to know yourself a little better.

For now, let's get to know them.

## ANTISOCIALS

Antisocial emotional vampires are addicted to excitement. They're called antisocial, not because they don't like parties, but because they're heedless of social rules. Antisocials *love* parties. They also love sex, drugs, rock 'n' roll, gambling with other people's money, and anything else that is thrilling or stimulating. They hate boredom more than a stake through the heart. All they want out of life is a good time, a little action, lots of money, and immediate gratification of their every desire.

Of all the emotional vampires, Antisocials are the sexiest, the most exciting, and the most fun to be around. People take to them easily and quickly, and, just as quickly, they get taken. Aside from providing moments of fun, these people don't have much to give back.

Ah, but those moments! Like all the vampire types, Antisocials present you with a dilemma: they're Ferraris in a world of Toyotas, built for speed and thrills. You're apt to be very disappointed if you expect them to be reliable or to tell the truth.

> Vampire Adam, the top sales rep for Nosferatu Software, is meeting with prospective clients: the regional VP, local manager, and representatives from the IT group. The meeting is an extravagant dinner, full of laughs, flattery, a few too many bottles of wine, and lots of talk about sports. Even though he is from out of town, Adam has always been a big fan of the local team. (Actually, he's never seen them play, but he did visit their website.) Everyone agrees that this year's prospects are good, if there are fewer injuries and better coaching.
>
> Finally, the conversation drifts to Adam's product.
>
> "Our system is so far out on the cutting edge that only a few select companies are using anything like it," Adam says.

"Since you are an early adopter, we can offer you a much better deal than we will be able to once it becomes the industry standard." (Really, the system has been out almost a year, but it isn't catching on. It's pretty much the same as what's on the market now, with a few bells and whistles that sometimes freeze up the whole system.)

"What about support?" the IT manager asks.

"Twenty-four seven by phone and remote, and onsite, in person within 24 hours of your request. (The tech support folks at Adam's company would be surprised to hear this, but don't try to tell them now; they're closed. You'll just get voice mail.)

"And the price?" the VP asks.

Adam hesitates a beat, and then he quotes a number. When there is no immediate response, he goes on. "The whole deal comes with a money-back guarantee, so there's no risk. We can send out a tech to set you up tomorrow morning, if you sign tonight." Adam slides a contract out of his Vuitton attaché case. He looks hopeful. (Needless to say, the guarantee is not exactly in writing.)

The VP, sensing a bit of desperation, leans back in his chair and suggests a number about 40 percent lower.

"Done!" Adam says as he proffers the contract.

Have you ever wondered why so many companies get stuck with bad investments and crappy software that doesn't work? Often, it is because of the seductive charm of antisocial salespeople like Adam.

On reading this, you might be thinking that Adam is not so different from other sales reps—aside from the fact that just about everything he says is a lie. Even then, we expect sales reps to be persuasive and to exaggerate a little. How would you recognize Adam as a vampire if he came to call on you?

The indications are there, and we will discuss them in greater depth in Chapters 4 to 7. The biggest clue is that the entire package he—or she—offers, his stories, his regular-guy friendliness, and the deal he offers, is all a little too good to be true. If you did some fact-checking, the whole charade might fall apart. But, like most people who are taken in by Antisocials, you just don't want to spoil the mood by checking facts. Antisocials offer an alternative reality tailored to what you want to believe. They are natural hypnotists, using, as we shall see, some of the same techniques as the folks up on stage who make people act like chickens. Hypnosis is emotional vampires' stock-in-trade. Antisocials are the smoothest hypnotists, but all the vampire types draw people in by offering alternative realities that are a little too good to be true. This brings us to the most important thing you need to know about personality disorders:

> Antisocials and all the other emotional vampires communicate differently than normal people. For most of us, communication is a way of conveying what we think, how we feel, or the specifics of a situation. When emotional vampires communicate, everything they say is directed toward achieving an effect in the person who is listening. The truth, as we understand it, is almost irrelevant.

The main thing Adam is selling is himself. He's a nice guy, a fan of the same team, so he must be selling a good product. He's exploiting the fact that we tend to like people we perceive as similar to us, and without real evidence we tend to attribute positive qualities to people we like.

Adam's main target is the decision maker, the VP, whose interest is deal making rather than software. The whole presentation is aimed at him.

Just a few paragraphs ago, I accused emotional vampires of not having empathy, yet Adam seems to be good at figuring out what's going on in the minds of the people at the table. What gives?

There is a huge difference between knowing and caring. Hunters know quite a lot about the behavior of their prey, but they do not see their quarry as being *like* them with respect to feelings and basic rights. This is how emotional vampires see the people in their lives: as a source of sustenance, but not having much of an existence beyond that. If vampires want something from you, they may say and do whatever it takes to get it. They may be able to read you well enough to figure out what that might be, but they give no thought to how you might feel about the process. If you expect them to think in the same way you do, you will be taken every time.

Antisocials are very good at discerning what feeds other people's egos and offering it up on an illusory silver platter. Adam sensed the VP's desire to be seen as the smartest guy in the room, and he played to it the whole evening. His feigned hesitancy and clearly inflated figure lured the VP into believing he was a big-time deal maker.

Later, when the system doesn't work, the VP will probably blame his subordinates for not doing their homework. We'll be discussing *his* personality type in a few pages. For now, the important thing to recognize is how skillful Antisocials like Adam are at picking up on hidden desires. To keep from being used, you have to know them well—and yourself better. As we will see in the next chapter, different types of people in every organization have different vulnerabilities that emotional vampires, especially Antisocials, recognize and exploit.

At work, Antisocials are not just sleazy sales reps. They are book cookers and con artists who lie for fun and profit, bullying bosses who love to see people cringe, con artists who run Ponzi schemes both legal and illegal, and everyone else at your office who makes a living or gets his or her kicks from seduction in all its forms.

## HISTRIONICS

Histrionic emotional vampires live for attention and approval. Looking good is their specialty. Everything else is an unimportant detail. Histrionics have what it takes to get hired into your business or your life, but be careful. *Histrionic* means *dramatic*. What you see is all a show, and definitely not what you get.

Vampires can't see their reflections in a mirror. Histrionics can't even see the mirror. They're experts at hiding their own self-serving intentions from themselves. They believe that they are wonderful people who never do anything unacceptable, like making mistakes or having bad thoughts about anyone. As managers, they avoid conflict but excel at creating discord by ignoring problems. They attempt to manage by magic, believing that what they don't pay attention to will just go away. Rather than concentrate on boring day-to-day details, they prefer to focus on what they consider to be big-picture concepts. *Motivation* is their all-time favorite. In the world of Histrionics, if people are motivated enough, all problems disappear.

Vampire Janine is having a conversation with Stacy, her boss.

"So, Janine, how are things in your department?" Stacy asks.

"Great! Couldn't be better," Janine says, flashing her 400-watt smile.

"That's not exactly what I hear. Lately there have been a few complaints."

The smile disappears. "From who?"

"I don't think that matters—"

Janine looks her boss in the eye. "Stacy, you know as well as I do that there are a few really immature people who are never satisfied with anything. They are always stirring up trouble instead of just doing their jobs. Was it Donna? She's the worst of the bunch."

"It wasn't Donna. The word is that you have it out for Donna and a few other people as well."

"That's not true. Who told you?"

"Never mind who told me. What I'm concerned about is the perception of differential treatment."

Janine looks exasperated. "Some people do nothing but complain. Are you going to believe everything they say?"

"I don't know what to believe. But I think there is enough of an issue that you need to do something about it, maybe bring in a consultant to help you sort things out, and maybe help you work with some of your more difficult people."

At Janine's next department meeting she announces a seminar with Cleve Gower, former basketball player, sports commentator, and nationally known motivational speaker. His topic will be "There Is No 'I' in Team." Janine is bubbling with excitement. She's heard Cleve before and finds him to be really inspiring.

Her team's lack of enthusiasm is clear evidence that a little motivation is just what they need.

If you have ever wondered who buys those glossy photos emblazoned with one-word synopses of Western Philosophy that hang in your hallways in lieu of art, you have your answer. It's Histrionic managers like Janine. To them, motivation has nothing to do with external contingencies; it comes from the heart. It is a spark of passion that can be fanned into flames of performance through rhetoric alone, eliminating the need for concern with pesky day-to-day details like managing conflict. Motivation is the magic that creates win-win situations for everyone all the time. Anyone who doesn't believe that is … well, *unmotivated.*

Midlevel management is full of Histrionics like Janine, with big smiles and can-do attitudes. Sometimes their infectious optimism can even get them promoted to CEO or elected to political office. Wherever they are, Histrionics manage to gain a great deal of control over the day-to-day operation of every organization in which they work. They are promoted because they look like what every manager hopes to see and say what every manager wants to hear. The cultures of businesses, nonprofits, the military, government, and politics are all strongly influenced by Histrionic personalities. In many organizations there is a layer of Histrionics in middle management. You will have to learn to think like they do and speak their language if you want to get anything done anywhere.

Histrionics come in two distinct forms: the Dramatic types who give the motivational talks and the more typical Passive-Aggressives, who deal with conflict by pretending that it doesn't exist. They themselves never get angry, but somehow people always seem to get angry at them.

Liz hurries to catch up with Vampire Gail in the hallway. "Gail, wait a minute. Do you have those projections I asked you to work up?

"What projections?"

"On the Lawton deal. You remember, we talked about them at the meeting last week, and I sent you an e-mail on Tuesday."

"I didn't get any e-mail."

Liz feels a cold prickle at the back of her neck. "Does that mean you don't have any projections on Lawton?"

"I have some rough figures, but you didn't tell me you wanted me to run projections."

"What do you mean, I didn't tell you? The whole department has been talking about nothing else but this deal for the past three weeks."

"I thought Jeff was supposed to get me a breakdown on those changes in production costs. I was waiting to hear from him."

"Gail," Liz hears panicky shrillness in her own voice. "I needed those projections yesterday. Go back to your office and get to work on them now."

"Okay," Gail says. "No problem."

> Two hours later, Liz is at her desk, feverishly trying to put together a credible proposal with no hard numbers in it, when she gets a call from her boss. "Liz," he says, "I need to see you right away. One of your people just filed a verbal abuse complaint with HR."

Histrionics hate dealing with boring details. They consider it tantamount to torture.

They always have good reasons why they cannot follow the same rules as everyone else. If you try to get them to do something they don't want to do, they can turn your office into a soap opera or a medical drama. They are famous for making illness into an art form.

Pity the poor manager who tries to write something in the "Needs to Improve" box on a Histrionic's annual review, or the team member whose demand to discuss real issues brands her as unmotivated.

The important thing to remember about Histrionics is that it is useless to try to get them to recognize their own hidden agendas. Their internal world is as foggy as a Transylvanian night. They don't recognize condescension either. To deal with them effectively, you must remember that they hunger for attention and approval as you slather on praise in doses that would nauseate other people. Think good to great to supercalifragilisticexpialidocious.

## NARCISSISTS

Have you ever noticed that people with big egos tend to be small everywhere else? All that Narcissistic emotional vampires want is to live out their grandiose fantasies of being the smartest, most talented, and all-around best people in the world. It's not so much that they think of themselves as better than other people as that they don't think of other people at all. Remember the deal-making VP mentioned earlier in the chapter? If he had been thinking about his company's needs rather than his own, he might have brought a little more due diligence to the table.

Narcissists in positions of power are legends in their own minds. Surely, you don't expect them to live by the rules of mere mortals.

> Michael, the CEO is paid about 50 times what you make, even though the company keeps losing money. He's kept the share price up—and with it, his compensation—by orchestrating two

huge rounds of layoffs. Difficult as it is, you can accept that that's the way it goes in business.

It's the little things that get to you, like the way Michael treats the people who work for him. If he passes you in the hall, stand aside, because he'll run you over. When somebody else is talking, he interrupts, looks at his watch, or plays with his phone. He always shows up late for meetings, never having glanced at the agenda. It hardly matters, because he'll forget what people said, anyway.

Michael's office is decorated with pictures of him shaking hands with politicians and movie stars. If you aren't one of those or on the board, he acts as if you don't exist—that is, unless he wants something from you. Then he's full of flattery and vague promises, but only until he gets what he's after. The rest of the time, you're lucky if he remembers your name.

Narcissists present a difficult dilemma. Though there is plenty of narcissism without greatness, there is no greatness without narcissism. Without these emotional vampires, there wouldn't be anyone with the chutzpah to lead.

Regardless of what they say, Narcissists seldom do anything that isn't self-serving. As long as you have something they want, they'll act as if you're just as great as they are. The minute they get what they're after, they forget you and move on to the next source of sustenance.

Narcissists' verbal contracts aren't worth the paper they're written on. If they want a favor, name your price and make them pay up front. Most other people would be insulted by this sort of venality, but Narcissists usually aren't. They assume everyone is looking out for number one, as they are. They think you're just being up-front about it.

Narcissists need to win. Don't compete with them unless you can just about kill them. Even then, watch out. They've been known to rise from the grave to wreak vengeance. Better you should sneak up on their blind side with an ego massage and learn how to give them the adulation they need without giving in.

If you have problems with sucking up, you will definitely have problems with Narcissists. Before dealing with them, you should have a heart-to-heart chat with your inner teenager about your own best interests.

## OBSESSIVE-COMPULSIVES

Obsessive-Compulsive emotional vampires are addicted to safety, which they believe they can achieve through scrupulous attention to detail and complete control over *everything*. You know who they are: anal-retentive people who can't see the forest because of the excessive number of superfluous, overabundant, and redundant trees. What you may not know is that all that attention to detail is designed to keep the Antisocial vampire inside safely contained.

Without Obsessive-Compulsives, none of the world's difficult and thankless tasks would ever get done, nothing would ever work the way it should, and none of us would do our homework, ever. For good or ill, Obsessive-Compulsives are the only people watching to see that the rest of us don't go too far astray. We may not always like them, but we need them.

For Obsessive-Compulsives, the most important conflicts are internal. They take no joy in hurting others, but they will hurt you if your actions threaten their sense of control. To Obsessive-Compulsives, surprises—even pleasant ones—feel like an ice-cold spray of holy water. They don't mean to hurt your feelings, but they do feel compelled to state their opinion.

Carly has worked for two weeks on the materials for the conference. She's finally done, and the result is great, even if she does say so herself. The PowerPoint presentation flows smoothly from one major topic to another, and the report that goes with it backs up all the facts and figures. It's artistic and rock solid. She can hardly wait to show it to Vampire Joanne, her boss.

Joanne's response is underwhelming, to say the least. Her only reaction to the 10-page report is to circle two grammatical errors. As Carly is going through the PowerPoint, Joanne stops her.

"I didn't know we had decided to go with the blue template. I thought we were going to try out the tan and the green and then make up our minds about which one to use."

"But ...," Carly is so choked up she can barely speak, "didn't we cover that last week?"

The second-longest wait in the world is for Obsessive-Compulsives to make a decision. The longest wait is for them to speak even a single word of praise.

Perfectionism, overcontrol, and attention to detail—Obsessive-Compulsive vampires indulge in vices that masquerade as virtues. They habitually confuse process with product and the letter of the law with its spirit. Your best protection from these vampires lies in continuing to keep your own eyes on the big picture and not getting lost with them in the dark forest of obsessive detail.

In Chapters 16 through 18, we will discuss strategies for dealing with micromanaging control freaks. The first step is to stop calling them that. The only way to get Obsessive-Compulsives to lay off is to see their fear rather than your hurt and irritation. This may require another heart-to-heart with your inner teenager.

## PARANOIDS

In common parlance, *paranoid* means thinking people are after you. It's hard to imagine that there could be anything attractive about delusions of persecution until you think about all the groups that pride themselves on being oppressed minorities.

What Paranoids offer is clarity in an ambiguous world. They know The Truth, and are happy to share it. As long as you accept their view of the world, you're on the team. The minute you disagree, you become a traitor. Regardless of your reasons for disagreeing, they will see it as you persecuting them and act accordingly. Other vampire types might make threats, but Paranoid bosses actually do fire people or drive them to quit.

Paranoids live by concrete rules that they believe are carved in stone. They expect everybody else to live by these rules as well. They're always on the lookout for evidence of deviation, and they usually find it.

Vampire Richard, the company owner, sees himself as a disciple of Ayn Rand, though Ms. Rand herself might have had some difficulty discerning her thoughts as a basis for his actions. His basic idea is that any restrictions on what an entrepreneur is allowed to do are crimes against reason. Richard's management style involves long discourses on philosophy and morality, and very little specific direction. If you are a member of his management team, he expects you to take personal responsibility for yourself and everybody who reports to you. This means reading his mind well enough to know what to do without being told. You'd better read *The Fountainhead* and *Atlas Shrugged*, too, if you know what's good for you.

Today, the management team is discussing an expansion project. It is the misfortune of David, the operations manager, to know that federal regulations apply.

"I hate to bring this up, guys," he says, "but before we start, we have to get a permit from the EPA."

Richard scowls. "What did you say?"

"I said—"

"I know what you said! You and your EPA, OSHA, and all the rest of those idiotic bureaucrats who want me to get a permit every time I take a crap. The question isn't who is going to let me; it's who is going to stop me."

There are murmurs of approval around the table, as there are every time Richard quotes the Words of the Prophet.

"Are you suggesting we go ahead without a permit?" David asks.

"That's your department," Richard says. "Take responsibility for it."


The magnetism of a Paranoid personality can disrupt your moral compass. The more disoriented you become, the more attraction you feel toward Paranoid certainty, and the more frightened you become of Paranoid wrath. It's easy to lose your way.

To make matters worse, sometimes paranoids *are* right. In their quest for clarity, they look below the surface of things to hidden meanings and deeper realities. Most great moralists, visionaries, and theorists (and any therapists worth their salt) have a touch of the paranoid. If they didn't, they would merely accept everything at face value.

Unfortunately, paranoia makes little distinction between great insights and delusions. The same motivation for clarity that led to the great religious truths of the ages leads also to poisoned Kool-Aid and suicide bombing. Truth or delusion? It will be up to you to decide.

To get your bearings, the question you need to ask yourself is, *who benefits?* Great truths benefit everyone. Delusions are usually self-serving. The benefit is confined to a small group of true believers, with the greatest benefit going to the Paranoid in charge.

Paranoia, like all forms of personality disorder, occurs at differing levels of severity. In small doses, Paranoia is the essence of charisma. In larger doses, it can be toxic. How much is too much? Again, that's up to you. Until you've thought it through, don't drink any Kool-Aid.

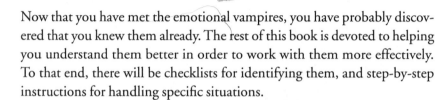

Now that you have met the emotional vampires, you have probably discovered that you knew them already. The rest of this book is devoted to helping you understand them better in order to work with them more effectively. To that end, there will be checklists for identifying them, and step-by-step instructions for handling specific situations.

An important part of protecting yourself from emotional vampires is understanding yourself. Since it is your own emotions they use against you, who you are and how you think will greatly influence how much damage they can do.

## RECOGNIZING EMOTIONAL VAMPIRES
## WHEN YOU SEE THEM

Emotional vampires usually make strong first impressions. Often, the best way to recognize them is by the feelings they evoke in you. One of the first signs that you are dealing with a vampire is thinking in superlatives. We tend to see them as the best, the worst, the most different, or all of the above. Vampires are hard to ignore. That's just the beginning of the spell that they cast.

Each vampire type tends to elicit specific responses. Antisocials are exciting. Whether they are amiable or mean, there is always that trembling feeling of being right on the edge. Sometimes they cause the hairs on the back of your neck to prickle. Histrionics can make you believe that your dreams are coming true, or they can outrage you with their blatant manipulation. Narcissists can arouse grudging admiration as well as out-and-out hatred for acting like they're better than you. Obsessive-Compulsives can turn you into a rebellious teenager who hates being told what to do. Paranoids evoke trust and blind belief. If you open your eyes, the trust can turn to terror.

Your own patterns of thinking and perception may determine the effect the emotional vampires you work with have on you and ultimately how much harm they can do. The first assessment device you'll encounter will help you to discover your own areas of strength and vulnerability.

## HOW EMOTIONAL VAMPIRES CAN CHANGE YOU INTO SOMEONE YOU DON'T RECOGNIZE

We all know from films and books that a vampire's bite can turn you into a vampire. Emotional vampires can transform you also. They infect you with their immature and predatory way of thinking as a way of getting you to meet their needs. Step by step, they move you farther away from your moral center, and they entice you or provoke you into thinking and acting in ways you never thought you would. It never happens all at once.

The psychological term for this stepwise process is *grooming,* which has a darker connotation than when it's typically used in a business setting. All emotional vampires groom their victims in one way or another, whether vampires or victims are conscious of it or not. Antisocial Con Artists are the most deliberate about the grooming process, and we will discuss it more fully in Chapter 6.

## VAMPIRE HYPNOSIS

Vampires are natural hypnotists. They use some of the same techniques you see hypnotists use onstage, but when they do it, it's not for entertainment, but to make you do their will. Hypnosis means using the power of suggestion to project an alternative reality that is too good to be true or too scary to ignore. Illusion is vampires' stock-in-trade, and unless you are very careful, you may find yourself ensnared in their web of deception.

### How to Break the Spell

The purpose of this book is to help you to avoid being taken in by vampires' hypnotic spell. The first step is to recognize emotional vampires when you encounter them. The checklists will help you, as will paying close attention to your own reactions.

Once you recognize emotional vampires, you need to know what to do to protect yourself. You do that by following a process that I call "stepping into their world and stepping out of the expected pattern."

Vampires operate based on instincts that are hardwired into the oldest parts of their brains. These instincts are programmed into your brain as well. They are automatic and very compelling unless you catch yourself and override your emotional responses using the newer, more rational parts of your brain.

Personality disorders, scary though they may be, are, at their heart, immaturity. The thing you must always remember is that emotional vampires, these frightening children of the night, are indeed children. To deal effectively with them, you will have to be more mature than they are. The next chapter will explain what maturity actually is, and how to maintain it in the face of vampires.

# Maturity and Mental Health

## Protect Yourself from Emotional Vampires by Thinking More Slowly than They Do

### IF EMOTIONAL VAMPIRES ARE CHILDREN, WHAT DOES IT TAKE TO BE A GROWN-UP?

IN MY OPINION, maturity and mental health are the same thing. Both are directly proportional to a person's skill at the process of *slow thinking*.

The latest neurophysiological research supports what's called *dual-process theory*. This is the idea that the brain operates in two separate modes, *fast thinking*, which is automatic and emotional, and *slow thinking*, which is more reasoned and rational. In poetry, the heart rules the head. In real life, it has to be the other way around or someone gets hurt.

*Fast thinking* is mediated by the programming that came in the box with our brains, much of which we inherited from our reptilian ancestors. Its basic subroutines have not changed much in the past 200 million years.

This dinosaurlike part of our brain is encoded with instincts that our ancestors needed to survive in the primordial jungle. In it are neural sequences for mating, defending territory, operating within a hierarchy, and responding to physical danger. This ancient part of our brain speaks to us without words, but its meanings are unmistakable. It communicates using direct neural connections in the emotional areas of the brain, and with powerful hormones like adrenaline and testosterone that affect every organ in the body.

*Slow thinking* involves using the newer areas of the brain to manually override the automatic programming and substitute rational analysis for physiological reaction. *The ability to analyze a situation and do what needs to be done rather than what we feel like doing is the very essence of maturity.* It is a skill that is hard won, and that requires regular exercise to remain viable.

Here is a simple example of how the fast and slow modes of thinking might operate in a work setting:

Say that, like many people, you experience some fear of speaking in front of a group. What this means is that the fast-thinking part of your brain reacts to delivering a PowerPoint presentation in the same way it would to a physical attack. Your instincts do not discriminate between the possibility of embarrassment and that of being eaten alive. Your instinctive fast thinking "protects" you by sending jolts of adrenaline and fantasies of escape every time you even imagine getting up in front of the group.

In order to give a presentation, you have to be able to use more rational slow thinking to override your fear.

The first and often the hardest step is convincing yourself that you really do need to make the presentation. This is where the interaction between fast and slow thinking gets confusing. The fast-thinking system can use this confusion to subvert your higher brain centers. The desire to run away can create any number of rational-sounding reasons why you really shouldn't do the presentation after all. Perhaps you are too busy doing something else, or a coworker is more adept at putting together a PowerPoint.

These rationalizations may fool you into believing that you are thinking when you are actually just reacting to your automatic programming. Different levels of your brain regularly play tricks on each other. This is why you shouldn't believe everything you think.

Mature, slow thinking, like a cricket on your shoulder, recognizes rationalizations and does its best to talk you out of them. You still feel the fear, but you don't let it make decisions for you. Once the back door is closed and you believe that the show must go on, you have an incentive to learn techniques to manage your stage fright.

Emotional vampires are less mature than you are. This means that they rely mostly on fast thinking. They are driven by their emotional needs. Instead of learning to use slow thinking to control their emotions, they fool themselves with clever rationalizations for letting their emotions control them.

They can fool you also and trick you into fooling yourself. Their emotions can connect directly with yours, causing you to act as immaturely as they do. Once they have you reacting without thinking, you are in their power. This is a game you cannot win. Even the dumbest vampires are better at immaturity than you are.

Instead, play to your strength. Be mature. *The secret to dealing effectively with emotional vampires is to think more slowly than they do.* Teaching you to do that, in a sentence, is why I wrote this book.

What follows is your first lesson.

## HOW TO TELL THE DIFFERENCE BETWEEN SLOW AND FAST THINKING

Our brains are always engaged in both fast and slow thinking. If your inner world seems to be a tangle of conflicts and mixed feelings, it means you're normal. Everybody thinks everything all the time, even if they're not paying attention. Slow thinking means using your mind to unravel these mixed signals from your brain and decide which of them to act upon. The more mature you are, the more variables you have to consider.

For people with personality disorders, the choices are more simple and automatic. One of the main functions of fast thinking is to narrow the options so that survival decisions can be made quickly. Emotional vampires don't struggle with difficult concepts like ethics and morality. They just go with their fast-thinking guts. Sometimes this can afford them a distinct short-run advantage.

Lives and careers are long games, however. Unless you are being chased by a wild animal, you will usually do better choosing slow thinking rather than fast. But which is which? Sometimes it's hard to tell.

Fast and slow thinking are not absolutes; they grade into each other and sometimes tangle hopelessly, but in four areas they tend to move in noticeably opposite directions. It is at these crossroads that the two types of thinking are easiest to identify. Whenever you recognize fast thinking in yourself or in the people you work with, you would do well to stop and slow down before you get lost in confusion.

The following are some signs that may help you find your way.

### Slow Thinking Moves Toward Gradations Rather than Dichotomies

Virtually everything in the real world is distributed along a continuum. Fast thinking dumbs down the complexity of existence into more easily understandable two-category systems. Regardless of what people call these two categories—good and evil, safe and dangerous, like me and different—they tend to mean just about the same thing. The important thing to remember is that *two-category systems are a manifestation of fast thinking rather than attributes of reality.*

Dichotomies can be useful simplifications to help us make decisions, but in the end, they are fingers pointing at the moon rather than the moon itself. Don't mistake one for the other.

Slow, businesslike thinking is most often a process of balancing forces, rather than choosing one as better than another. Work decisions are usually dilemmas that require compromises rather than problems with a solution that is right or wrong.

### Slow Thinking Moves Toward Internal Rather than External Control

Slow thinking begins with yourself. The more mature you are, the more clearly you realize that the most effective way to control your life is to control your own thoughts, feelings, and actions.

Fast thinking looks outward. It is reactive, based partly on instinctive programs for survival and partly on habits, which are thought and behavior sequences that we have learned, mostly automatically, based on the contingencies in our lives.

A contingency is an *if-then* situation. *If* you do a particular thing, *then* certain consequences follow.

Contingencies operate by rules that, like instincts, are programmed into the brain.

The first and most important of these is: *whatever is rewarded will happen more often.* Rewards can be either getting what you want or avoiding what you don't want. The second is by far the stronger motivator, especially in fast thinking.

Please note that there is no rule that says *what is punished will happen less often,* because that is simply not true. Despite the universal popularity of punishment, any psychologist will tell you that punishment does not work. Its effects are unpredictable. Rather than teaching people to refrain from doing what is punished, punishment is more likely to teach them to be sneaky, to hide their actions from punishers. You know this if you have ever been a teenager. If punishment actually worked as intended, your kids would always do their homework, there would be no market for radar detectors, and people would not go back to prison for committing the same crime.

Punishment does occasionally work as a deterrent, but it works mostly on people who don't need it because their actions are determined by internal rather than external contingencies.

Here's what I mean: ask yourself why you don't steal.

If you said it's because you don't want to go to jail, let's look a little deeper. What you think is an external contingency, avoiding punishment, is actually an internal contingency, avoiding guilt. If it were only fear of jail that kept you from stealing, you'd have little compunction about taking things if you were pretty sure you wouldn't get caught. An emotional vampire, especially an Antisocial, might steal, but you probably wouldn't.

The biggest difference between normal, healthy people like you and people with personality disorders is that, whether or not you're aware of it, most of your actions are determined by internal contingencies rather than external ones. Internal contingencies are based on following the unwritten social rules that define the group you are a part of. Emotional vampires are a group of one.

## Slow Thinking Moves Toward Connection Rather than Separateness

Emotional vampires don't follow social rules because they see themselves as separate from the social group. To them, their needs are greater than anyone else's could possibly be. It's not that they consider themselves better than other people, although some certainly do. It is because fast thinking is by its very nature self-serving. Its purpose is individual rather than group survival. It takes slow thinking to recognize that if the group doesn't survive, none of its members survive either.

Mature, slow thinking appreciates the fact that everything is connected to everything else. Human beings are social creatures. We experience full humanity only when we are a part of something larger than ourselves. The larger the group to which we feel connected, the healthier and more mature we are. We demonstrate this connection by following social rules. These are some examples.

**OTHER PEOPLE ARE JUST LIKE ME:** This rule is the basis of all the others.

Fast thinking divides all of humanity into two categories: *like me* and *different*. For many emotional vampires, the *like me* group is extremely small, often only one. As normal people grow, they become more acutely aware of their similarity to others. Empathy is what maturity is all about. Vampires just don't get empathy. To them, other people were created to supply their needs.

**WHAT'S FAIR IS FAIR:** Social systems are based on reciprocity in everything from back scratching to telling the truth. Mature, slow-thinking adults use their sense of fairness as a yardstick for measuring their behavior. Vampires don't do reciprocity; their idea of fair is that they get what they want when they want it.

**WHAT YOU GET IS WHAT YOU PUT IN:** Adults understand that the more you give, the more you get. Vampires take.

**OTHER PEOPLE HAVE THE RIGHT TO SAY NO:** Human relationships depend on a clear perception of the psychological line between what's mine and what's yours. Robert Frost said it well: "Good fences make good neighbors."

People with personality disorders pay no attention to boundaries. They believe that whatever they want already belongs to them, so you'd better hand it over or else. Emotional vampires wrote the book on *or else*. They are far better than other people at intimidation. They have no compunctions about using any strategy to look out for number one, because in their world, there are no other numbers.

People with personality disorders play by different rules than you do. They're not fair, but they're fairly consistent. Here are the social rules that emotional vampires follow. Study them well, so you won't be blindsided.

**MY NEEDS ARE MORE IMPORTANT THAN ANYONE ELSE'S:** People with personality disorders operate with the selfishness of predators and young children. Regardless of what they say, most of what they do is guided by their desires of the moment rather than by any moral or philosophical principles. As we'll see in later chapters, if you understand the momentary need, you understand the vampire.

If your needs coincide with theirs, emotional vampires can seem fairly normal. Everything changes when your needs conflict with theirs. That's when the fangs come out.

**THE RULES APPLY TO OTHER PEOPLE, NOT ME:** The technical term for this belief is *entitlement,* and it is one of the most exasperating characteristics of emotional vampires. At work, on the road, in relationships, or wherever, normal people follow the basic rules of fairness they learned in kindergarten. They take turns, wait in line, clean up after themselves, and listen while other people talk. In kindergarten, emotional vampires learned how easy it is to take advantage when you're not bound by the rules that other people follow.

**IT'S NOT MY FAULT, EVER:** Vampires never make mistakes; they're never wrong; and their motives are always pure. Other people always pick on them unfairly. Vampires take no responsibility for their own behavior, especially when it leads to negative consequences.

**I WANT IT NOW:** Vampires don't wait. They want what they want when they want it. If you get in their way, or try to delay their gratification, they'll come at you snapping and snarling.

**IF I DON'T GET MY WAY, I THROW A TANTRUM:** Emotional vampires have elevated the tantrum to an art form. When they don't get their way, they can create a sumptuous array of miseries for the people who tell them no. As we'll see in later chapters, each vampire type specializes in a particular kind of manipulative emotional explosion. Many of the annoying and draining things that vampires do make sense when you see them as tantrums.

Emotional vampires may look like ordinary people. They may even look better than ordinary people, but don't be fooled. Vampires are, first and foremost, different. To keep yourself from being drained, you must always be aware of what those differences are.

The main difference is that they act as if they are separate from the social group and therefore not bound by its rules. This perception of separateness can be a competitive advantage, but it is also the reason for emotional vampires' internal pain. The universe is a cold and empty place when there is nothing in it that is larger than your own need.

## Slow Thinking Moves Toward Challenge Rather than Expediency

Each day, we stand at the crossroads between fear and boredom. Viewed through the lens of fast thinking, it may seem that the choice is between safety and danger, and that safety lies in avoiding what is difficult or frightening. This is an illusion. If we avoid what we fear, our lives shrink to safe but unsatisfying routines. We get bored, and eventually we get depressed. Slow thinking recognizes that everything in life changes and that we must change with it or be left behind.

As we will see throughout this book, dealing effectively with emotional vampires will require you to switch off your autopilot, think new thoughts, and take unaccustomed actions. At times that may be scary, but facing fear is the kind of challenge that will make you grow.

### WHAT CAUSES PEOPLE TO BECOME EMOTIONAL VAMPIRES?

Just as some of the newer stories about real vampires ascribe their delicate condition to a blood-borne virus, so there are many theories about the personality disorders that afflict their emotional cousins. Presently, some of the most fashionable involve unbalanced brain chemistry, early trauma, or the long-term deleterious effects of growing up in a dysfunctional family.

Forget the theories; they will hurt you more than help you in your quest to understand vampires. There are two reasons for this. First, understanding where a problem comes from is not the same as solving it. Second, emotional vampires already see themselves as the innocent victims of forces beyond their control. If that's how you see them, their past can distract you from paying attention to the choices that you and the vampires are making in the present.

Many self-help books have long sections about how difficult people got to be that way. This one doesn't. After years in the therapy business, I have come to believe that it is far more important to understand the mechanics of human problems, how they operate, and what to do about them than it is to speculate about what causes them.

## IMMATURITY VERSUS EVIL

Emotional vampires are not intrinsically evil, but their immaturity allows them to operate without thinking about whether their actions are good or bad. Vampires see other people as potential sources for whatever they happen to need at the moment, not as separate human beings with needs and feelings of their own. Rather than evil itself, vampires' immature perceptual distortion is a doorway through which evil may easily enter.

The purpose of this book is not to consider the morality of emotional vampires, but to teach you how to spot them in your life and give you some ideas about what to do when you find yourself under attack by the forces of darkness.

## ABOUT ASSESSMENT

Throughout this book, you will encounter checklists for assessing yourself, your organization, and especially the emotional vampires you work with. You've probably seen hundreds of such checklists in books and magazines and on the Internet. They work because small samples of behavior can be accurate indicators of the underlying social rules that people follow. These rules are what define a personality or an organizational culture.

The checklists here are rough measures, not precise psychological instruments, but they can still offer you some useful insights into how people think and what they are likely to do.

All psychological tests are subject to the *Everybody and Nobody Rule*. Human beings don't fit neatly into diagnostic categories, no matter how elegant or well-conceived. As you read further, you'll probably discover that everybody you know, including yourself, has some characteristics of each of the vampire types. Everybody has some; nobody has all.

*Most difficult people are a blend of two or more vampire types.* The chances are good that you will find your bullying boss or your supercilious coworker scattered all over the pages of this book. Feel free to use the techniques that seem most appropriate, regardless of which chapter they appear in. Many of the techniques are introduced in the earlier chapters and refined later in the book. You'll probably find it most helpful to read straight through so that by the time you reach the later, more complex types of vampires, you'll have a whole arsenal of techniques from which to choose.

What if you see yourself among the vampires? If you do, take heart; it is a very good sign. We all have some tendencies in the direction of personality disorders. If you recognize your own, they are apt to be less of a problem than if you have no insight.

I hope you'll find this book useful at work and everywhere else in your life. Beyond that, I wouldn't be in the least upset if it gave you a chuckle here and there—and, if it would not be too much to wish for, the occasional glimmer of hope for the human condition that comes with understanding.

# Who Are You?

**3**

MOST OF US DEFINE ourselves by the groups we belong to. Such groups are characterized by similarities, perhaps in ethnicity, nationality, occupation, or, more important in a psychological sense, by the values we hold and our typical patterns of perceiving the world and the people in it.

In Chapter 1, I suggested that different patterns of thinking and perception have particular strengths and weaknesses in dealing with the various types of emotional vampires. In order to deal effectively with them, you must first know yourself. In this chapter, I hope to offer you that opportunity.

Most of you have been to workshops that use various tests like the Myers-Briggs to classify your personality type. I find these tests to be useful but rather cumbersome. Here, I would like to go about it somewhat differently.

Rather than classifying whether you are an introvert or extrovert, or whether you process information through sensing or feeling, for our purposes, I believe it would be more useful to know which of three differing attitudes you hold about work.

Throughout 30 years of organizational consulting, I have been profoundly influenced by Terrence Deal and Allan Kennedy's work on corporate cultures. Following their lead, I try to observe organizations as an anthropologist might, looking at social structures and rules. Very early, I discovered that, within most overall organizational cultures, there seem to be three separate and often competing subgroups that are remarkably similar in thoughts and behavior from one organization to another.

1. *Rebels,* who pride themselves on their technical skills and ability to handle crisis but do not like being told what to do.

2. *Believers*, who work hard and play by the rules, expecting that their effort and responsibility will help them get ahead. Usually they are disappointed, because hard work, in and of itself, is seldom rewarded.

3. *Competitors*, who live by the unwritten rules. They understand and use politics to get things done. Sometimes politics uses them.

All of these subgroups are necessary to run a successful organization, but the members of each group believe that they are the only ones who are doing things correctly. They regard the other two groups with suspicion, condescension, and sometimes open derision. Each of these groups has its own particular strengths and weaknesses in dealing with stress in general, and emotional vampires in particular.

The rest of this chapter consists of a self-scoring test that will help you to decide whether you are a Rebel, Believer, or Competitor.

Each of these groups has its own automatic ways of thinking and acting at work. Each is good at some tasks and not so good at others. Knowing where you fit can help you understand yourself in relation to other people. Even more important, recognizing your automatic responses may help you slow down your thinking enough to decide whether they are working for you.

Whichever group you belong to, it will be to your advantage to learn to think like the other two. No one group has the whole story.

This test, like every other psychological measuring device, follows the Everybody and Nobody Rule, discussed in the last chapter. Everybody has some aspects of everything we measure, and nobody can be placed neatly into any particular category. Tests are just trying to find what fits best.

## ARE YOU A REBEL, BELIEVER, OR COMPETITOR?

For each question, choose the response that best describes you most of the time. At the end of the quiz, you will find a scoring guide and discussion of the responses you chose.

1. Pick the statement that is most true of you:
   (a) It really bothers me to have to do things that should not be part of my job.
   (b) I pride myself on doing all parts of my job as well as I can—including the parts I don't like, and the ones that no one checks.
   (c) I focus my effort on the parts of my job that my organization considers important.

2. Choose the one that is most true of you:
   (a) I know how to tell where I stand with my boss.
   (b) I wish my boss would leave me alone.
   (c) I wish my boss would give me more feedback.

3. Indicate which of the following best describes your viewpoint:
   (a) I wouldn't like to be considered conceited.
   (b) I am responsible for making people aware of my skills and accomplishments.
   (c) I don't care what people think.

4. What is success?
   (a) Success is mostly a matter of luck and who you know.
   (b) Success is mostly a matter of motivation and hard work.
   (c) Success is mostly a matter of knowing the system and using it to accomplish your goals.

5. Which is most true of you?
   (a) I'd rather be right than be happy.
   (b) I'd rather be happy than be right.
   (c) I don't see a connection between being happy and being right.

6. Which best describes you?
   (a) I have been reprimanded for not doing something I was supposed to do.
   (b) I make it my business to avoid being reprimanded.
   (c) If you've never been reprimanded, it means you've never taken any risks.

7. In an unfamiliar situation, you usually figure out what to do by:
   (a) Asking someone, or reading about the subject.
   (b) Watching the people in charge and doing what they do.
   (c) Figuring out the situation, and trying things that might work.

8. Which is most true of you?
   (a) I sometimes bend the rules.
   (b) I play by the rules.
   (c) It depends on what rules you mean.

9. Choose one:
   (a) I like the excitement of a crisis.
   (b) I perform best in stable, predictable situations.
   (c) I perform best in the spotlight.

10. With which do you most agree?
    (a) The means are as important as the ends.
    (b) The ends sometimes justify the means.
    (c) Who cares?

11. Choose the one that is most true of you:
    (a) I want to be seen as highly skilled and independent.
    (b) I want to be seen as intelligent, motivated, and hardworking.
    (c) Sometimes it's an advantage to have people underestimate you.

12. Which of the following bothers you most:
    (a) People who say one thing and do another.
    (b) People who don't understand how organizations really operate.
    (c) People who don't know what they're talking about.

## How Did You Score?

Review your answers, and use the following scoring guide to record your points for Rebel (R), Believer (B), and Competitor (C). As you will see, each answer represents a way of thinking and acting at work that can be strength or weakness.

Emotional vampires always approach from your weak side, so be warned. To get stronger, what you need to exercise is the ability to shift your perception, to see things in the way other people might see them—especially people who may not see things the way you do. This is the very skill that people with personality disorders lack. Insularity is everyone's weak side.

1. Pick the statement that is most true of you:
   (a) It really bothers me to have to do things that should not be part of my job.

(b) I pride myself on doing all parts of my job as well as I can—
including the parts I don't like, and the ones that no one checks.
(c) I focus my effort on the parts of my job that my organization
considers important.

If you chose *a*, score **R**: Rebels often have a strong focus on the
technical aspects of the job. Ask yourself if the tasks you tend to
avoid are really unimportant or if they are actually things you
don't like, don't do well, are afraid of, or don't understand.

If you chose *b*, score **B**: Your maturity and work ethic are showing. You can be proud of them. Your naïveté may also be showing. Ask yourself why no one checks. Could it be that part of
your job doesn't warrant being done well?

If you chose *c*, score **C**: Competitors focus their efforts on what
is rewarded, most often paying attention to this quarter's bottom line. This is the clear path to getting ahead at work. Unfortunately, some of the tasks that aren't as closely monitored may
still be important in the long run. Are you being efficient, or are
you cutting corners?

2. Choose the one that is most true of you:
   (a) I know how to tell where I stand with my boss.
   (b) I wish my boss would leave me alone.
   (c) I wish my boss would give me more feedback.

If you chose *a*, score **C**: Competitors know that pleasing the
boss is job number one. They are experts at figuring it out on
their own, since they also know that when bosses are pleased,
they generally feel no need to say anything. To Competitors,
praise is for wimps.

If you chose *b*, score **R**: Rebels like to be left alone to do their
jobs. Being independent is generally a good thing, but seeing
your boss as a pain in the butt is not.

If you chose *c*, score **B**: Believers like feedback, so they know
how they're doing. Studies show that feedback, especially
positive reinforcement, is the best way to get the most from
employees. Unfortunately, your boss may not have read these

studies. Competitors think of feedback as hand-holding. If you ask for it, they may give it, but they may also write you off as a player.

3. Indicate which of the following best describes your viewpoint:
   (a) I wouldn't like to be considered conceited.
   (b) I am responsible for making people aware of my skills and accomplishments.
   (c) I don't care what people think.

If you chose *a*, score **B**: Believers know that there is no *I* in TEAM. What they don't realize is that if you don't tell them, nobody will know what a good job you're doing. Likewise, if you don't ask, you don't get. Ask yourself where you learned that being conceited was bad.

If you chose *b*, score **C**: Competitors have no problem promoting themselves. Sometimes this can be irritating to the rest of the team. There is a time and a place for everything. Know when it is appropriate to blow your own horn and how to do it subtly.

If you chose *c*, score **R**: Rebels are proud of their independence. They often believe that they don't care what people think. Actually, this is not possible for a social creature. Everybody has a reference group. What about the people who would call you a brown-noser if they caught you having lunch with the boss?

4. What is success?
   (a) Success is mostly a matter of luck and who you know.
   (b) Success is mostly a matter of motivation and hard work.
   (c) Success is mostly a matter of knowing the system and using it to accomplish your goals.

If you chose *a*, score **R**: Rebels often believe that they have little control over what happens to them. They may be right, or they may just not be paying attention. Controlling what you can is essential to mental health. Worrying about things you can't control will drive you crazy. You have to find the balance point.

If you chose *b*, score **B**: This is what Believers believe in. If they didn't, everything would come crashing down. One of the great tragedies in most organizations is that hard work is not valued as much as it should be. It's not how hard you work but what you work hard at that will determine your rewards.

If you chose *c*, score **C**: This is the Competitors' core belief. It is correct, as far as it goes. Often, it goes too far. Only you can draw the line.

5. Which is most true of you?
   (a) I'd rather be right than be happy
   (b) I'd rather be happy than be right.
   (c) I don't see a connection between being happy and being right.

If you chose *a*, score **B**: Believers stand up for principles. If they didn't, who would? Unfortunately, they tend to see moral issues even when none exist. Believers also forget that being right is a competitive sport. If you win, someone loses.

If you chose *b*, score **C**: Competitors like to be right as much as the next guy. They also recognize that being right and being happy are often mutually exclusive. If you go too far into the gray area of moral relativism, you can lose your way.

If you chose *c*, score **R**: Rebels think that *right* and *correct* are synonyms. They are good at being correct, but they sometimes miss the distinction between technology and morality.

6. Which best describes you?
   (a) I have been reprimanded for not doing something I was supposed to do.
   (b) I make it my business to avoid being reprimanded.
   (c) If you've never been reprimanded, it means you've never taken any risks.

If you chose *a*, score **R**: Was it worth it?

If you chose *b*, score **B**: Believers try to stay the straight and narrow. Sometimes this leads them to avoid risk and try to please everyone. How much are you willing to pay for safety?

If you chose *c*, score **C**: Competitors know that in most organizational situations, it is easier to apologize for making a mistake than it is to ask permission.

7. In an unfamiliar situation, you usually figure out what to do by:
   (a) Asking someone, or reading about the subject.
   (b) Watching the people in charge and doing what they do.
   (c) Figuring out the situation, and trying things that might work.

If you chose *a*, score **B**: Believers do their homework. This strategy works well if someone will tell you or if what you're looking for is written down somewhere. Unfortunately, the answers you get may be wrong, or at least incomplete. Read everything you can, both on and between the lines; then think for yourself.

If you chose *b*, score **C**: Competitors learn by watching successful people and doing what they do. This is a good way to succeed. It is also a good way to learn bad habits.

If you chose *c*, score **R**: Rebels are independent and creative, and they often come up with new ideas. They can also spend a lot of time reinventing the wheel. At least, read the directions.

8. Which is most true of you?
   (a) I sometimes bend the rules.
   (b) I play by the rules.
   (c) It depends on what rules you mean.

If you chose *a*, score **R**: Rebels sometimes bend rules because those rules can get in the way of an elegant solution. But sometimes they bend rules because they don't like to be told what to do. Before you start bending, consider your motivation, and check out what's happened to people who have bent rules in the past.

If you chose *b*, score **B**: Believers follow rules because they *are* rules. This makes them good citizens. Following rules can also make you vulnerable, if no one else is following them.

If you chose *c*, score **C**: Competitors can figure out which rules are important and which ones are there just for show. Unfortunately, you may have a tendency to think that good citizens are chumps.

9. Choose one:
   (a) I like the excitement of a crisis.
   (b) I perform best in stable, predictable situations.
   (c) I perform best in the spotlight.

If you chose *a*, score **R**: Rebels shine in crisis situations, but they can get bored with day-to-day routine. If you feel bored, try to stay out of trouble.

If you chose *b*, score **B**: Believers take pride in doing day-to-day tasks well. There is honor in this, but no glory.

If you chose *c*, score **C**: Competitors go for the glory. Who you are is also determined by what you do when you're not in the limelight.

10. With which do you most agree?
    (a) The means are as important as the ends.
    (b) The ends sometimes justify the means.
    (c) Who cares?

If you chose *a*, score **B**: Believers are ethical to a fault. Ask yourself: *How small does a moral issue have to be for me to ignore it?*

If you chose *b*, score **C**: Competitors believe that ethics are relative. Ask yourself: *How big does a moral issue have to be to warrant my attention?*

If you chose *c*, score **R**: Rebels wonder why people stand around discussing philosophy when there's work to be done.

11. Choose the one that is most true of you:
    (a) I want to be seen as highly skilled and independent.
    (b) I want to be seen as intelligent, motivated, and hardworking.
    (c) Sometimes it's an advantage to have people underestimate you.

If you chose *a*, score **R**: Rebels believe that their skill should earn them independence. Maybe it should, but it doesn't.

If you chose *b*, score **B**: Believers generally *are* intelligent, motivated, and hardworking. Just realize that these virtues are their own rewards.

If you chose *c*, score **C**: Competitors are Machiavellian. To decide whether this is a strength or a weakness, read Machiavelli.

12. Which of the following bothers you most:
    (a) People who say one thing and do another.
    (b) People who don't understand how organizations really operate.
    (c) People who don't know what they're talking about.

If you chose *a*, score **B**: Believers are addicted to integrity. Their drug of choice is looking down on hypocrites.

If you chose *b*, score **C**: Competitors divide the world into Players and Nobodies. Nobody is too small to cause you problems. This sentence can be read two ways: make sure you do.

If you chose *c*, score **R**: Rebels value expertise above all. Too often, they consider expertise outside their own area as an oxymoron.

Count your total number of **R** (Rebel), **B** (Believer), and **C** (Competitor) responses. Compare your totals to see which of the three groups you are most like and which is most different from you. The ideal score is a balance among the three types, though most people tend to score significantly higher in a single one. The summaries below should give you an idea of where you are now, and how you automatically approach a number of situations at work. As we shall see throughout this book, each of the groups has different strengths and vulnerabilities in dealing with specific types of emotional vampires.

## REBELS

If you are a Rebel, you tend to focus on the technical aspects of your job. Rebels pride themselves on know-how, which to them means skill, knowledge, experience, creativity, and ability to handle emergency situations. This is the traditional culture of frontline first responders, people who prefer to think on their feet rather than in a brainstorming session.

Rebels are the people organizations want to have around when something breaks down, but the rest of the time, authority issues can get in the way. Rebels do not like to be told what to do, especially by people who don't have the technical knowledge and expertise that they do.

Rebels generally do not consider management or sales to be skills. For all the various forms of political behavior, they have only one word: *brown-nosing*.

Most Rebels have a touch of the Antisocial about them. They thrive on excitement and have a hard time making themselves do boring, everyday tasks. This creates problems with Obsessive-Compulsive emotional vampires who work with them. The term *control freak* is a Rebel invention, as are the self-destructive power struggles in which they tend to engage.

Rebels often have a good sense of humor, which they think the entire world shares. They are genuinely surprised when their joking offends other people.

Rebels' greatest strength is their bravery. When they feel something needs to be done, they do it, regardless of personal cost. They make decisions quickly and live with the consequences.

Rebels are great at seeing through everybody's affectations but their own. They have no patience with Histrionic motivational rallies or the political games so beloved by Narcissists.

If you are a Rebel, you need to approach interpersonal difficulties with the same sort of careful analytical thinking you would use to solve technical problems. Always use the right tool for the job. For people problems, the tools are alternative ways of thinking. Don't try to drive a screw with a hammer.

## BELIEVERS

If you are a Believer, you believe in truth, justice, hard work, fairness, motivation, and work ethic. Believers are the core of any organization. They don't just talk the talk; they do their best to walk the walk.

Believers share some of the more positive traits of Histrionics and Obsessive-Compulsives. They try to be positive, and they pay attention to day-to-day details. Believers do their homework, even when no one is checking.

When Believers make a promise, it means something. Unfortunately, this makes them easy prey for all the emotional vampires whose promises are merely manipulative devices.

Believers' greatest vulnerability is thinking that everyone else is playing by the same rules that they are. They react to perfidy around them with moral outrage rather than seeing it as a learning opportunity. To Believers, playing politics is evidence of a character flaw. They don't realize that in any office, politics is a game that you can't *not* play. You can only play well or play badly.

In addition to the steadfastness and reliability of Believers, their great strength is their openness to new learning, if someone will teach them. At work, however, many of the most important things are never taught.

They must be learned through observation, since much of what is taught is actually misdirection. You can thank emotional vampires for that. Misdirection is their stock in trade.

If you are a Believer, to deal effectively with emotional vampires, you need to observe their behavior carefully and hold off moral judgments as long as you can. When you start thinking about concepts like lying, unfairness, and hypocrisy, you are limiting your options for response by assuming that vampires, like you, are moved by internal contingencies and that it means something to them to see themselves as fair and honest. If someone accused you of being hypocritical, you might be concerned enough to examine your own behavior. Vampires will merely lash out.

Emotional vampires are better than most Believers at recognizing external contingencies, the material rewards and punishments in a given system. They know how to get what they want, and they are not usually hampered by concerns about ethics or morality. If you want to deal effectively with vampires, you have to look for the contingencies that motivate them.

## COMPETITORS

If you are a Competitor, you recognize external contingencies. You understand and use politics. You naturally think in terms of hierarchies, alliances, and knowing whom you need to influence to get things done. To Competitors, politics is merely basic human relations. You give people what they want; they give you what you want. There is nothing inherently exploitative about this process.

Competitors' great strength is their ability to make things happen. They are masters of observational learning. They figure out what to do by watching people who are effective and copying them. This skill is absolutely essential if you want to get ahead in any kind of organization, because more than anything else, your success will be determined by your ability to discern and live by rules that no one will tell you.

Competitors are pragmatism personified. They are always on the lookout for what works. They excel at picking up good ideas and running with them.

Observational learning is also Competitors' greatest weakness. When vampires are in charge, Competitors learn to act like vampires. It is through this imitation that emotional vampires in power tend to create cultures that mirror their disordered personalities. In the following chapters, we will take a look at some of those cultures.

If you are wondering why we are bothering with this introductory material about cultures and patterns of perception, and why I'm not just describing emotional vampires and telling you how to deal with them, you have a point.

I have one also. The way people with personality disorders get you is not so much by doing things *to* you as by using your own weaknesses to control you. To protect yourself, you need to know what those weaknesses are.

You also need to know the written and unwritten rules of your organization. The rest of this book will also address those.

Once you know yourself and recognize the cultural context in which you work, you will be able to confront emotional vampires on their home ground.

Now that you know some of your own strengths and weaknesses, you're ready to meet the vampires.

# Antisocials

4

ANTISOCIALS ARE THE SIMPLEST of emotional vampires, and in many ways they are the most dangerous. All they want out of life is a good time, a little action, and immediate gratification of their every desire. If they can use you to accomplish these goals, nobody is more exciting, charming, or seductive. If you stand in their way, nobody can be more threatening.

Antisocials, like all vampires, are immature. On their best days, they function emotionally at the level of early teenagers. On their worst, they can give infants a run for their money—which, come to think of it, is true of teenagers also.

To be technically correct, we're talking about people who have tendencies in the direction of what has been called *Antisocial Personality Disorder.* Antisocial, in this case, means unsocialized—heedless of normal social constraints. The name is unfortunate. Like its predecessors, *sociopath* and *psychopath,* it harks back to the days when psychiatric diagnoses were moral judgments rather than personality descriptions. A hundred or so years ago, when this diagnosis was first formulated, it was considered to be the personality type of criminals. It still is.

Of all the emotional vampires, Antisocials are the most likely to be involved in illegal behavior. There are a number of reasons for this, all simple and direct. Antisocials want what they want when they want it. Like small children, they are untroubled by forethought or guilt. They don't consider morality or legality. If you have what they want, they will do whatever it takes to get it, including lying, cheating, and stealing.

Most of the Antisocials you encounter at work are not criminals. Personality disorders exist along a continuum. At one end are criminals; at the other are exciting, adventurous, grown-up teenagers still heavily into sex, drugs, and rock 'n' roll.

The other problem with the name is that the colloquial meaning of *antisocial* suggests people who don't like parties. This is definitely not true of Antisocials. They like being around people, and they love parties for all the opportunities they present. Antisocials are energetic extroverts. Whatever room they're in, they work it. They are experts at making a good first impression. They appear friendly, attractive, and highly motivated. They have what it takes to get hired or promoted. Unfortunately, they usually don't have what it takes to do the job. They do what comes easily, and the rest they ignore.

What comes easily to Antisocials is manipulation and subterfuge. They suck up to the people above them, and they terrorize the people below. They often manage to keep their jobs much longer than they should because they at least appear to produce. If numbers are what counts, they will make them by hook or by crook. The people who should check up on them don't because they are so charming and reassuring.

Antisocials are extroverted, but in another sense, they are loners. They have a hard time making any sort of commitment because they don't really trust anybody. Antisocials are convinced that the only human motivation is self-interest. They are predators to the core, and proud of it. They are perfectly comfortable with selfishness because they don't think there's any other form of motivation.

Antisocials are often damnably attractive, and a hell of a lot of fun. Imagine taking a regular person, doubling the energy level, tripling the love of excitement, then switching off the circuitry for worry. Wouldn't you hire someone like that? It's so easy to think that because they excel in one area, they will excel in all.

## THE FERRARI-TOYOTA DILEMMA

Antisocials are expert hypnotists. They present you with illusions, both positive and negative, that are much more vivid than actual reality. Whoever you are, they know exactly what you want.

I put together a composite of employment ads that I believe sums up many people's fantasy of the personality characteristics of the ideal employee:

> High-energy, enthusiastic self-starter wanted. We're looking for an independent person who doesn't need to be told what to do every minute of the day, someone with an entrepreneurial spirit who creates his or her own security by being quick, decisive, flexible,

and able to think outside the box. Good social skills and political savvy a must. Apply only if you can turn setbacks into opportunities and are willing to handle a little risk in return for big rewards. No whiners.

If in your mind you can see this applicant standing there with a big smile, a firm handshake, and a two-stroke handicap, what you're looking at is an Antisocial vampire. A Ferrari in a world of Toyotas.

Toyotas are safe and practical, but they're not much fun. Ferraris are dangerously powerful, fabulously expensive, and in the shop more than they are on the road. Still, they're what we dream about when we buy Toyotas.

After a few months on the job, the person hired from the above ad might deserve (but not necessarily get) a performance review that looks like this:

Unreliable and at times even dishonest. Does not accept being told what to do. Convinced that most rules are silly, confining, and made to be broken. Easily bored with day-to-day routine to the point that he or she often cuts corners and leaves important tasks undone. Takes advantage of others, and often throws tantrums to get his or her way. Little ability to plan ahead or learn from mistakes. On the personal side, is going through divorce, has financial difficulties, and is rumored to have problems with alcohol and drugs.

The most important thing to remember about Antisocials is that the ad and the evaluation represent two parts of the same personality. You rarely see one without the other.

Emotional vampires' traits, both positive and negative, hang together in identifiable clusters. If the positive traits are there, the negatives are there also, whether you see them or not. This book is full of descriptions, examples, and checklists that will teach you more than you ever wanted to know about which traits goes with which personality type. You will be amply warned.

It may not make any difference. Impractical as Ferraris are, people want them. Those who own Ferraris love them enough to pretend that they're sensible. Aficionados may talk themselves into believing that the Ferrari-Toyota dilemma doesn't really exist, or is the result of an anomaly that can easily be corrected by a skillful-enough mechanic. I know that this is true because, for more than 40 years in my work as a therapist and business consultant, people have brought me countless human Ferraris to repair. They think I can somehow get rid of the bad parts and keep the good. I tell them it isn't possible, but most of the time they don't believe me.

In making your own existential choices between Ferraris and Toyotas, it doesn't matter so much which one you pick, only that you know the difference. The people most damaged by emotional vampires are people who believe they can have the speed and exhilaration of a Ferrari with the safety and reliability of a Toyota.

### HOW TO RECOGNIZE AN ANTISOCIAL VAMPIRE

Now we come to our first vampire identification checklist. I'll be the first to admit that the test is crude in that it relies more on opinions, impressions, and value judgments than on objective fact. The reason for this is that in most cases, impressions are all you'll have to go on.

The purpose of the checklists is not to make a medical diagnosis, but to help you recognize emotionally draining people before they suck you dry. Your first line of defense is always your own subjective impression that something is amiss. If you're in doubt, check out your intuitions with other people. This is a good idea even if you are absolutely certain.

Remember the rule from Chapter 2: *nobody is all or none*. Nobody fits a category completely or not at all. Everybody is made of a set of characteristics that make him or her unique, but some of those unique people are considerably more emotionally draining than others.

### THE ANTISOCIAL EMOTIONAL VAMPIRE CHECKLIST

True or false: Score one point for each *true* answer.

1. This person believes that rules were made to be broken.    T   F

2. This person regularly avoids doing things he or she does not want to do.    T   F

3. This person is rumored to have had legal or ethical problems.    T   F

4. This person regularly engages in dangerous activities for their thrill value.    T   F

5. This person can turn on brilliant bursts of charm to get his or her way.     T F

6. This person acts very differently toward people above and below him or her in the organizational hierarchy     T F

7. This person's "jokes" often hurt other people's feelings.     T F

8. This person is an enthusiastic drinker, smoker, gambler, adrenaline junkie, or all of the above.     T F

9. This person has a stormy relationship history.     T F

10. This person blames others for his or her mistakes or shortcomings.     T F

11. This person is a bully.     T F

12. This person sees no problem with lying to achieve a goal.     T F

13. This person sees no problem with taking advantage of customers and coworkers.     T F

14. This person throws tantrums if he or she doesn't get his or her way.     T F

15. This person makes impulsive decisions.     T F

16. This person has a lot of people fooled.     T F

17. This person has been fired from a job or has quit impulsively.     T F

18. This person gets angry, blows up, calms down, and then wonders why others are still upset.     T F

19. This person regularly makes promises that he or she never keeps.     T F

20. Despite all these faults, this person is still one of the most exciting and interesting people I have ever met.     T F

Scoring: Five or more true answers qualifies the person as an Antisocial emotional vampire, though not necessarily for a diagnosis of Antisocial Personality Disorder. If the person scores higher than 10, watch your back and hold onto your wallet.

## WHAT THE QUESTIONS MEASURE

The specific behaviors covered on the checklist relate to several underlying personality characteristics that define an Antisocial emotional vampire.

### High Need for Stimulation

At the core of the Antisocial's personality is a lust for stimulation of all sorts. All the other characteristics arise from that central drive for excitement. At any crossroads, Antisocials will usually choose the path that leads to the most excitement in the least time. They may be completely unaware of this dynamic, yet it serves to explain a good deal of their behavior.

On the positive side, Antisocials are not held back by doubt and worry. They act as if they were bulletproof, embracing risks and challenges that terrify ordinary people. Most of history's great deeds of exploration, financial daring, and physical courage have been done by people who would meet the criteria set down here for Antisocials. From the beginning of time, we have loved them, thrilled to their exploits, and built monuments to honor their names. We just can't live with them. Heroes are often as dangerous to their friends as they are to the enemy.

### Boredom with Everyday Life

The same drive that leads to courage on battlefields, in sports arenas, and on trading floors leads to boredom with everyday life. The landscape of the Antisocial world is made of scattered peaks of pulse-pounding exhilaration with wide deserts of mind-numbing boredom in between.

Throughout the long hours when more mature people content themselves with delaying gratification in order to live up to their obligations, Antisocials are pacing like trapped beasts looking for any way to escape. Antisocials are perpetually doing things to alleviate their boredom. They see themselves as looking not for trouble, but only for the chance to be free. Freedom for them often means trouble for everybody else.

### Low Frustration Tolerance

Antisocials want what they want, and they want it now. If you stand in their way or make them wait or ask them to do what they don't want to do, they tend to get irritable very quickly. They often pick fights just to liven things up.

## Addictions

When Antisocials are bored, they want to feel better right away. They are drawn to all things addictive as are lemmings to cliffs. Sex and drugs are always popular, as are gambling, overuse of credit cards, and risky investments with other people's money. The drug of choice may vary, but the purpose is the same. Under the skin, all addictions are alike in that they provide a rapid change in neurochemistry that is the central striving in Antisocial lives.

## Impulsiveness

Antisocials seldom reflect on why they do the things they do; they just do them. Planning or consideration of alternatives, to them, is unnecessary and boring. On battlefields and playing fields, they are more beautiful than the rest of us could hope to be because they are free from the worry and doubt that slow us down. They seldom find fault with themselves, but they are quick to find it in others. Sometimes they can be openly aggressive. Driving for them is a competitive sport.

## Lack of Internal Direction

Only over time does it become apparent that most Antisocial decisions are simply a roll of the dice. From the inside, Antisocials don't see themselves as making decisions at all. Life to them is a series of inevitable reactions to whatever is happening at the moment. Give them what they want, and they're cheerful. Frustrate them, and they throw a tantrum. Put them in a boring situation, and they stir up a fuss. They are the personification of fast thinking. They truly believe that their actions are caused by what happens to them. This belief frees them from responsibility and guilt, but it also robs them of the perception of control over their own lives—a view that is one of the essentials for mental health. Worry and doubt may slow us down, but they also provide meaning and continuity to our lives.

## Charm

Despite their faults, Antisocial vampires are lovable. You'd think that such predatory people would be hated and shunned, but that is far from the case. Immaturity is the wellspring of attraction and the source of all charm. Antisocials make their emotional living by using other people. To survive, they have to be very good at convincing you that they have exactly what you want. They *do* have what you want, but seldom for as long as you want it.

## Sales Skill

At work, you're likely to find Antisocials in sales, where their charm, extroversion, and lack of inhibition help them succeed. Studies have shown that Antisocials are less sensitive to the effects of punishment than are normal people. If you think about it, this is an important trait for success in sales. Antisocials are better than most of the rest of us at picking themselves up, dusting off, and starting over.

## Machismo

Something you may have noticed about Antisocials is that their personality style sounds like stereotypic masculinity on steroids. They are sports stars and action heroes who have no idea what to do with themselves after the game or when the movie is over. This is not to say that there are no female Antisocials. There are plenty; they just act like men with regard to sex, drugs, excitement, aggression, and avoidance of responsibility. As we will see later, the Histrionic style is more stereotypically feminine.

### HOW DO SUCH IRRESPONSIBLE PEOPLE END UP IN POSITIONS OF RESPONSIBILITY?

Being likable and having so many qualities that are highly valued in organizations often blinds people to Antisocials' faults. They may have great sales numbers or be cool under fire, but as leaders their skills are abysmal. This does not always stop them from getting promoted. Even when people doing the promoting actually need Toyotas, they often prefer Ferraris. In the next chapters we will look at some of the techniques Antisocials use to get hired and promoted into positions in which they can do quite a bit of damage. I also hope to give you a few suggestions about how to protect yourself.

# Antisocial Bullies and Substance Abusers

5

THE ANTISOCIALS most likely to give you trouble at work come in two basic models, Bullies and Con Artists. Their approaches may differ, but as we shall see, the underlying pattern is quite similar. Antisocials of either kind are high risk for drug or alcohol abuse.

Knowing what you do about Antisocials, how dishonest and unreliable they are, you might be surprised at how many find their way into management. Quite a few of them have the kind of charm it takes to get promoted way beyond their level of competence. From above, they look great. From below, it's an entirely different story, as you probably know if you have the misfortune of reporting to one.

In our discussion, we might as well start at the top with Antisocial Bullies, the most menacing of the emotional vampires. If you can learn to handle them, the others will be easy. Well, easier.

The most critical skill needed to deal with emotional vampires is the ability to think rather than react when subjected to emotional pressure. If you work for a Bully, the good news is that you'll get plenty of opportunities to practice.

There are few experiences more emotionally draining than being verbally abused. It's not just the yelling and name-calling that gets you, but the constant walking on eggshells and the endless replaying of attacks in your mind, adding all the things you *should* have said. Your ultimate goal with Bullies, as with all the rest of the emotional vampires we will discuss, is to limit the damage they do to you. To protect yourself, you have to understand them, so you can think your way through stressful situations rather than just react to them.

Like the rest of the Antisocial types, Bullies are hooked on excitement. Their drug of choice is intimidation. As bosses, they delight in making their subordinates squirm. Fear has the same effect on them as blood in the water does on sharks. I mean this literally. Instinctual patterns are enforced by internal psychoactive drugs that are more potent than anything you can buy on the street. If you follow the patterns, you get a jolt right in the pleasure center. If you deviate, you get kicked in the gut by anxiety.

Just as alcoholics look for excuses to drink, Bullies look for reasons to attack. The cause is unimportant. They do it because it feels good.

Bullying Antisocial bosses often create fear and confusion in the crudest way possible, with profanity, harsh teasing, and name-calling. They never pick on anyone their own size. They delight in doing whatever it takes to throw underlings off balance, then kick them when they're down. In some organizational cultures, they probably urinate on them as well. It is the air of smug satisfaction when attacking that differentiates Bullies from other Antisocials who throw tantrums when they're frustrated, and from normal people who might occasionally lose their tempers. For other people, angry outbursts have a purpose; for Antisocial Bullies, they are an end unto themselves.

## THINKING INSTEAD OF REACTING TO BULLIES

People are always telling you to stand up to Bullies, but what does that actually mean? There's no way you can match their raw aggression, so why try? Instead, do what they *don't* do: think slowly.

The adult version of standing up means picking a course of action and sticking to it no matter how difficult it becomes—in other words, courage.

I can help you pick some actions worth sticking to. The courage you'll have to supply for yourself.

If there is a single secret to dealing with Antisocial Bullies and other emotional vampires, whoever and wherever they are, this is it: *Every hurtful and annoying thing vampires do follows a pattern. Intentional or not, they do what they do because it gets them the responses they expect and the outcomes they want. The best way to defend yourself is to recognize the patterns and step out of them.*

With Antisocial Bullies, stepping out of the pattern means taking the fun out of abusing you and turning it into work. This isn't easy; you'll have to use everything we've discussed so far.

Clara is in a meeting with Chuck, her boss, and the other managers on the team. This quarter's numbers look grim, and Chuck is royally pissed. What else is new?

Even though the shortfall is not the team's fault—you can't sell products that aren't made—Chuck doesn't care. Numbers are numbers, and bad ones get him in trouble with his boss, which is as good an excuse as any to ream somebody a new one.

One by one, he lays into the members of his team. "What is the matter with you?" he says to Kevin. "Are you lazy or just stupid? If you had the brains God gave a turd, you would have seen this coming and done something about it."

"But, but ..." Kevin sputters.

"But nothing. You're supposed to be thinking, not making excuses."

Clara has had enough. Chuck is being a complete asshole. She feels she has to do something, but what?

She summons up her courage and attempts to change the tenor of the meeting.

"Chuck, I know things are really bad, and we're all sorry," she says. "Maybe if we put our heads together we can figure out what to do about it."

For a second, everything is quiet.

Then Chuck turns toward Clara and smiles. Everybody recognizes that look. She knows she's the next victim.

"You want to know what we can do about it, Ms. Nicey-nice-put-our-heads-together?" Chuck starts softly and slowly, then builds to a crescendo. "I'll tell you what we can do. We can get our heads out of our asses and move some goddamn product. And you, Clara; you want to know what you can do? You can stop acting like such a whiney bitch every time somebody asks you to get off your butt and do a little work for a change."

Clara feels like she's been slapped in the face. He called her a bitch! Nobody deserves that. And, speaking of butts, she works hers off for this department while Chuck sits on his.

Now, it's personal!

Here is your test: What should Clara do?

Actually, we don't have enough information to answer the question, but that may not have stopped you. Your first response to this scenario can reveal some of your own automatic ways of thinking. We are looking for patterns here, and your responses have a part in creating them.

Rebels usually think Clara should fight back. Maybe hit Chuck over the head with her laptop. Or better yet, with a lawyer. She could sue him for creating a hostile work environment.

Believers might be thinking that she should report the incident to Chuck's boss, hoping he will enforce the rules against harassing employees.

Competitors are probably trying to figure out what I think the correct response might be.

Whatever it is, your first response in an emotional situation is usually your own habitual kind of fast thinking. Often it plays right into the vampire's hands. In stressful situations, your first idea is rarely your best. Even if you do have a good idea, it can benefit from further thought and consideration. This cannot happen if you are talking.

Here are some suggestions that might help Clara survive Chuck's attack.

**ASK FOR TIME:** The first thing Clara needs to do to get some control over what's happening is to slow it down. One of the best ways to do this is by asking for a minute to consider her answer. This is absolutely the last thing a fast-thinking Bully like Chuck expects, so it disrupts the pattern of his attack. At the same time, asking for time to think models more adult behavior for the rest of the people in the room.

**REPEAT, IF NECESSARY:** Chuck will, of course, try to lure Clara back into fast thinking with further insults. If he keeps it up, she should just repeat herself, saying that she needs time to think about what he's saying before she responds. Chuck will eventually have to stop. How can he criticize her for taking him seriously?

If you learn nothing else from this book, this one little trick might be enough to save your sanity: *in emotional situations, before you say anything else, ask for a moment to think.*

**Know Your Goal:** So, Clara has her moment. What should she think about?

She needs to decide what she wants to happen in the short run. Her fast-thinking brain may be clamoring for revenge, perhaps looking for the perfect rejoinder to put Chuck in his place. Slow thinking will tell her that revenge is a dish that is best served cold. She may decide later to pursue longer-term goals like making a formal complaint or even filing a lawsuit. Those things can wait. If she is considering them at all, she needs to keep her options open by not descending to Chuck's level.

Clara's short-run goal should be to calm things down. To do this, she needs to consider the situation from Chuck's point of view. If she has read up on Antisocial Bullies, she knows that attacking people is their idea of fun. An effective strategy is to spoil their fun by turning it into work.

**Maintain Control by Asking Questions:** One way of turning Bullies' fun into work is by ignoring attacks and asking questions. This was Clara's first idea before Chuck attacked her, but her timing was off. Now that she has broken Chuck's stride, she can try again.

> "Seriously, Chuck, this is a tough situation. What do you think we ought to do?"

Whatever Chuck says, and it will certainly be another attack, Clara should treat it as an answer to her question, and ask for further clarification.

> "I don't give a shit what you do. It's your job to figure it out for yourself."
> "I know it is, and I think that as a team we are capable of doing that. We just need some parameters from you. What do you want to happen?"

With any luck at all, the rest of the team will recognize a good strategy when they hear one, and follow up with questions of their own in response to Chuck's attacks. He probably won't give helpful suggestions, and he may just end the meeting in disgust, which, if you think about it, is a positive outcome for all concerned.

Now, the team can decide what to do about the numbers, and Clara can decide what further action she wants to take about Chuck's bullying.

Being a Believer, Clara wants justice for herself and her teammates. To make a realistic plan, she will have to think like a pragmatic Competitor and decide what is possible. First, she'll have to consider the unwritten rules of her organization. What happens when someone complains about a boss? The most common answer is *nothing*. Organizations generally support the highest-level person regardless of the facts. As to a lawsuit, before thinking about that, she should consult an attorney, preferably one who is bigger and nastier than the one the organization will hire to defend Chuck. She should also look into what happens to the careers of people who sue their employers.

Clara may not be able to find justice. She should also consider self-interest. Is it possible to get a transfer or to find another job? To answer these questions, she will have to know something about the culture of the organization and the job market.

I don't know what Clara will ultimately decide to do. I have faith in her resourcefulness, and I do know that the best way she can defend herself from attacks by Bullies and other emotional vampires is by using knowledge and slow, careful thinking to control whatever part of the situation she can. That is all any of us can do in dealing with adversity. Usually it is more than enough.

## THE PATTERN TO STEP OUT OF: DOMINANCE

Most conflicts with Bullies are really about dominance. Content hardly matters; everything is determined by rules of engagement that are literally programmed into our brains. Everybody knows them, not as words in the head, but as feelings in the gut, buttons that, when pushed, activate automatic behavioral sequences.

Dominance is about hierarchies. The rules are simple: alphas are alphas because they are bigger, stronger, and more aggressive. They get a bigger share of everything, and they can attack you, but you can't fight back. If you do, it is a clear signal that you are trying to take their place. To maintain their status, they have to beat you down to a position that is clearly below them. Bullies get off on beating people down, especially people who can't fight back. To the people above them in the hierarchy, they are as obsequious as they expect you to be.

This dominance pattern is the same one that wolves follow; your position in the hierarchy is maintained by snapping and snarling and escalating threats of physical aggression. It is fully programmed in all our brains. We all respond to it, whether we are aware of it or not. When we are attacked, our emotions tell us to submit or assert our own dominance. Either will serve as a releaser to the attacker, and the sequence will intensify. Stepping out of the pattern means breaking the rules and actively choosing a response that is neither fighting back nor running away.

Antisocial Bullies are not particularly subtle. Snapping and snarling is good enough for them. Bullying Narcissistic and Paranoid bosses, as we shall see later, are much more circumspect, but the basic dominance pattern is the same. Now is a good time to learn the rules, so when you encounter them at work you can make conscious choices rather than letting your own instincts take over.

## The Dominant Order; the Submissive Obey

This rule is simple and direct, at least on the surface. The boss gives the orders, and the subordinates follow them. Below the surface, there is more to it. Being told what to do is, in effect, a put-down. We don't like it even from people who have the right to give orders. We absolutely will not tolerate it from people like spouses and coworkers who have no formal authority over us.

Rebels are most likely to make an issue of being told what to do by acting visibly surly, but even Believers might feel a little bit insulted, especially by being ordered to do something that is not really part of their job. Antisocial Bullies, who are always looking for an excuse to attack, will set you up by ordering you to do bogus tasks until your irritation shows, then you are fair game.

The way to step out of this part of the pattern is to accept orders and ask for clarification so you will be sure to do it right. Keep asking. Bullies may call you stupid for doing this, but they can't call you insubordinate.

## The Dominant Talk; the Submissive Listen

We have to listen to our superiors, but they do not have to listen to us. This explains the almost universal dislike of long-windedness, as well as how irritated we get when people look at their watches or their smartphones while we are talking. This is one rule you just have to accept without getting bent out of shape.

### The Dominant Joke; the Submissive Laugh

Laughter at work has much more to do with who is telling the joke than how funny it is. Before you let fly with a zinger, no matter how hilarious, remember Freud's pronouncement about humor being aggression in disguise. Making a joke is a way of fighting back, and will be dealt with accordingly. Bullies laugh at you. They never laugh at themselves.

### The Dominant Are Right; the Submissive Are Wrong

It is no accident that right and wrong mean both correct and incorrect, and good and evil. The concepts are inextricable because ascendancy is ascendancy, regardless of what hierarchy we happen to be talking about. Remember, fast thinking divides everything into two categories that mean the same thing regardless of what you call them. Even if your facts are incontrovertible, superiors, even if they aren't Bullies, will not be wrong for subordinates. This is why, in most companies, if there is a dispute between you and your boss, upper management will support your boss regardless of who is correct.

In order to step out of this pattern, you have to subtly structure the situation so that your boss stumbles over the correct conclusion on his or her own. To do this, you will have to use the one rule of dominance that you can safely break if you do it carefully.

### The Dominant Ask Questions; the Submissive Answer

In general, the person asking questions is asserting dominance over the person answering them. However, most people habitually answer questions when they are asked, regardless of who asks them. In the gray area between these two conflicting rules lies your best defense against Bullying bosses or anyone else who is trying to take advantage of you. Get control by asking questions.

Whatever point you have to make will be more effective if it is presented as a request for information. Why do you think your therapist always answers questions with questions?

Please note that I said a request for information, not an interrogation. Interrogation is a *demand* for information, like when your mother would ask you where you'd been until three in the morning. The questions that work are phrased as sincere appeals for clarification that can allow you to lead a conversation by appearing to follow. Think: *that's a great idea, but I'm just not clear on one little detail.* If you want to see this technique done by a master, watch a video of the late Peter Falk playing *Columbo.* It has never been done better.

Even if you don't have a rumpled raincoat, you can use the technique, if you do it with finesse. When your boss concludes a speech and asks if there are any questions, be careful. Subordinates can request clarification, but not justification. Make sure you know the difference.

Most of the conflicts you are likely to experience with emotional vampire bosses, whether they are Antisocials or any other type, begin as struggles for dominance. We will be coming back to these rules again and again, so you might want to mark this section for future reference.

**BULLIED TO THE DARK SIDE:** Antisocial Bullies can do worse things than fire you or undermine your self-esteem. Most corporate scandals begin with a conversation like this. How would you respond?

> "Your figures are way off," Chuck says. "Run them again. Now."
>
> The figures are accurate, but not very heartening. You've run them every way you can think of, and you're absolutely certain. There is no way short of cooking the books that can make the numbers more favorable.
>
> Chuck also knows that the figures are accurate. Is he suggesting that you change them without actually saying anything incriminating?
>
> If you comply with a vaguely threatening suggestion like this, Chuck will own your soul.

It is in ambiguous conversations like this that white-collar crimes begin. What would you do?

Having talked to a number of people who wish they had chosen otherwise, I can offer the following advice.

**CHECK YOUR MORAL COMPASS:** Facts, especially in the financial area, are facts. Always let your work show that they are. Never let anyone persuade you to alter numbers. This is a real moral issue worth losing your job over. If you make even a tiny change now, Chuck's demands will never end.

**PLAY DUMB:** Do exactly as Chuck asks, no more, no less. Run the figures again and tell him you got the same result. If he wants something besides deniability, make him ask for it.

**BE SMART:** Don't merely accept purportedly new numbers or any other new information you may be offered; check everything thoroughly. Ask how numbers were calculated and where new information came from. Ignore implied threats or promises. Take strength in knowing that if you refuse to alter anything, Chuck can do you far less damage in the long run than if you comply. Also remember that no matter how hard he makes it for you, it's easier than being indicted.

**DON'T KEEP SECRETS:** When you are confronted with a moral dilemma, always share it with someone you trust. Your own moral compass may be influenced by the magnetic pull of Chuck's demands. A close friend, preferably one outside the organization, can help you keep your bearings.

I am not suggesting that you inform on Chuck, or talk about his veiled demand with coworkers or managers. You have nothing but easily denied speculations. If you make them public without an airtight case, he will know and can eat you alive.

**SAY NO, EVEN IF YOU ARE TERRIFIED:** If a Bully like Chuck gives you a direct order to do something that is illegal or immoral, tell him no directly. If he orders you to alter the figures, ask for some time to think, which will at least break his rhythm. When the time is up, say you're sorry, but you are unwilling to make the changes. This will take courage, because he may fire you on the spot. Or not.

If Chuck can get away with firing you for refusing to do something illegal, you are probably better off being gone, because it is likely that the rest of the management team supports his clandestine maneuvers. If his illegal activities come to light, it will be people at your level who take the blame and take the fall. Chuck, like every crooked boss before him, will claim he had no idea of what was going on in his department.

**Before You Go Public, Contact an Attorney:** If you are considering blowing the whistle on Chuck, you will need expert advice. Find an expert before you say anything to *anyone* in the organization. Your attorney will tell you that everything you say is on the record.

## THE ALCOHOLIC BOSS

> Colin is a party animal. He'll be the first to tell you that, because to him, it's the best thing you can possibly be. Work hard, play hard—that's his motto. Every day at five on the dot, he's at happy hour. Want to come? You'd better, if you want some face time.

For many people, the word *alcoholic* conjures up the slurring, staggering, reeking image of someone who drinks most of the time to the exclusion of all else. That's what the disease is like in its late stage, but most of the alcoholics you know are more like Colin. They drink too much too often, but they still manage to get to work and do their jobs, at least after a fashion.

Should you ask them—and you probably shouldn't—they will maintain that they are not alcoholics because they don't drink all that much, they still work regularly and get lots of things done, and, besides, they can stop any time they want. Let's not quibble about who is and isn't an alcoholic, and say instead that many emotional vampires are unrepentant substance abusers, and that Antisocials, with their high need for stimulation, lead the pack. We might as well discuss alcoholics here, because so many of them act like Bullies.

Substance abusers think that alcohol, or whatever other drug they're into, doesn't affect their performance or their day-to-day behavior. The people who have to work with them know otherwise. You don't have to be drunk on the job for drinking to be a problem.

Drugs subtly dictate the thoughts, actions, and even the schedules of their devotees. Try to discuss something important with Colin before he's had his sixth cup of coffee in the morning, or at 10 minutes before happy hour, and you'll see what I mean.

Happy hour starts at five for a reason. Drinking is part of the culture of work in many places. You will have to make your peace with it somehow, because you will not be able to avoid it, even if you don't actively participate.

With an alcoholic boss, there are several traps you can fall into. Believers tend to think of alcoholism as a moral or medical problem. They assume that there is someone in the organization who can make their boss get treatment, which there probably isn't. Instead of dealing with the situation as it is, Believers keep hoping that someone in authority will do something about it, while delaying the process by heroically trying to hold the department together.

Rather than becoming enablers, Rebels and Competitors may get into drinking themselves, though at different places and for different reasons. Competitors are apt to go to happy hour with their boss. Rebels will go to happy hour at a different place to get away from their boss. Either way, substance abuse can be contagious.

If you have an Antisocial party guy like Colin as a boss, here are some ideas.

**IF YOUR BOSS GOES TO HAPPY HOUR, YOU PROBABLY SHOULD, TOO:** Like it or not, the department will be divided between those who go and those who don't. Colin will regard the people who go as his real team, and act accordingly. If you want him to take you seriously at work, he needs to see you at the bar.

If you go, you don't have to stay long, as the only thing people will remember is who was there and who wasn't. You don't have to drink either. Surreptitiously tip the bartender and tell him or her that your "usual" is iced tea on the rocks with a slice of fruit. If you do drink, never let it be more than one.

Needless to say, if you are in recovery yourself, the dangers of going far exceed those of staying away. Be proud of your recovery; don't hide it. But don't talk about the details unless you're at an AA meeting.

If you are a Rebel sitting in the bar down the street, bitching about your boss, what are you thinking?

**KNOW THE SCHEDULE:** Alcoholics have times during the day when it's safe to approach and times when it's best to stay away because they are distracted or irritable or both. Unless drinking starts at midday, a couple of hours before or after lunch are usually the best bets for actually getting some work done.

**DON'T COVER FOR YOUR BOSS:** An alcoholic boss will make mistakes that affect the whole department. Tempting as it is, don't step in and correct them. The most dangerous place to be is between an Antisocial and the consequences of his or her behavior. If there are no consequences, there will be no change.

**KEEP MINUTES:** Antisocials have lousy memories, and alcoholics are even worse. When your boss tells you something, write it down, preferably in an e-mail that says: "Just want to clarify: at our meeting today, you said ... Let me know if I misunderstood. If I don't hear from you, I will assume that I am correct about your intentions." Cc whoever is appropriate. If your boss is an emotional vampire of any type, this sort of simple, respectful e-mail can be a lifesaver. We will come back to it many times.

**DON'T EVEN THINK ABOUT AN INTERVENTION:** Unless they are handled with utmost skill, interventions only make people angry. Interventions are unduly popular because normal people think: *that would work on me*. As I have said many times, the biggest mistake you can make with emotional vampires is assuming they think the same way you do.

In doing an intervention, everything is against you. Alcoholics are in denial, and people with personality disorders don't care how others feel. Interventions are risky even for therapists with years of experience. The only ones you hear about are the ones that work.

**DON'T COUNT ON HR:** In most organizations, the human resources department can help people who want to be helped, but they do not have much power to intervene when someone is not following the rules. Worse yet, HR may be obligated to investigate reports of substance abuse, which usually means asking your boss if he or she has a drinking problem. The net effect, though unintended, may be to report you for reporting.

I bring this up because I am appalled at how many columns about dealing with difficult people at work advise going to HR. Unless HR in your organization has a track record for setting things right and maintaining confidentiality, you will be much better off carefully approaching your boss's boss asking for advice on how to handle a specific situation. If your boss's boss is not willing to give advice, get out quickly. It's not likely that anything will be done, and you may get in serious trouble for being there.

**Focus on Behavior, Not Alcohol:**  If you have to confront your boss or attempt to go up the line, don't be the one to bring up drinking. Your boss will deny that alcohol is a problem, and his or her boss may not want to open that can of worms until it is wriggling all over her desk. If mistakes have been made or things haven't been done, focus on those, rather than the drinking that may be the cause. Even if you know alcohol is the problem, nothing will happen until someone else figures it out for him- or herself, that someone being your boss or your boss's boss.

## MORE SUGGESTIONS ON HOW TO HANDLE A BULLYING BOSS

What can you do if you report to a Bully or any other type of Antisocial? Obviously, the first and best answer is to look for another job. If this is not an option, then you're left with trying to make the best of a bad situation. The most important battle you have to fight is in your own head, not the conference room.

　　Antisocial Bullies are the least complicated of emotional vampires. The rules by which they operate are simple, direct, and clearly visible. The power that vampires have is in the emotion they elicit in you. The more you are able to override your emotional reactions and think, the less control they have. This is easy to say; it's harder to do, but not as hard as you may think. Here are some ideas to consider. They will help you deal with Bullies, alcoholics, and most of the other vampires you may have the misfortune of working with.

**First, Ask Yourself, "Why Am I Still Here?"**  No one deserves to be treated like chattel. To keep your sanity when you work for a Bully, you need to look into your own heart to find the reason you stay, and that reason is what you need to hold onto. If it's for money or power, or because it's a necessary step in your career, go for it. In the dark times, that's what you will need to remind yourself. If the only reason you're staying is that you're afraid to look for another job, it's time to go. Your own fear will do you more damage than any Bully ever could.

**Forget Justice:**  The most dangerous strategy I can imagine is going over your bullying boss's head to complain, hoping that his or her boss will side with you. Often tyrannical bosses do quite well with the bottom line, and their bosses tend to allow them quite a bit of leeway. If you go, let it be to ask for advice on how to be a better employee. If you do attempt to attack from above, realize it is a kill-or-be-killed situation.

In most organizations there are grievance procedures on the books. Before you consider using them, get some information about the fate of people who have used them in the past.

**Be Realistic:** Emotional vampires rarely change. There is nothing you or anyone else can say or do to make them see the error of their ways. You will have to adapt; they will not.

Don't believe for a moment that if you do everything correctly, there will be an end to criticism. Criticism is the source of a bullying boss's power in addition to being an end in itself.

**Transcend Temper:** Bullying bosses get off on attacking employees in front of others. When this happens to you, you need to endure it with dignity. The only safety there is lies in controlling your emotions.

Many office tyrants say that they want employees who will stand up to them. I have never known any that would tolerate it.

**If You are Getting Chewed Out, Never Ever Explain!** Bullies will attack you for no good reason. Every fiber of your being may be crying out for you to explain the situation. Don't. This urge, no matter how rational it seems, is an emotional reaction coming straight from your dinosaur brain.

All explanations boil down to this: *if you know the facts, you will see that I am right and you are wrong.* Do I need to say more?

Do not explain anything unless you are specifically asked to do so. Even then, it is often best to admit a mistake and state what you are going to do to fix it.

**Avoid the Temptation to Gripe:** There is nothing more tempting than getting together with fellow employees and talking about a Bully's latest atrocities. This feels good while it's happening, but it makes the situation harder to live with in the long run. Your goal is always to calm your emotions, not to stoke them up. Rebels should pay close attention to this advice.

Even if you are a Believer and right is on your side and it seems like everyone agrees with you, don't become a leader of resistance unless you are willing to die for the cause. Before you charge, look behind you. There may be no one there. They're all in the break room griping.

**BE A COLLABORATOR AT YOUR PERIL:** Bullies love getting the dirt on everyone. They offer the illusion of safety to informers. Competitors can get caught in this trap, not realizing that if there's trouble, Bullies expect their allies to take the fall. Believers can get caught also, but for an entirely different reason. They may think they are representing the concerns of the team when they are actually ratting out dissidents.

**BECOME INDISPENSABLE:** If at all possible, develop competence in an area with which your boss is unfamiliar. This is your best protection, especially if you are a Rebel with authority issues.

Don't compete in your boss's area. If you get too competent, you might get disappeared.

**KEEP YOUR DUCKS IN A ROW:** Know what is going on in your area and be ready at a moment's notice to cite facts and figures. Bullies love to get their information by cross-examining rather than by listening to presentations. Be ready at any time to give information when subjected to the third degree.

When you are told to do something, make sure that what you are asked to do is clear. Log conversations and directives. You may need to refer to them later. Use the e-mail trick I referred to earlier in the chapter.

**BE ABLE TO ASSESS YOUR OWN PERFORMANCE:** Bullies are quick to blame and slow to praise. To keep your own sanity, you have to be able to know how well you are doing without being told. Pay close attention to your goals and objectives and how well you meet them. This is partly a way to defend yourself, but it also is a way to convince yourself you are doing a good job, even if you are unappreciated.

**DEMAND TOP DOLLAR:** Many tyrants are willing to pay for the privilege of pushing their employees around. If you are going to stand up and stand firm in any area, it should be salary. Make a coherent case, and don't be afraid to push. This is one area in which your boss is likely to be reasonable.

If you can't ask for money, you probably shouldn't be there.

**WARN YOUR FAMILY:** Let your family know that your boss may ask you to do things at inconvenient times, such as the middle of the night or two days into your vacation. Make sure you share your mixed feelings, and your reasons for staying. Resist the trickle-down temptation to treat your family members the same way your boss treats you. Likewise, resist the temptation to make your boss into the family villain and come home every day and talk about the awful things he or she did to you. It will only make you feel worse, and there will be subtle pressure from home for you to stand up to the asshole.

Finally, if after reading these suggestions, you find yourself coming up with reasons that they won't apply in your situation, maybe today is the day you should turn in your resignation.

# Con Artists

**6**

Con Artists, like other Antisocials, crave excitement and the adrenaline rush of living on the edge. Their internal dynamics are quite similar to Bullies, but from the outside, the two couldn't look more different from each other. Bullies are rough; Con Artists are smooth operators who prefer putting one over to putting people down. The excitement they crave is persuading people to do their will. Unlike Narcissists, who use some of the same techniques to create big-time Ponzi schemes, Con Artists usually have no grand designs; they just want what they want when they want it. They believe that whatever they want is theirs already; if it happens to belong to you, all they have to do is talk you into giving it to them.

Con Artists read people, not as biographies, but as instruction manuals, paying attention to hidden doubts or desires that can be used to manipulate. They know what you want, often better than you do yourself, and they dangle it in front of you as an enticement. At least, that's what it sounds like.

> Jake, your boss's boss, puts a hand on your shoulder and leans close to your ear. "If you make us look good on this project, there could be some big things in store for you. I can't say who told me, but I just thought you'd like to know."

Before you get too excited about big things in store, think about what Jake actually said. That's right, nothing. But it is a beautiful nothing, the stock-in-trade of Con Artists everywhere.

Though it has no substance, it sounds delicious, and if ladled on thickly enough, it may entice you to do whatever it takes to "make us look good," even if it is against your best judgment.

In the first chapter, we saw that emotional vampires communicate differently from normal people. Everything they say is for effect. For Con Artists, the effect is everything. You recognize them not so much by what they do as by what they make you feel—as if something big is about to happen unless you're dumb enough to mess it up. To protect yourself, you have to know yourself and sometimes ask yourself difficult questions.

When someone like Jake is ladling on praise and promises, instead of lapping them up, you have to ask yourself: *Why is he telling me this? What's in it for him?* Only you can decide if the promises are real and the flattery genuine, or if you are being asked to give something for nothing. Remember, if a deal seems too good to be true, it usually is.

Con Artists are born hypnotists. They create enticing illusions that make you eager to do their will. At work, you're likely to find them in sales, where hypnotic abilities are rewarded with big commissions, but you may find them anywhere you can get to by talking a good game.

Perhaps you remember Adam, the Con Artist sales rep in the first chapter. You may still be wondering what makes him any different from other salespeople you have encountered. The techniques he uses are legitimate. They're taught in sales seminars everywhere. What's different is the spirit in which he uses them.

Normal sales reps develop a relationship with their clients that goes beyond the immediate sale. They want to sell people something they actually need so that they will come back and buy again.

Con Artists live for the moment. They want what they want right now, and will say whatever it takes to get it. They will persuade you, or simply wear you down by continuing to ask. Con Artists are not concerned with relationships. To them, other people are prey, put before them to be exploited. If customers discover they've gotten the short end of the deal, Con Artists are either nowhere to be found or right there making excuses, promising the world, or putting the blame on someone else. What they're really doing is setting up their mark for the next sting.

Normal people have real empathy; they see others as like them and deserving of the same treatment they are. Emotional vampires of all kinds, especially Con Artists, may be good at reading people, but they use their understanding to exploit rather than cooperate.

The rest of this chapter is about specific techniques for hypnosis and persuasion. My hope is that you will recognize them when you see them and be able to make conscious decisions to avoid being exploited. The techniques can also be used to exploit. What you do with them is up to you.

## THINKING INSTEAD OF REACTING TO CON ARTISTS

Con Artists get what they want by eliciting reactions in you. To get a feel for what this is like, let's go back a few years and sit in on the job interview that got Con Artist Jake, your boss's boss, hired in the first place.

As Bill, the VP for operations, ushers Jake into his office for a job interview, Jake begins searching for cues about who Bill is and what he wants.

Jake sees lots of books and pictures of Bill shaking hands with various dignitaries. One looks like the late, great Stephen Covey. Behind the credenza, in a place of honor, hangs a row of plaques: continuous Quality Improvement awards from 2007 to the present.

"Quite a collection," Jake says. "It looks like you're the man to beat when it comes to quality."

Bill shakes his head. "Not me. As far as I'm concerned, these plaques belong to the team." He gestures at the busy workers outside his door. "Those are the folks with the guts; they deserve all the glory. I'm just the guy who keeps things organized."

Jake recognizes the rhetoric of management by humility. He figures the guy in the picture really is Stephen Covey.

"You know," Jake says, "that reminds me of something I read in *First Things First*. Uh, what was it exactly—?"

"Oh, you're a Covey fan," Bill says.

"Absolutely! We'll all really miss him."

After an appropriate moment of silence, Bill swivels around, and points to his bookshelf. "Every word Stephen Covey ever wrote." Bill pulls out *Seven Habits* and reverently turns to the title page. "This one's autographed."

"You actually knew him?" Jake gasps, as if anyone who associates with Stephen Covey sits at the right hand of God.

Bill beams. "I wouldn't say I knew him, but I talked to him a couple of times."

"That must have been great," Jake says. "I wish I'd had that chance. What an opportunity." This opens the door for Bill to tell about his dialogues with Covey.

After an hour of stimulating conversation like this, Bill feels that he really understands Jake and can develop a real win-win working relationship with him.

If Bill had asked himself what Jake really said and why he said it, Bill might have realized that he actually found out very little about Jake's qualifications for the job, except for his admiration for Covey and his skill at ego massage.

Nevertheless, Bill is sure enough of his judgment to offer Jake the job on the spot. He doesn't even check references. He should have.

Of course Con Artists are good at job interviews! For emotional vampires, almost every conversation is an interview for something. Jake has developed instinctive skills born of long experience. Whether you call it hypnosis or putting your best foot forward, it still works.

Does Jake really think about what he's doing in the way I've described? Probably not. He does know that interviewers usually believe that the candidate they like best is the one who'll do the best job. Really, that's all he needs to know.

Jake's secret for making people like him is to get them to talk about themselves. This is a good plan, based on years of psychological research, about which Jake is completely unaware. He just knows what works.

In his quest to be likable, Jake stumbles over the fact that Bill, a dyed-in-the-wool Believer, has a hard time acknowledging his own ego, at least directly. Jake uses this information to create an instinctive, but nonetheless elegant bind. How can Bill not like somebody who sees him as a superior human being because of his tenuous association with a disciple of humility?

Neither Bill nor Jake may know what to call it, but what's happening is hypnosis.

## THE PATTERN TO STEP OUT OF: HYPNOSIS

Con Artists are natural hypnotists. To protect yourself, you have to know what that means.

When I say hypnosis, many people envision a guy in a turban swinging a watch and convincing people on a stage to believe that they are chickens. Hypnotic techniques can be used for entertainment, but they can do so much more.

The first thing you need to know about hypnosis is that what it looks like is not what it is. Stage hypnosis is not about turbans, watches, and making people act like chickens. It is about reading people, finding aspiring performers in the audience who will do whatever it takes to be part of the show.

Hypnosis involves creating an attractive alternative reality and offering it up as an enticement for specific actions. Stage hypnotists imply that only really intelligent people have what it takes to act like a chicken. Con Artists like Jake want you to give them whatever they're trying to get. No matter what the goal is, for hypnosis to work, you have to be a willing participant, even if you aren't quite sure what you are participating in. Enthusiasm and confusion are both part of the process. The idea is for you to stop thinking and just go along because it feels good.

Emotional vampires' specialties are the kinds of illusions that entice people to stop thinking and just go along. To protect yourself, you have to start thinking again. Here are the warning signs that someone may be trying to hypnotize you.

DEVIATING FROM STANDARD PROCEDURE: Bill's first clue that something was amiss should have been the fact that he wasn't following his typical job interview pattern. In other interviews, Bill would have been trying to elicit information; in this one, he seems to be doing most of the talking.

THINKING IN SUPERLATIVES: If Bill had asked himself why he was doing things differently in response to Jake, the answer would probably have been phrased as some sort of superlative. Jake was the *best* or *most promising* candidate Bill had seen in 20 years. Bill should have asked himself how he came to such a far-reaching conclusion so quickly. If he had, Bill might have realized that Jake was the best, not because of his own qualifications, but because he saw Bill in precisely the way he wanted to be seen.

**INSTANT RAPPORT:** Bill felt that Jake understood him immediately, but the feeling wasn't exactly accurate. What Jake understood was that Bill wanted someone to see him in the same way Bill saw Stephen Covey. Jake was just giving Bill what he wanted, in the hope that Bill would reciprocate. He did.

**SEEING THE PERSON OR SITUATION AS SPECIAL:** Not only did Jake charm Bill into giving him the job, Jake also set the stage for a working relationship with Bill that would be different from the relationship Bill has with other people. Jake presented himself to Bill as a prospective disciple, someone who would stop in for advice and guidance from Bill's vast store of business knowledge. Jake won himself not only the job but also a special place in Bill's heart.

**LACK OF CONCERN WITH OBJECTIVE INFORMATION:** Somehow, Bill decided that he didn't need to know much about Jake's history. Maybe he didn't want to know. If Bill looked too closely at the facts, he might discover something that would break the pleasant spell.

Your two most important sources of objective information about another person are the details of that person's history and the opinions of other people. If for some reason you find yourself avoiding those sources or thinking that they don't apply, watch out.

**CONFUSION:** If you asked Bill how he drew so many unusual conclusions from a single interview, his answer would probably be rather vague. Bill's haziness about the details of the conversation, and how they led him to make the decisions he did, would probably not affect his certainty that his decisions were correct. That last part is the dead giveaway.

Hazy understanding of the reasons for your own reactions, coupled with unusual certainty, is a pretty clear sign that somebody has been messing with your mind. The main purpose of this section is to help you discover who it was, how they did it, and how to step out of the pattern.

In dealing with hypnosis, you have to look behind the curtain of illusion to see the objective facts. Sometimes that means admitting to yourself that your impressions were wrong. This is extremely hard because of *cognitive dissonance*. Once we have made a decision, we look for evidence that the decision was right and ignore evidence that it may have been wrong. All of us do this unconsciously, and it makes us likely to persist in our mistakes.

> Over time, Bill keeps getting feedback that suggests that Jake isn't doing a good job. The numbers look bad, and several people have commented about Jake's lack of follow-through. When Bill brings these issues up, Jake always has an excuse—usually that his subordinates are not sophisticated enough to understand the great truths that he and Bill know—and a promise that everything will work out. Bill is inclined to give him the benefit of the doubt because he wants to believe that Jake is actually the guy he thought he hired.

Con Artists cause all kinds of problems both above and below them on the organizational chart. Needless to say, your position dictates the kinds of actions you can take to protect yourself and your organization.

If you are below Jake, you have to watch out for manipulation by threats or promises. He may try to get you to do extra work or manage information so he doesn't have to face consequences. Try to get everything out in the open and in writing. As with Bullies, it's a good idea to do what I've called "keeping minutes." Send e-mails requesting clarification about what was said. Carbon copies can be helpful, but only if the recipient is directly involved.

Wherever you are on the org chart, another trick to watch for is purposely trying to make you angry at someone else. If Jake can stir up enough conflict, it may distract from his own poor performance and convince Bill that his department is a bunch of malcontents. Watch out if a Con Artist tells you someone else is ticked off. *You* are the one he wants to make angry.

No matter how clear it is to everyone what Jake is doing, bear in mind that it is not clear to Bill. He's entranced. The more you criticize Jake, the more Bill will believe that it's a personality conflict rather than a legitimate complaint. In order to break the spell, he has to discover the problem for himself—and then have the courage to recognize his mistake and fix it.

Your best bet is to get Bill to focus on the numbers. He's a manager; numbers may be more real to him than anyone's opinion, even Jake's. Ask questions that prompt Bill to study the spreadsheet, and hope he can draw his own conclusions.

If you are in Bill's position and you hear the rumblings of discontent, don't assume you know what's going on. Check it out.

"Jake, have a seat," Bill says, drawing a chair close to his desk and turning his monitor so both of them can see it.

"Is there something wrong?" Jake asks.

"You could say that," Bill says as he moves his mouse to bring up the spreadsheet for Jake's department. "You've seen these figures, haven't you?"

Jake lets out a sigh of relief. "Oh, those. Remember, I told you last week that this data is incomplete. The software's been down and we've still got a stack of production reports to input. Not only that, but—"

"Jake, you've been here seven months, and you still haven't been able to give me an accurate picture of what's going on in your department."

Jake laughs. "Bill, I don't like to point the finger, but the way Tim Norton set things up when he was managing this department before I came makes it almost impossible to tell what's going on. I've been trying to do a little re-engineering. You know, like Hammer and Champy said. Having the team question every single process to see what we're trying to do and how we're trying to do it. With the way Tim left things, what can I tell you?" Jake shrugs. "It's pretty slow going."

When Con Artists get caught, they start throwing out alternative realities faster than the SyFy Channel. Their major skill is talking a good game, which in many cases is more than enough to get hired and promoted and to keep their bosses from looking too closely at objective data. The greatest danger is believing them rather than the numbers or what their coworkers say. The truth is out there, but Con Artists will do whatever they can to discourage you from looking for it.

"Well," Bill says, leaning back in his chair, "if you're having that much difficulty, I think we'd better make this re-engineering into priority one."

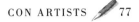

Jake gives Bill the thumbs-up sign. "Can do, boss!"

"Oh, I don't expect you to do it by yourself," Bill says. "I'm willing to help."

"You've been a big help already. The example you set—"

"I intend to help with more than an example. Monday morning I want to meet with you and your whole department to see if we can work together to figure out what's going on. Have your people put together whatever data they have, and we'll go through it line by line."

Jake shakes his head. "I'm not sure the team would take that very well. It's like a vote of no confidence. After all the problems in the past, it might undo all the progress we've made."

"I'll take that risk," Bill says.

Vampires operate best in the dark, and they like to keep it that way. As managers, they build structures in which they are the only conduit of information coming in or going out. It takes courage for an executive like Bill to turn on the lights. But courage is what being a leader is all about, especially when you have made a mistake.

## CON ARTIST GROOMING

A vampire's bite can turn you into a vampire. Con Artists can are adept at getting normal people to do things that they know are wrong. It always happens a little bit at a time. As mentioned in Chapter 1, the psychological term for this process is *grooming*. It means using praise, intimidation, or both to subtly coerce victims to act in the way that meets the vampire's needs. What the process does to the victim is of no concern to the vampire. To people with personality disorders, other people exist only to meet their needs.

All emotional vampires groom. Bullies do it with intimidation, but Con Artists are more subtle, and more effective. Gently, they entice their victims to take the first step away from their moral center. From there, it's easier to persuade them to take the next step, then one after that.

Before the victims know it, they are lost in the fog with a vampire as their only guide.

Grooming is hard to detect; it has to be. Con Artists do it instinctively, and their victims respond instinctively as well. It begins, as do normal relationships, with establishing a connection. As we have seen, Con Artists are experts at seeming to be just like you.

> Mark, an account rep, is in the break room, pouring himself a cup of coffee. In walks Vampire Angela Magnano, his new boss. "Hi Angie," Mark says. "The coffee's fresh for a change. Want some?"
>
> "You call that coffee?" Angie says. "With a name like Mark Rossi, I think you'd know that the stuff in that pot is not coffee." She shakes her head. "I'm not sure what it is. Hey, Paisan, it's a nice day. What say we go down to Luigi's cart for some real espresso with lemon peel?"
>
> Mark immediately agrees. He's flattered that the boss wants to go out with him for coffee.
>
> Sitting on the bench next to Luigi's cart, Angie sips her espresso. "Now this is more like it. Reminds me of my old neighborhood in South Philly. Kind of tough place, but you learn quick on the street, and the food and the coffee were great. Where'd you grow up, Mark?"
>
> "New York."
>
> "Brooklyn?"
>
> "Well, no. Upper West Side, actually. But I used to hang a lot with my cousins on Staten Island," Mark says, trying to sound streetwise.
>
> "Well, wherever. At least you learned to appreciate good food and good coffee. Not like some of the white bread and mayonnaise types back at the office." She puts a hand over her mouth. "Don't tell anybody I said that."
>
> "Fuggedaboutit," Mark says, and they both laugh.

A friendly conversation, or something darker? Sometimes there's no way of knowing. The first stages of grooming are hardly distinguishable from what ordinary people do when they like you. Mark's first clue might have been that Angie emphasized not only their similarity but also their difference from others. Then there was her almost joking suggestion that he keep her secret. For grooming to work, vampires need to move you closer to them, and away from anybody who might break the spell.

Was there enough in this one conversation to alert Mark that Angie was setting him up? Probably not. Yet, looking back, it's easy to see that this is where it all began.

After that day at Luigi's, Angie and Mark would talk about Italian food and joke with each other doing bad imitations of movie Mafiosi. Other people begin to wonder why the boss seemed so tight with one of the more junior members of the department. To make things worse, at least for the people watching, Angie would occasionally assign Mark projects that were a little above his pay grade. If there was talk, Angie would say it was just jealousy.

Mark didn't question his good fortune. To him, it seemed that Angie recognized his talent and was mentoring him. *Grooming* was more like it.

Mark was the only one who wasn't surprised when Angie asked him to head up the new marketing effort for the whole department. After all, that *was* what he studied in business school.

As with any deal made with an emotional vampire, there was a catch.

"I don't have to tell you that her highness isn't completely sold on this marketing stuff," Angie says. "You know how she is about the bottom line. Anything that doesn't turn a profit in 10 minutes flat isn't worth doing. *Capisce*?"

Mark sits up straighter in his chair. "That's the whole point of marketing. If we know what our clients want, we can tailor our products, and our reps can sell more."

Angie smiles. "I know that, but to get this thing off the ground, we're going to have to convince the powers that be. Can you put together a presentation in, say, six weeks?"

"No problem. I can plan a research project and—"

"Not research, results."

"How do we get results when we haven't done the research?"

"Paisan, we're talking politics here. I don't have to tell that to an Italian, do I? No way. You'll know what to do. That's why I picked you for the job. So tell me, are you with me on this?"

It's clear that Angie expects some payback for giving Mark the job. She implies that if he is worthy, he will figure out what she expects and do it without being asked directly. This will give her deniability later on, but in her relationship with Mark, it will have a more significant purpose. If he crosses the line here, Angie will have changed his view of himself. Their playing at being Goodfellas will move a step closer to reality.

Angie puts the pressure on by asking for an immediate answer. She doesn't say what will happen if he says no. She doesn't have to. In Mark's confusion between reality and fantasy, the next step toward being a made man seems like his only choice.

In the last chapter, we saw how Bullies get people to cross over to the dark side using intimidation, and how it takes courage and toughness to maintain your integrity. Protecting yourself from Con Artists' grooming requires even more. Con Artists draw you in by seeming to see you in just the way you hope to be seen. Mark, who is more than a little green, is flattered at being seen as a tough guy.

To protect himself from this sort of subtle persuasion, Mark has to consider the possibility that he may not be as cool as Angie seems to think he is. This is difficult, but absolutely necessary.

If you seem to be receiving what some people might see as inordinate attention from a powerful person in your organization, here are some suggestions.

**SWITCH OFF YOUR AUTOPILOT:** Emotional vampires exploit automatic responses, the things we say and do just to be friendly or polite. At work, it's always a good idea to stay conscious. When someone says something, before you answer, always ask yourself, *why is he or she telling me this?* In human interactions, nothing happens without a purpose. On your own time, perhaps you can imagine that you are just chatting for no particular reason. At work, you have to pay more attention to business.

**KNOW THYSELF:** Take a tip from the Oracle of Delphi. If you want to know anything at all, you need to know yourself first. This means having an accurate view of your strengths and an even more accurate view of your weaknesses. Con Artists know that vulnerabilities often lie in areas about which people feel most certain. They are especially good at getting people to do things they think they'd never do in a million years. They know that people don't defend against what they think will never happen. You should know this too.

All emotional vampires strive to be your main source of information about yourself. They can convince you that they know you better than anyone else does. This is deadly. Everyone should have at least one trusted friend to whom they give permission to tell it like it is. If you don't have a friend like this, ask your mother.

**RECOGNIZE A SALES PITCH WHEN YOU HEAR IT:** The main reason to stay alert at work is that people are often trying to sell you something. Unless you know who it is and what they are selling, you can end up buying stuff you don't really want.

No one understands sales pitches like Robert Cialdini,* a social psychologist who has made a career of studying the ways that people influence one another. He points out that there are seven basic sales pitches, all of which rely on people choosing the automatic, socially acceptable response, rather than thinking closely about what they're being asked to do.

> *Do It Because You Like Me.* The main reason that people get to like other people is that they perceive them to be similar to themselves. Con Artists, as we have seen, usually begin their approach by establishing a perception of similarity. They watch you closely. They ask questions about what you think and what you like, and then they profess to like the same things. Before you know it, they are acting like you're their best buddies. This is how Angie got to Mark.
>
> Con Artists' probes and ploys can seem like ordinary friendliness, but at an artificially accelerated pace. Remember that instant rapport is a danger sign of hypnosis.
>
> Watch out if someone starts complimenting you on whatever you are most proud of. Or, especially if you are a Believer, what you are most sensitive about. Hard as it may be when you are basking in the light of synthetic admiration, ask yourself how you got there so quickly.
>
> *Do It to Reciprocate.* Reciprocity is the foundation of normal relationships. When someone gives us something, we feel obligated to give back. Con Artists like Angie take advantage of this automatic response. They don't like you or give you anything for free. They always expect a big return on their investment. Often, like Mark, you may not know the price until you've already signed on the dotted line.
>
> *Do It Because Everybody Else Is Doing It.* This is the sales pitch that really gets to Competitors. Just tell them that all the hip people are breaking the rules, and if they don't, they'll be left behind. If smart, high-

---

*Robert B. Cialdini, *Influence: The Psychology Persuasion,* 5th ed. New York: Prentice-Hall, 2008.

achieving people didn't regularly fall for this pitch, there would have been no bank collapse, and nobody in sports would use steroids. *Capisce?*

Rebels fall for this as well. Hip to them is not being chicken.

***This Offer Good for a Limited Time Only.*** Fast talking leads to fast thinking, the primeval belief that if you don't get it quick, it will disappear. This is how Angie got Mark to cross the line.

The limited offer pitch gets to everyone, but Rebels are particularly susceptible. They pride themselves on making quick decisions based on common sense, rather than screwing around with a bunch of stupid details. They sometimes forget that devils can hide in the details.

***Do It to Be Consistent.*** Cognitive dissonance, that amazing force that bends reality to conform to what we already believe, is the foolish consistency that Emerson called the hobgoblin of small minds. Con Artists know how to sic your own hobgoblins on you.

Cognitive dissonance is the psychological principle that makes grooming possible. People try to maintain an internal sense of consistency between their actions and beliefs. This is hard enough to do with careful thought. It's almost impossible with a vampire trying to confuse your perceptions about who you are and what you believe after you've crossed one little line after another.

Was talking like Mafiosi a deliberate choice on Angie's part? Freud always said there are no accidents. For an Italian, it is an obvious, albeit stereotypic ploy.

***You Can Believe Me—I'm an Authority.*** Vampires know that, no matter what, people are likely to do what authority figures tell them.

In the most chilling social psychology experiment of all time, Stanley Milgram* demonstrated that average people would administer what they believed were potentially lethal electric shocks because someone in a white coat told them it was okay.

The exact same disastrous effect can be achieved by doing the opposite of what authority figures say. Rebels, are you listening?

---

*Stanley Milgram, *Obedience to Authority,* New York: Harper & Row, 1974.

***Do It to Get Me to Stop Bugging You.*** This is not one of Cialdani's sales pitches, but it is used so often and so successfully that I thought I'd add it to the list.

***Do It or Else.*** The threat is the simplest sales pitch of all. As we saw in the previous chapter, intimidating managers use it all the time.

At work, many people do what their vampire bosses want because they are afraid they'll be fired if they don't. This is true sometimes, but not usually. The best way to know what the contingencies are where you work is to find out what happened to people who have said no in the past.

If you can get fired for doing the right thing, are you working in the right place?

Let's get back to Mark and Angie.

Against his better judgment, Mark slapped together a few focus groups. He interviewed clients and sales reps and discovered that the two main reasons cited by clients for investing in the company's financial products were to have money for their own retirement and to improve their children's future. He came up with a sales presentation that addressed both issues, complete with graphs of how much money regular monthly investments could yield when clients were ready to retire or send the kids to college. Angie was less impressed than he had hoped.

"Mark, let's think outside the box here. People believe in saving for their retirement or their children's future. They mean to save, but when it comes time to plunk down the money, there's always something else they can spend it on. According to your research, these folks want to feel like they're being responsible. That's what we have to capitalize on. What if we get the reps to tell people that the only way they can be responsible investors is to be absolutely sure they're getting the best possible return on their money? Otherwise, they're screwing over their own children."

"Uh, there's a little problem with that. The clients aren't sure they're getting the best possible return on their money, and the reps say that in a lot of cases they aren't."

Angie shakes her head. "The real problem is that the reps are having trouble interpreting the programs—the printouts are too complicated. They can't explain what they don't understand. What they really need are some simple, easy-to-understand ways to show clients that they are getting the best return. That's the kind of marketing effort we need."

"Uh, there's more." Mark takes a deep breath and goes on. "The reps are saying that the quotas are so high that there's pressure on them to churn their present accounts, to sell stuff and buy stuff unnecessarily just to make enough commission to live on."

The irritation Mark expects doesn't materialize. Instead, Angie settles back in her chair and lets out a huge sigh. "Welcome to management," she says. "The first thing you'll discover is that there are a lot of people out there who just can't cut it, so they always blame the system. You've done okay with commissions. You know how it works."

How it works is that Mark, like most of us, is not completely pure. He probably did a bit of churning to keep his totals up. In Angie's world, everybody does, and anybody with management potential knows it.

Since he is a manager now, Mark figured he ought to act like one. He gave Angie what she wanted, and of course she kept asking for more. A couple of years later, when some investors initiated a class action based on misleading information, Angie testified that Mark went rogue, and she had no idea what he was doing.

Unfortunately, neither did he. Angie's grooming took care of that.

With Con Artists, as with any vampires, you have to decide where to draw the line. Then you have to draw it and defend it. Some of the same techniques that work on Bullies will help you with Con Artists, but only if you are not so lost in the fog that you forget who you are and what you believe in. If you feel like you're losing your bearings, talk it over with someone you trust. The more hesitant you feel about getting things out in the open, the more you need to do it.

# Antisocial
# Cultures

7

**O**RGANIZATIONAL CULTURE is a set of rules, mostly unwritten, that define a group. These rules are so basic to how the culture operates that even if people can't say specifically what the rules are, they still follow them. Group members think, act, and behave in certain predictable ways. People who don't are considered outsiders.

Emotional vampires in upper management create organizational cultures in their own image. To be a part of things, you have to think and act the way they do.

The unwritten rules that define an Antisocial culture should already be familiar to you if you've ever seen a movie about the mafia. If your organization follows these rules, you're part of a crime family, or at least a group that acts like one.

## IT'S ALWAYS US AND THEM

In an Antisocial organization, there are always good guys and bad guys, but the bad guys might well be considered good guys by the rest of the world. The enemy to Antisocials is anyone who tries to stop them from doing whatever they want. Another *us* and *them* is the organization and the customers and investors it freely exploits to make money. Yet another *us* and *them* divide is between upper management and the people in the rest of the organization whose role is to shut up and keep selling.

## THE MONEY IS GOOD, EVEN IF THE JOB ISN'T

Money is the lure of antisocial organizations. People work for them and stay with them against their better judgment because the pay is much better than what they might make anywhere else. The handcuffs are made of gold, but they're still handcuffs.

## EVERYTHING IS SECRET

Knowledge is closely guarded by people at the top. You're told what to do, and you're expected to know how to do it. Questions are not welcome.

## NOTHING IS IN WRITING

Documents can be used as evidence. Most Antisocial organizations are not engaged in criminal activity. At least, there are no specific laws against what they do. As organizations, they are deceptive and exploitative, but they do whatever it takes to keep those aspects hidden. From the outside, they are just legitimate businessmen.

## YOU'VE GOT TO MAKE YOUR BONES

To be part of an Antisocial organization, you have to do something illegal, immoral, or exploitative to show you're part of the group.

Whether the job is cooking the books, falsifying information to make a sale, or covering a mistake, in an Antisocial organization, you are expected to make it happen. No one will tell you directly to lie, cheat, or steal. You are expected to do it on your own initiative. If you should be so stupid as to blow the whistle, you're the one who'll take the fall.

### Omerta

Nobody talks, even after they leave the organization. If they do, the rest of their career sleeps with the fishes.

### If the Godfather Asks for a Favor, You Do It

If you are told to do something, you do it now and don't ask questions. *Capisce?*

## You Break the Rules, You Get Whacked

These days, most organizations use lawyers as their hit men. They cost more, but on the whole, they're more effective and less messy.

All kidding aside, if your organization follows these rules, you're in over your head. As if you need me to tell you that. What you do need is to discuss your career with a knowledgeable person that you really trust.

My best advice is to get out quietly and on good terms, then go straight.

# Histrionics

8

**H**ISTRIONIC MEANS DRAMATIC. The most important thing to know about Histrionics is that they are always putting on a show. It's not like your high school musical. After that was over, you took off your costume and went back to being yourself. For Histrionics, the show never ends. They become the role they are playing, in their own minds, if not in yours.

Just as Antisocials are addicted to excitement, Histrionics are hooked on attention and approval. They are extroverts for whom the only reality is the audience. They want good reviews, and they are willing to work hard to get them. Given half a chance, they'll sing and dance their way into your heart. They invented musical comedy. They do more subtle performances too. Histrionics are virtuosos of polite conversation, so interested that they make you feel interesting. One of their finest inventions is small talk, the miracle glue that holds conversations together. They also invented gossip.

Histrionics have what it takes to get hired into your business or your life. You want good looks? They've got them (or they'll spend hours trying to get them). You want motivation? They bubble with enthusiasm and sparkle with wit. You want positive attitude? Can do! The attitude, that is, not the substance. What Histrionics can't do is tolerate boring day-to-day responsibilities. They'd rather put on a show instead, or maybe a motivational rally.

Usually, Histrionics are quite skilled at the roles they play, but their range is limited. They're always the good guy, at least until the reviews are bad or the audience loses interest. Then they switch to their other role, the victim. Medical dramas are a specialty, as are soap operas with you as the persecuting villain.

These vampire performers have tendencies toward the diagnosis formerly known as *Histrionic Personality Disorder*. The condition is old, but the name keeps changing. This name, which will soon go out of style, is an attempt to replace the less politically correct *hysterical.* Ancient Greek physicians like Galen and Hippocrates thought that the dramatic emotional shifts and vague physical complaints they saw in Histrionics were caused by the migration of a childless womb (hystericum) to other parts of the body.

Unfortunately, a Histrionic personality has long been considered to be primarily a disorder of women, which is what creates the political problems with the diagnosis. The misperception arises from the fact that the Histrionic types most often seen in psychiatric clinics are somewhat passive and stereotypically feminine. Most of them were referred by frustrated physicians who refer them because they don't know what else to do. Think of your Aunt Sadie, who's been dying of an undiagnosed disorder for the last 30 years. Histrionics, when they have problems, never see them as mental. Most of them never see themselves as having problems at all, only the misfortune of being surrounded by insensitive, unmotivated people.

Stereotypic Histrionics are often referred to as Drama Queens. They explode into emotion at the slightest provocation. I think that by and large, psychiatry has not recognized the less flamboyant Histrionics, female and male, who are out there working, sometimes driving the people who work with them to seek treatment.

Most often missed by psychiatry and psychology are the Histrionic men, for whom any kind of treatment would be a sign of weakness. We might not see them, but you certainly have. Male-pattern Histrionics play good guy roles like fifties dad, avid sports fan, joke-telling raconteur, or highly motivated businessman. Histrionic women at work often play these same roles, usually better than men do.

Regardless of sex, Histrionics are often promoted over their more qualified peers because their enthusiasm and positive attitude can easily be mistaken for ability. They look like perfect middle managers, the kind who can keep everybody happy and not create problems for the people above them. This is what they're hired for and what they valiantly try to do. Unfortunately, the pesky technical demands of the job often get in the way. Histrionics are not detail people. They firmly believe that if everybody is motivated enough, the details will take care of themselves.

If you work for a Histrionic, you're part of the show, whether you like it or not.

The role you're supposed to play is the happy, motivated employee who just does what he or she is supposed to and doesn't ask too many embarrassing questions. Woe unto you if you don't stick to the script. First, you'll likely be sent to a social skills class or motivational seminar. If that doesn't fix you, well, you're just not a part of the team, and you deserve what you get. Histrionics all have black belts in passive aggression.

Nobody can victimize like a victim.

If this characterization sounds familiar, it is because the middle levels of many organizations, and sometimes the upper levels as well, are full of Histrionics who have gotten there because of their social skills. This is so pervasive that many organizational cultures have taken on aspects of the Histrionic personality. Extroverts who perform well in meetings are valued above more introverted people who prefer to stay in their cubes and get the job done.

You will find Histrionics at every level of every organization. When things are going well, they are great to have around, cheerful and enthusiastic, but when there's a problem, it's likely to be seen as someone else's negative attitude. If the problem doesn't go away in response to positive thinking, Histrionics decompensate quickly. They get very upset or they get sick. Either way, the people who work with them end up suffering at least as much as they do, and the problem may never get addressed.

From the outside, Histrionics look like a mass of contradictions. They can't stand conflict, but they excel at creating it. They are really nice, but they can also be incredibly cruel. They espouse playing by the rules, but regularly bend them when the need arises. The list goes on and on. Histrionics seem like phonies and hypocrites, but if that's how you see them, you are likely to make the biggest mistake you can possibly make with a Histrionic: attempting to end their self-deception and make them see reality the way you do.

Unless you want to bring suffering down upon yourself, what you say to Histrionics must be consistent with what they believe about themselves. If you try to tell them that they aren't who they think they are, the least that can go wrong is that they won't hear you. To deal effectively with Histrionics, you have to understand how their minds work and operate within those constraints.

Histrionics were Freud's favorite patients. They taught him everything he knew about the unconscious. Histrionics invented *repression*, which means banishing disturbing thoughts from awareness. Repression is, by definition, an unconscious process. If you know you're doing it, it doesn't work. Telling a Histrionic that he or she is in denial is worse than useless.

In the world of Histrionics, you *can* be a vegetarian who eats fish and chicken, or a manager who has no clue that there are real problems in his or her department.

The secret to dealing with Histrionics is to know them better than they know themselves. Even in their most positive and enthusiastic moments, somewhere in the back of their minds is a vague feeling that something is amiss that could cause the attention and approval they crave to vanish. This is the fear you must speak to but never name. Though Histrionics can never be wrong or bad, they are always eager to do better and be better. This is the drive you must tap into to be effective. If you are wondering how to do it, turn on the TV or open any magazine. The art and science of advertising is based upon this very premise.

To communicate effectively with Histrionics, you have to speak in the language of commercials and ad copy. In the next chapter, we'll discuss this further. For now, your first task is to recognize Histrionics in all their various forms. The following checklist should help you, since, as we shall see, the Histrionic style manifests itself in so many different ways.

### THE HISTRIONIC VAMPIRE CHECKLIST

True or false: Score one point for each *true* answer.

1. This person usually stands out in a crowd by virtue of looks, dress, or personality. T F

2. This person is outgoing, friendly, enthusiastic, entertaining, and absolutely wonderful in social situations. T F

3. This person likes meetings. T F

4. This person often speaks in superlatives. T F

5. This person treats superficial acquaintances as if they were close friends. T F

6. This person loves to chat, gossip, and tell stories. T F

7. This person is rarely found at his or her desk actually working. T F

8. This person's eyes glaze over when anyone talks about technical details. T F

9. When asked for specifics, this person often responds with vivid but vague clichés, buzzwords, or sports metaphors.　T　F

10. This person believes that attitude is everything.　T　F

11. This person often talks behind people's backs.　T　F

12. This person acts shocked and betrayed if anyone talks behind his or her back.　T　F

13. This person does not claim to be smart, but cannot conceive of being wrong.　T　F

14. This person is unpredictable in stressful situations. He or she may overreact, completely withdraw, or both.　T　F

15. This person cannot tolerate criticism.　T　F

16. This person doesn't admit to being angry, even when his or her anger is quite apparent to everybody.　T　F

17. This person often spaces out day-to-day details.　T　F

18. This person sends a lot of e-mails that are hard to decipher. You can tell if he or she is upset about something, but you may not be able to figure out what it is or what he or she wants you to do about it.　T　F

19. This person has one or more unusual ailments that come and go according to no discernible pattern.　T　F

20. This person fervently follows several television shows or sports teams.　T　F

Scoring: Five or more true answers qualifies the person as a Histrionic Emotional Vampire, though not necessarily for a diagnosis of Histrionic Personality Disorder. If the person scores higher than 10, be careful. What he or she doesn't know can hurt you.

## WHAT THE QUESTIONS MEASURE

The specific behaviors covered on the checklist relate to several underlying personality characteristics that define a Histrionic Emotional Vampire.

## Extroversion

Histrionics are social creatures to a fault. They score at the far end of the introversion-extroversion continuum. This means more than being outgoing, though they are definitely that. The introversion-extroversion continuum actually refers to where people's reality is located. For introverts, reality is inside their heads; for extroverts, reality is out there in their relations with other people. We all fall somewhere on the continuum, usually in the moderate range. As we mature, we acquire some of the skills that the other group comes by naturally, because both sets are essential. Introverts learn to socialize, and extroverts learn introspection.

It takes considerable skill for an introvert to act like an extrovert and vice versa. Histrionics don't make that effort. They are so far out on the extroverted side that they can hardly conceive of anything below the surface. This handicap can be a tremendous advantage, at least in the short run. The world is biased in favor of extroverts. We like them more and attribute abilities to them that they may not have. Nowhere is this more apparent than in the world of business, where attitude and motivation are everything.

Antisocials, Histrionics, and Narcissists all tend to be extroverted, Histrionics most of all. Obsessive-Compulsives are introverted. We may need them, but we are not drawn to them.

Most of us enjoy Histrionics' company, at least most of the time. They can be cheerful, cordial, witty, sexy, exciting, or anything else you want, except substantial. Without Histrionics, the world would be a less friendly place, all business, devoid of drama and style.

## Need for Approval

Histrionic vampires love attention when it's positive. They strive for social acceptability and work hard to live up to everyone's expectations—unless those expectations involve taking care of boring day-to-day details.

Histrionics believe that everybody should think they're wonderful. They regard criticism either as meaningless grumpiness to be charmed away or as an affront to natural law. Either way, they will not hear anything but unqualified praise. Even when they appear to find fault with themselves, they ascribe it to low self-esteem rather than accurate perception. If you are a good friend, you are expected to talk them out of it.

If you dare to criticize, you will be astounded at how quickly their perceptions of you can change from being the most wonderful person in the world to evil incarnate.

## Unpredictability

Histrionic reality is defined by gut feelings rather than objective facts. A butterfly flapping its wings in China is sufficient to change a Histrionic's mood. Even less is required to change his or her mind.

In high-stress situations, Histrionics become confused and erratic. It's a toss-up whether they will overreact or deny that there is any kind of problem.

## Belief in Magic

Histrionics believe that if they want something enough, it will somehow come to them. They may not state the belief in this way, but it can be inferred from their words and actions. The mechanism by which this magic happens may involve a specific supernatural entity or an undefined force that requires little effort beyond absolute faith and sincere desire. This Histrionic belief has manifested itself in countless forms and traditions. Letters to Santa, the New Age movement, and motivational rallies at your office are all based on the fond hope that if you want something enough, it will happen.

There is truth to this statement, but it is metaphoric rather than literal. Histrionics do not distinguish between the two. For them, the magic is real.

## Lack of Concern with Details

Histrionics don't think much about how or why things happen. They just do.

Histrionics often know less about their own motivation than about that of their favorite celebrities and sports figures.

## Vague Communication

Histrionics love buzzwords and sports metaphors. The way they think of sports is all pep talk and no playbook.

## Physical Symptoms

Histrionics invented the undiagnosable illness. Their lives are confusions of reality and fantasy, obsession and repression, impulse and inhibition.

When they are under stress, they experience it in their bodies rather than in their minds. Illness to them is a form of expression to be interpreted like poems as well as treated with medicine and surgery. Histrionics get backaches when they can't stand up to somebody.

Or constipation when they can't take any more crap.

It rarely occurs to them that the kind of treatment they need is psychological rather than medical. Their idea of the cure for stress is tranquilizers or antidepressants rather than changing thoughts or behavior.

The Histrionics you will encounter at work come in two basic styles: Hams, who crave attention and will do whatever it takes to get it, and Passive-Aggressives, who want approval so much that they cannot possibly think or do anything that is unacceptable.

Under the skin, the two types are quite similar. There is only one show business.

9

# The Magical World of Histrionic Hams

**T**HINK OF THE HISTRIONIC personality as a tangled mass of unrecognized contradictions that is plastered over, covered with a glossy coat of paint, and presented to you as the new, improved model of whatever you want to see. It's magic—unless you look below the surface.

Histrionics are best at looking good. They run into some difficulties when it comes to knowing who they are and what they're doing. The important thing for you to remember in dealing with Histrionics is what you see is definitely *not* what you get.

The simplest and least dangerous Histrionics you'll meet at work are the ham-it-up performers who crave attention so much that they overdo everything. Let's say that subtlety is not their long suit. They can't seem to figure out the difference between an office and reality TV.

You've seen them: a common version is the Barbie-wannabe with stiletto heels, short skirt, and skintight blouse so tiny that you can see the top of her tramp-stamp when she bends over, which she does quite often in front of gullible guys who are only too happy to do her work for her. You may find this hard to believe, but Histrionic Barbies really have no idea that anyone would mistake their sassy friendliness for a real sexual come-on. Pity the poor fool who does.

The people who are most often drained by Barbies and other Histrionic Hams are those few who are actually taken in and Believers who get overly annoyed at their flagrant phoniness and unprofessional behavior.

If Barbies bother you, remember that, like all Histrionics, they are not trying to deceive you or anyone else. They are deceiving themselves. Barbies are far less aware than you are of their blatant sexuality or manipulativeness. If their outrageous behavior outrages you, you will be the one who suffers. It's best to enjoy the show, but don't join the cast.

Male Histrionics also come to work in costume. There are *Mad Men*–wannabes wearing swanky suits from the discount place at the mall and way too much aftershave. Another favorite persona is the lovable dork from just about any sitcom you could name. Depending on where you are, you might even find a cowboy or two, but they're never the strong silent type.

Male-pattern Histrionic sexuality is usually verbal rather than visual. They all seem addicted to off-color attempts at humor. Sometimes they can be really funny, but even then, they border on the pathetic.

Whatever you do, don't laugh. Histrionics mistake polite chuckles for guffaws.

Histrionic stand-up comedians can be annoying, but they are not usually dangerous unless you make an issue of their behavior. I know that there are rules about sexual harassment, but I'd think twice about trying to invoke them unless your lawyer happens to be present as a witness. Remember Anita Hill at the Clarence Thomas hearings.

There are some sexual harassers who definitely need to be stopped. Histrionics just need to be ignored.

If you just want these guys to quit bothering you, the most effective response is no response at all. If possible, just walk away without saying anything.

Histrionic Hams can hurt you only if you are fooled or outraged. Then, you can get hurt badly indeed. The same is true about the Passive-Aggressives we will meet in the next chapter.

Enjoy the show, but don't join the cast, or, better yet, just walk away.

Unfortunately, there are Histrionics you can't walk away from, like your boss.

## MANAGEMENT BY MAGIC

Histrionics believe in magic. They can make problems disappear by ignoring them. Their personalities are structured around the conviction that if they are cheerful and positive enough, everything will work out. Don't ask them how, just shut up and believe.

Histrionic managers are extroverts. They don't spend much time inside their heads balancing alternatives and thinking things through. Instead, they focus outward, trying to inspire their subordinates. If everybody has a positive attitude, complications disappear; the difficult becomes easy, and problems go away. It is also makes great theater.

The name they give this magical approach to management is *motivation.*

Cleve Gower, former basketball player, sports commentator, and renowned motivational speaker (and Histrionic Ham), is already sweating beneath the lights. You can see every crystalline drop on the huge video screen behind him.

"I played against Jordan," Cleve thunders over the PA. "Michael Jordan is my friend. A great athlete and an even greater human being. One day, Michael Jordan and I were talking. 'Cleve,' he said, 'there are a lot of guys out there with talent, but you and I know that the guys who really make it are the ones with the right kind of attitude.'

"I don't have to tell you that Michael Jordan lived what he preached. *He* had the right attitude. The question I'm here to ask today is: Do you have the same kind of attitude as Michael Jordan?" Cleve pauses for the question to sink in. His giant eyes scan the people in the audience, looking, it seems, into their very souls.

"It's like Michael said, 'The ones who really make it are the guys with the right attitude. If *you* have the right attitude, no one is big enough to block your shot at success.'" There is a smattering of applause, but Cleve waves it away.

"Take me. I wasn't born a successful athlete. I admit I had a little talent when I was growing up dirt-poor in the slums of San Diego. That talent counted for absolutely nothing. Why? Because I had asthma. It was so serious that the doctor told my mother I wouldn't live to graduate from high school." Cleve nods gravely. "That's right; he said I wouldn't live through high school. But now that doctor is dead, and here I am talking to you. Why? Because I had the right attitude!" The applause is louder this time. Cleve waves it away again.

"I *refused* to believe that even asthma could hold me back. And that's why I'm here today. Here to tell you that *attitude is everything! If you have the right kind of attitude, nothing and nobody can hold you back!*" Now the cheering starts.

Motivational speakers retell the central heroic myth of sports and business: if you have the right attitude, anything is possible. The concept is indispensable for success, but it is metaphor and not literal fact. Attitude is not really everything. Training, ability, specific knowledge, and clear direction all count for something. In the minds of Histrionics, however, magic is always preferable to complicated details.

Sometimes the magic works, but not exactly in the way Histrionics think it does. In order to deal effectively with Histrionics, we need to do what they don't and look more closely at the technical aspects of how things are done rather than how people are feeling when they do them. Bear with me on some details.

In addition to being endowed with natural talent, Michael Jordan spent countless hours practicing every detail of his art, especially the parts he found difficult. I'd guess that he went about it in the way most high-achieving people do. First, he figured out what specific goals he needed to accomplish. Also, he probably had quite a few skilled coaches to help him with this task, because that's what coaches are for. Pep talks in the locker room may be good theater, but they work only after long hours of training and practice.

Next, Michael Jordan had to make himself put in those long hours. To do this, he had to create internal contingencies, encouraging and rewarding himself to keep going. He may have called this process "having the right attitude," but it would not have worked if he didn't have specific goals and direction.

Heroic motivation became popular in the less technical days when honest salespeople (not the Con Artists in Chapter 6) rode out in the blue on a smile and a shoeshine. It evokes an element of spirit that is necessary to bounce back after being turned down a dozen times in one day. In that sense it is useful and admirable. From sales, the concept has pervaded the culture of many organizations, spread by Histrionic managers, who embrace the magic because their personalities are long on spirit but short on specific details.

Pep talks can be beneficial as an adjunct to the technical aspects of management, but there is nothing as demotivating to employees as attempting to use the magic of motivation as a substitute for the decisions, support, and guidance that management actually requires. The unintended message that Histrionic managers send to their subordinates is that the only reason they have problems is that they are not motivated enough to make them go away.

At the 7:30 Monday morning team meeting, Gene kicks things off by playing a motivational talk. He must have hundreds downloaded to his phone.

Today it's Cleve Gower, one of his favorites. Every time Cleve makes a good point, Gene writes it on the electronic blackboard, in quotes and underlined. At the end of the meeting, each member of the team will get a printout.

After Cleve is done, Gene steps up to the plate. "Continuous Quality Improvement is the way we become a full-time, customer-driven, learning organization. Creativity! Flexibility! We always need to be on the lookout for ways to do more with less. Like Cleve says, we've got to use our hearts, not just our heads. If we have the right attitude, we can do it all. With the new management information system, we can track our performance, increase our sales, and improve the already excellent service our customers expect."

Steve holds up his hand. "How much improvement are we talking about?"

"No more than we can handle, big guy," Gene answers. "If we just learn to work smarter instead of harder."

Jamal chimes in. "What about the downtime while we're switching to the new system? It's so much more complicated than the old one. There are bound to be glitches."

"I'll be honest with you," Gene says, shaking his head. "Corporate doesn't think you guys can do it all. They said it was way too—what did they call it?—ambitious. But I told them that we had what it takes to come from behind and win."

*Get to the point, already*, Gwen thinks. She lets out a sigh and raises her hand. "I assume there are some specific goals and timelines. Are there some estimates about how much disruption this changeover will actually cause?"

"You know, that could be the problem right there," Gene says. He gets up and writes the word ASSUME on the board, then draws lines on either side of the U, so that it reads ASS/U/ME. "When you assume, you make an ASS out of U and ME."

Sometimes at these meetings Gwen feels as if she's fallen down a rabbit hole into Wonderland. Nothing makes sense, and there are a lot of big, empty smiles.

What is Gene getting paid those big bucks to do?

The answer is *look good*. He does that really well. When it comes to management, he falls short, but nobody important seems to care.

Real management is a balancing act. Histrionics like Gene are terrible at balancing. They are afraid that if they are too specific about what's needed in one area, it will limit performance in other areas. This is true, but it is the lot of managers everywhere. No matter how motivated you are, nobody can get everybody to do more of everything all the time.

Histrionic managers get around this difficulty by assuming that everyone is like them. Histrionics really believe they can do it all, because they repress everything they can't do. Their internal world is simple; imagine it as a single dial with settings that go from Good to Great to Excellent and on up to the stratosphere. The other end of the dial is labeled simply *Don't go there*.

Gene's simple world can be dangerous to people who don't understand it. His idea of employee performance evaluation is two big boxes. One is for "good guys" with good attitudes who can do their jobs without requiring much besides pep talks and an occasional attaboy or attagirl. Then there is the bottomless pit for "bad guys." If Gwen doesn't watch out, she could wind up there.

One of the many contradictions in the Histrionic personality is in the way they classify people. They think you're wonderful until they think you're terrible. All you have to do to cross the line is criticize them. Histrionics hate conflict, yet they create far more than their share of it. Of course, they don't see it that way. To them, it's *your* negative attitude that causes the problems.

So, what should Gwen do? All she really wants is to get Gene to do his job by giving some straight answers, engaging in a discussion about what goals are possible and realistic, and then making a decision and sticking with it for more than 10 minutes. How do you get a Histrionic manager to actually manage?

Gwen is not the only one who has this problem. Middle management in many organizations is full of Histrionics like Gene, who got where they are by being positive and motivated, and stay there by seeing that nobody rocks the boat. It's easy to be irritated or even to make fun of them, but you do so at your peril. Hell hath no fury like a Histrionic scorned.

Histrionics can be influenced to do a better job, but it requires clear, slow thinking and some careful stagecraft.

## HOW TO GET YOUR HISTRIONIC MANAGER TO ACTUALLY MANAGE FOR A CHANGE

If you want to get your manager to manage, you have to start with a clearer idea than he or she has about what management is and how it's done.

Managing is more a way of thinking than it is the performance of specific tasks. It involves integrating a large, ever-changing set of personal and organizational needs. Managing is a large-scale version of the task that Histrionics have such a hard time doing within their own personalities. Instead of integrating conflicting forces, Histrionics tend to focus intensely on some of them and ignore others, not seeing that there are relationships between them. In their own lives, and in their jobs, Histrionics devoutly wish for everything to run smoothly. Of course, it never does. Problems keep coming up, raising unpleasant anxieties that Histrionics try to calm down as quickly as possible by playing the nice guy and telling everybody whatever they want to hear. Needless to say, solving problems in this way ensures that problems will increase exponentially. This is the dilemma that Histrionics face as individuals and as managers. Unfortunately, Histrionics don't understand dilemmas.

As a therapist, one of my first goals with Histrionic patients is to help them recognize that many of the things they see as problems are actually dilemmas. This insight helps them make better choices by recognizing that each choice affects all the others, which to them is often a completely new idea.

Here's how I explain it to Histrionic managers: A problem can be solved, and with luck it goes away. Once you've figured out how to get an order out the door on time, the shipment is gone and the problem with it. Dilemmas are not solved; instead, they must be continuously balanced. More of one means less of the other. Some examples are quality vs. cost, speed vs. accuracy, or profit vs. market share. If you "solve" a dilemma by moving too far in one direction, you create problems that can only be solved by moving in the other.

In order to get a Histrionic manger to do his or her job, you have to do some of the same things I do as a therapist. This is undoubtedly an unfair burden to place on your shoulders, but it is either that or submitting to an endless series of contradictory directions plastered over with motivational talks.

This is the dilemma you face with a Histrionic boss—or with a boss of any other vampire type, for that matter. You shouldn't have to do things that aren't part of your job to get them to do theirs, but if you don't, you have to face the consequences.

The sad truth is, everywhere you go, at work or elsewhere, you will have to deal with powerful people who are not as mature as you are. You can't tell them what to do, but you can influence them if you are willing to make the effort. The effort involves understanding how they think well enough to communicate within their own frame of reference.

The basic pattern for getting people to act in a more mature fashion is the same one that therapists use: you step into their world, and from there, encourage them to think more rationally by asking well-crafted questions that gently lead them in the direction you want them to go. We have already used this approach in dealing with Bullies and Con Artists. With Histrionics, we can look at the technique in a more sophisticated way and make a few refinements.

## HOW TO ENTER THE EMOTIONAL VAMPIRE WORLD WITHOUT BECOMING A VAMPIRE YOURSELF

We've talked about stepping out of a behavioral pattern by avoiding the response vampires expect, thereby causing them to stop and think instead of merely reacting. This is the essential strategy for calming emotional situations, especially those involving the fight-or-flight response. What we are discussing now is actually an expansion of this technique that may help you prevent the emotional situations before they happen.

Entering the vampire world does not mean becoming a vampire yourself. It does mean being able to think like them and doing some of the same things they do, but in slightly different ways and for different reasons. The most significant difference is that you are acting consciously to achieve a goal instead of merely reacting emotionally as vampires do. Slow thinking will keep you safe.

The one thing you have to let go of to be able to enter another person's world safely is making judgments about whether that world is right or wrong. If you can't let go of the judgments, you must recognize them and keep them to yourself. The minute you start lecturing, you're dead.

In interpersonal relations, the most useless conflict you can engage in is a dominance struggle over who is right and who is wrong. As we have seen, these struggles cannot be resolved, and once they start, they never end. Despite their futility, they are the easiest conflicts to fall into, if you aren't paying attention. Not paying attention in this case means mistaking your own assumptions for natural law.

Based on the Rebel, Believer, or Competitor test in Chapter 3, you already know something about your assumptions about how to think and act at work. You also know that yours are not the only assumptions possible. Remember this as we go forward.

Stepping into someone else's world means accepting, but not necessarily agreeing with, their assumptions, and using those as a basis for communication. To be effective with difficult people, you have to be able to think like they do and use their strengths to counteract their weaknesses.

In the Histrionic world, the most important commodities are attention and approval. They are so important that Histrionics believe that they are always on stage and they cannot even imagine doing anything that their audience would not applaud. This is the world that managers like Gene live in.

If you are a Rebel, you may see Gene as full of bullshit. If you're a Believer, you might see him as lacking integrity. Competitors may see him as incompetent. All of these judgments may be accurate, but none of them will be useful to you in getting him to do his job.

To influence emotional vampires, you have to imagine a world in which their assumptions apply, and speak and act as if you live there. With Histrionics like Gene, this will not be too hard because you've actually been there. His world is called "high school."

Most Histrionics were really successful in high school, where their social skills and positive attitudes were rewarded with popularity, good grades, and leadership positions in student government. While you were out partying, or at your desk trying to figure out algebra, they were at pep rallies, sports practice, and meetings of the drama club.

In high school, Histrionics learned about a psychological principle called "halo effect." They didn't call it that, but they certainly benefited from it. Countless social psychological studies have shown that authority figures, like teachers and coaches, see likable, extroverted people as smarter, more talented, more responsible, and all-around better than their more introverted or rebellious peers. Needless to say, "halo effect" carries over to the corporate world. It is the secret to Histrionics' success. That's why there are so many of them in management. Histrionics believe they were promoted because of their school spirit, which is what halo effect is called in their world.

In order to communicate effectively with Histrionics, you have to, in effect, go back to high school. Now, you will be going not as the teenager you were then, but as the adult you are now. Perhaps you'll learn a few tricks you didn't pick up the first time around. Here are some of the things Histrionics did then that may be useful to you now in dealing with them and with other vampire authority figures.

## TREAT THEM THE WAY THEY TREAT IMPORTANT PEOPLE

Regardless of whether you were a nerd, a jock, a stoner, or someone who was just not paying attention, if you want to be effective with bosses, especially Histrionics, you have to treat them in the same way the popular kids treated their high school teachers.

Histrionics call this "being respectful." Just about everybody else calls it "sucking up."

Regardless of what it's called in your world, sucking up is a useful skill. Your disdain may have prevented you from learning how to do it in high school. If so, you may need some remedial work.

Here are some of the specific techniques those popular kids used on their teachers. Call them whatever you like, but you will find them helpful in dealing with all kinds of bosses. The more dysfunctional your boss is, the better these techniques will work. Try them and see.

**ENGAGE YOUR BOSS IN CONVERSATION:** Popular kids talked to adults as if they were regular people. Rebels in high school did not fraternize with the enemy. They still don't. Believers didn't want to bother busy people, and Competitors didn't bother to talk unless they had something to say. Histrionic Populars just chatted away about anything and everything, as they did with their friends. The assumption teachers made based on these behavioral choices was that the Populars liked them and the other kids didn't. Bosses today make that same assumption.

**LISTEN WITH INTEREST:** Populars always sat in the front of the room and took notes. Rebels sat in the back and still do.

**DEMONSTRATE LEARNING:** Believers and Competitors attempted to demonstrate learning by doing well on tests. Rebels often did it by correcting the teacher's mistakes. Popular kids talked to teachers about what they learned in class and how they used it. They would also ask their teachers for advice and actually take it. Then they would come back and tell the teachers how well it worked.

Histrionic bosses see themselves as teachers dispensing pearls of wisdom. If you want them to listen to you, listen to them. Don't be a swine.

**BE POSITIVE:** Do I need to explain this one?

The skill formerly known as sucking up essentially involves treating authority figures as if you like and respect them. Emotional vampires excel at recognizing how people want to be seen and using that as the basis for communicating with them. This is something we can learn from them. It is one of the most effective ways of getting people to listen to you and do what you want them to do. Sucking up works just as well for cooperation as it does for exploitation. How you use it is up to you.

**PUTTING IT ALL TOGETHER**

If you are as frustrated with your Histrionic manager as Gwen is with Gene, here's how you might step into his or her world, and use the techniques we've discussed to coax out a little real management for a change.

**Know Your Goal:** Real management involves resolving dilemmas. The goal you should try for is to get your Histrionic manager to define a balance point between the horns and stick with it rather than jumping back and forth. The product you should go for is a rank order of priorities that you can count on, meaning one that your manager will defend before his or her manager.

This goal is possible to attain if you are willing to step into the Histrionic's world and put on a little performance of your own.

**First, Suck Up:** The idea is to create your own halo effect by doing the things a popular high school kid would do. If Gwen wants Gene to listen to her, she has to have built up a track record of appearing positive and motivated.

**Write Your Manager a Heroic Role:** Histrionics are actors, but the roles they invent for themselves are rather thin. You can do better if you put your mind to it. What you want is a metaphor a manager like Gene will take literally. An excellent choice is "shepherd watching over his flock." If you're looking for metaphors, you might as well go all the way to the top.

To see what Gwen might do, let's go back to the team meeting, just after Cleve Gower finishes his spiel and before Gene starts his.

Gene has just turned off the motivational talk on his phone. He's still nodding and smiling at the wisdom of Cleve's words.

> Gwen raises her hand, and Gene points to her. Just like in high school. "Those are some great ideas!" she says. "The other day, I was reading an article in *Fortune* about leaders as servants. How does that relate to what Cleve was saying?"
>
> "Good question!" Gene says, and he launches into an explanation. What he says doesn't much matter, because Gwen's purpose is to connect these two admirable concepts in Gene's mind and set him up for a third.
>
> "Oh, I get it," she says. "A leader as servant is like a shepherd watching over his flock."

Yes, what Gwen is doing is blatantly manipulative. One of the assumptions you have to let go of if you are to safely enter the vampire world is that manipulation is bad. Believers, pay attention! This information could save your sanity. Manipulation itself is neutral. Moral judgments apply only to the way manipulation is used. We all manipulate people all the time. Some of us are better at it than others. Some of us are even good enough to go pro. Like all therapists, I get paid for manipulating people.

**WRITE A ROLE FOR YOURSELF:**  If Gene is a shepherd, Gwen needs to play the little lost lamb.

> Later in the meeting, Gwen shakes her head, but she continues to smile, showing that her heart is still in the right place. "Gene, all this change is so confusing. There are so many choices. I really want to do the right thing, but I just can't figure out what to do first."

Do you see where this is heading? Gene will undoubtedly respond first with platitudes. Gwen will, of course, listen and nod as if they made sense. Then she will ask the real question:

> "What would you do if you were me?"

Gwen is leading Gene toward coming up with a rank order of priorities, but she is getting him to do it as her rather than as himself. In this way, according to Histrionic logic, any mistakes will be hers, not his. Asking a Histrionic to understand you is a waste of time. Asking one to play you often yields a totally different response.

Like all emotional vampires, Histrionics have very little real empathy, but they can easily pretend to be another person. This is what acting is all about. Don't ask how it works; just use it.

Gwen and the other members of her team can ask Gene to play each of them in turn, thereby yielding the priorities they need to do their job. All they need to do is write them down as goals and objectives. Some subtlety is needed, but not so much as you might think.

So far, so good. The final act of this little drama is designed to make it more likely that Gene will defend the priorities he's been tricked into setting when he's questioned about them by his boss.

> Gwen continues her own performance by helping Gene to write a script for his. "So, we're all in agreement that this changeover is so important that we need to be as careful as possible. No rushing through it. What will they say upstairs if you tell them it's going to take longer and maybe even set us back a little? Will they think the product is worth the wait and the expense? Do they believe that quality is job one?"
>
> "Of course they do," Gene says. "They say it all the time."
>
> "Excellent!" Gwen says. "We can put all this together on PowerPoint so you can present it."

Preposterous as this scenario may seem, I can tell you based on years of experience that tactics like this work better on personality disordered managers than more direct and businesslike approaches. I can't guarantee that everything will go according to the script I've written here. The words may vary, but the basic idea, transparent as it may be, will work surprisingly well with Histrionics and, as we will see, with some other types of vampire bosses.

Emotional vampires may be dangerous and powerful, but they all have vulnerabilities that you can use to trick them into being more mature and doing a better job.

One final word on this matter: take a tip from Gwen. When a vampire boss is going to present your case to his or her superiors, always make the PowerPoint presentation yourself, if you possibly can. Your boss will be happy to let you do the work; believe me, that work is worth doing.

## BOSS OR BFF?

Histrionic bosses are not good at boundaries. They tend to see all their relationships as much more intimate than they actually are. Like best buddies in high school. The same kind of bosses who emphasize professionalism and high motivation at team meetings can drop the façade the minute they get into your cube, and can turn before your eyes into an insecure and dependent 15-year-old. The trick here is stepping out of the pattern and not turning into a 15-year-old yourself.

Marge, Brenda's boss, lets out a huge sigh as she lowers herself into Brenda's visitor chair. "It feels so good to sit down. I walked all the way over here from a management meeting on the other side of campus.

"These shoes." Marge takes off one of her Blahniks and begins rubbing her feet. "You'd think that for what they cost, they'd at least be comfortable. I really should get some shoes like you wear." She leans over to get a better view of Brenda's feet. "Yeah, like those. They are so cute, and they look like you could actually walk in them. Are they comfortable?"

Brenda nods. "They really are."

"Where did you get them?"

"There's this shoe boutique on Sixty-Eighth Street that I go to," Brenda says. "They have lots of styles at pretty reasonable prices."

"Really?" Marge sounds excited. "Maybe we should check it out at lunch tomorrow."

Is there anything wrong with going shoe shopping with your boss? Of course not. People form friendships with coworkers all the time. If your boss is a Histrionic, however, it might be a good idea to think about what that friendship could be like before you get too deeply involved in it.

Do you remember the popular girls in high school? Sometimes their friendships were like a queen and her court, in that there was a dominant person at the center, with retainers around her who were expected to take care of her and do her will.

Marge is already in a dominant position with regard to Brenda. The question is whether the rules of dominance that apply at work would carry over into the friendship. I listed some of those rules in Chapter 5. If you have a question about being friends with your boss, it might be a good idea to go back and review them.

Bear in mind also that relationships with emotional vampires generally follow the grooming pattern discussed in Chapter 6. They start out innocently enough, but once you are in them, you find yourself crossing one little line after another until you find yourself in over your head. Grooming is generally not a conscious or planful process on either side. It just happens because vampires don't recognize boundaries. They just keep asking for more and more.

What Histrionics keep asking for more and more of is emotional support. Beneath the shiny exterior, they are often a mass of insecurities that they do not completely understand or acknowledge. They need someone more stable to keep telling them that they are who they think they are, and to demonstrate that they are worthwhile by catering to their needs for conversation and entertainment. Unlike with more mature friendships, with Histrionics, relationships are unbalanced. It's all about them. Not only that, it's about them as they think they are. You can't level with them about parts of them that they don't want to see. As we have seen, Histrionics are fickle. They think you're wonderful until they think you're terrible.

Being friends with your boss can be a positive experience, or it can be like taking on a dependent 15-year-old who has control over your livelihood.

If you, like Brenda, are surprised and perhaps flattered by unexpected attention from your boss, how should you decide whether to go shoe shopping? Here are some suggestions.

**SWITCH OFF YOUR AUTOPILOT:** Deciding whether to have an outside work relationship with your boss requires slow, careful thinking. There are definitely pros and cons to consider. If you are a Believer, your first impulse may be to be polite and just go ahead. Competitors may see a career-enhancing opportunity, thinking that they can maintain control of the relationship. Rebels may miss the opportunity through inattention or because it isn't part of their job.

At the beginning, there is no way to tell where the relationship will go. It could be a rewarding friendship or a good career move, or both. It could also be a tremendous mistake. Whatever starting a friendship with your boss might be in the future, at the beginning it is an important decision that needs to be carefully considered. Ask yourself a few questions before you decide.

**Is Your Boss an Emotional Vampire?** One way to make an informed decision is by using the checklists in this book. If your boss qualifies as one of the vampire types, it might be a good idea to keep a formal distance.

If you decide to decline offers to do things, the most tactful way to do it is by being too busy. It would be hard for your boss to fault you for being too serious about your job.

Be cheerful and friendly but emphatic. Your boss may think you're stuffy and no fun, but in the long run, that might be a positive outcome.

**Is There Any Possible Sexual Attraction?** Histrionics are often unaware of their own sexual feelings. All the more reason you should be.

**Can You Say No?** If your boss doesn't take no for an answer about a shopping excursion, think about what it will be like when the stakes are higher later.

If your boss fits the Histrionic pattern, beneath the energetic cheerfulness there is a lot of neediness and very little compunction about demanding that you fill it.

**Is the Relationship Reciprocal?** Is your boss as eager to run your errands with you as he or she is to have you accompany him or her? (Male Histrionics are less likely to ask you to go shopping. They usually want to do guy things like going to sports events or checking out cars or electronic gadgets.)

Reciprocity is a good indicator of overall maturity. Brenda cannot know the answers to all these questions when Marge first suggests shoe shopping. One way Brenda might get a rough idea about how the relationship will go is by suggesting a second stop on the excursion to do something she wants to do. Marge's reaction, especially if it's negative, will yield useful information about what the future might be like.

I am not saying that you should never be friends with a Histrionic boss. I am pointing out that problems with boundaries are a typical part of the overall picture. You need to be careful.

One final word of warning has to do with gossip. Histrionics love it, and they cannot keep secrets. They will pump you for any juicy information you may have. A good rule to follow is never tell a Histrionic anything you wouldn't post on Facebook.

In the next chapter, on Passive-Aggressives, we will deal with gossip in more detail.

# Passive-Aggressives

## 10

**B**EING PASSIVE-AGGRESSIVE means never having to say you're sorry. That's because you're never aware of doing, or even thinking, anything that you need to be sorry about.

*Passive-Aggressive* is a term that is used to describe many different behaviors ranging from procrastinating and forgetting to rumor spreading or even illnesses. All involve irritating actions (or inactions) that are not perceived as antagonistic by the person performing them.

The most common form of Passive-Aggressive behavior is getting out of doing something unpleasant by forgetting or misunderstanding instructions. You don't have to be a vampire to use this strategy; everybody does it.

Next, there are people with authority issues who respond to being told what to do with surliness and foot-dragging. Several vampire types and many Rebels are afflicted with this chronic form of adolescent rebellion.

Most Passive-Aggressive behavior at work falls into these two categories. Such infractions usually fall short of the requirements for taking formal disciplinary action. If you make an issue of them, you're the one who ends up looking bad. However, as we'll see later in this chapter, these forms of Passive-Aggressive behavior can often be controlled through judicious use of contingencies.

Histrionic emotional vampires raise Passive-Aggressiveness to another level entirely. Their irritating actions are a by-product of their own internal struggle to win acceptance and approval from everyone everywhere. They are not merely unaware of their own hostility; they think they are always being supernice. If you seem irritated at their behavior, you will be cast as an abuser, and they will become victims, a role that they play with chilling authenticity. In their world, victims get to defend themselves against their abusers. Bear in mind that most of the great atrocities of history were perpetrated by people who perceived themselves as victims who were acting in self-defense.

Needless to say, Histrionic Passive-Aggressives are by far the most dangerous nice people you will ever meet. At work, if their hidden hostility is not handled correctly, it can lead to general disruption, morale problems, rampant factionalism, and even lawsuits.

Most Passive-Aggressive Histrionics are merely annoying, but they can be treacherous. All of them are confusing and complicated. Nothing is ever direct, and nothing is what it seems to be. Let's start with a typical example.

> Eileen makes more mistakes than anyone on your team, but she never admits to them. Somehow, it's always someone else's problem.
>
> You ask her to do something she doesn't want to do. You can tell she doesn't want to do it by the snorting, which she says is from sinus problems, or the eye rolling, which according to her is the result of staring at a computer screen all day. Nevertheless, she agrees, then either forgets, misunderstands, or goes ahead with whatever she wanted to do in the first place. Or she does absolutely nothing because she is sure you gave her the wrong instructions. If you say something to her, she will be offended and explain how it's your fault for not being clear. She may even cry because you're picking on her.

Eileen, like most Passive-Aggressive Histrionics, is a headache waiting to happen.

Passive-Aggressives are among the hardest people in the world to work with. They never admit to being angry themselves, but they have no trouble getting other people angry at them. Always unjustly.

You may wonder how someone like Eileen, who is actually no dummy, can be so utterly clueless about her effect on other people. What can she possibly be thinking?

Actually, that is the relevant question, but not in the exasperated way people usually ask it. It is your frustration at Eileen for not acting the way you think she should rather than her behavior that causes the pain in your head. Remember, if you are outraged by outrageous people, you will be the one to suffer. To ease the pain, let's go back to the original question, this time taken literally: What is she thinking?

Eileen thinks that she is a really nice, very competent person who is repeatedly mistreated by people demanding that she do things that either make no sense or are not humanly possible.

To you, and to just about everybody else, these herculean labors are merely parts of her job that she doesn't feel like doing. You're right, of course, but being right won't help you a bit, especially if you try to convince Eileen that she's wrong.

## PASSIVE-AGGRESSIVE MARTIAL ARTS

Passive-Aggressives like Eileen practice a peculiar kind of martial art that looks like just being nice but feels like being hit upside the head with a two-by-four. If you approach them directly, they will use the force of your attack against you. To defend yourself, you have to practice a martial art of your own. It requires the Zen-like calm of a Jedi knight and the chutzpah of a Jewish mother.

Let's start with the calm. Here are some suggestions that might help you keep the Force with you.

**UNDERSTAND THAT SHE ISN'T LYING:** Don't work yourself up by judging Eileen by your standards. If you were acting as she does, you'd have to lie to bring it off. Eileen doesn't. The fact that she's angry at you and is fighting back with obstinate behavior may be apparent to everyone else on earth, but it is indiscernible to her. In that peculiar Histrionic way, Eileen has divided herself into what is all sweetness and light and what isn't there. Nothing you can say will change that. Forget any attempt to make her admit to what she's doing. It will only make her cry and give you an even worse headache.

As with all Histrionics, to communicate effectively with her, you have to step into her world. You cannot say anything that conflicts with her view of herself.

**CONTROL YOUR THOUGHTS:** Passive-Aggressives are like those woven finger traps we had as kids. The harder you pull, the harder it is to get out.

The more intense you are, the more likely they are to retaliate with misunderstanding, forgetting, or sabotage. If you get angry, you will lose.

You need to recognize that getting angry is something you do, not an inevitable reaction to someone else's behavior. To control yourself, you have to be aware of the traps you can fall into that will lead you to react emotionally rather than think.

If you're a Rebel, your first impulse might be to get back at Eileen by doing some of the same things to her that she seems to be doing to you. Sarcastic rejoinders and mimicking are the weapons of choice. The rationale, if you can call it that, is to show her how it feels to be messed with, so she'll know better than to mess with you. To the best of my knowledge, this strategy has never worked on anyone, ever. It is direct, unfiltered dinosaur brain thinking that always leads to escalation.

If you're a Believer, you can make yourself so angry at Eileen's dishonesty and lack of work ethic that you are tempted to lecture her on how responsible people are supposed to behave. Sermons, no matter how well crafted, have no more effect on Passive-Aggressives than blunt sarcasm.

Competitors, who prize inside knowledge, are likely to treat Passive-Aggressives as idiots who are beneath contempt.

Any of these immediate reactions will increase your irritation, which will be clearly apparent to Histrionics like Eileen, who are extremely sensitive to anger in others, but not in themselves. The situation will escalate, and you will suffer even more.

As in dealing with all emotional vampires, the only way to win is by using slower, less emotional thinking. Passive-Aggressive behavior is a problem to solve, not an affront to redress.

The following suggestions will help you to deal more effectively with garden variety Passive-Aggressive behaviors at work as well as with Histrionics like Eileen.

DON'T LECTURE: When you think back on your own work ethic, to how you made the transition from adolescence, when goofing off was a reward and work seemed like a punishment, to your present state in which the values have shifted, your memory can play tricks. You may recall a specific time that you didn't work up to your capacity and got a real stem-winder of a sermon, probably from your dad, that really made you change your ways. You might be tempted to re-create this same sort of sermon as a way of instilling virtue into children, coworkers, and other benighted heathens.

Unfortunately, your memory is not reliable. This was not what actually happened. We tend to remember dramatic events and pithy sayings that crystallize what we have already learned rather than the schedules of reinforcement that actually taught us.

That stem-winder sermon most likely occurred within a context of rewards for doing your work well and punishments, usually in the form of lectures, for goofing off. The epiphany you experienced was at least in part the realization that it was easier to do your work than it was to hear the same damn sermon every time you cut corners. For most of us, avoiding sermons, rather than the sermons themselves, is the genesis of the work ethic.

As we saw in Chapter 2, avoidance paradigms are always the most powerful teachers. Passive-Aggressives have learned many of their most annoying behaviors because that conduct has helped them to avoid unpleasant tasks without feeling guilty. They use avoidance paradigms to teach as well as learn. Their snorting, eye rolling, and general obstinacy are actually an avoidance paradigm that teaches hardworking people like you that it is easier to do the job themselves than to get them to do it. This is not a skill you want to learn, because you are giving them big rewards for being Passive-Aggressive.

**USE PUNISHMENT CAREFULLY OR NOT AT ALL:** Slow thinking must be goal directed. The point is to get Eileen to do her job, not to get back at her for not doing her job. Punishment is usually an emotional reaction rather than an actual strategy. It is rarely useful with anyone, but with Passive-Aggressives it can be spectacularly ineffective.

If you are going to use any kind of punishment strategy, it should be completely by the book. Follow the procedures in the employee manual for warnings, documentation, and eventual termination. Don't start on this path unless you are willing to follow it to the end, and have organizational support to do so. If it's a bluff, Passive-Aggressives will call it, thereby demonstrating to themselves and everybody else that the procedures are meaningless.

The worst possible thing you can do if you are in a position of power over a Passive-Aggressive is to be Passive-Aggressive yourself, hoping that they will change their ways or just quit. Believe me, they are much better at this strategy than you are, and they will get you back faster than you can say "hostile work environment."

If Passive-Aggressives think they are being treated unfairly, they are much more likely than other workers to get unions or lawyers involved in disputes, because they are so absolutely sure they are right. They may not win, but they can cause tremendous disruptions that hurt themselves and everyone around them.

If you are in a position of authority and have to deal with someone whose performance is below par, you must decide whether to fire that person or keep him or her. There is no middle ground. Many organizational nightmares have been caused by the mistaken belief that it will be easier to get employees to quit than it will be to fire them.

Believers may avoid firing people because they are trying to be nice. Competitors in cultures that emphasize cost avoidance may see driving a person to quit as a way of saving on unemployment. Such savings will be completely wiped out by the cost of a few hours of legal time.

Enough dire warnings about what will not work with Passive-Aggressives. Let's focus now on what *will*. A useful cliché that will keep you on the right track is that an ounce of prevention is worth a pound of cure. Speaking of clichés, how about accentuate the positive and eliminate the negative? However you phrase them, these time-tested techniques will help you minimize the damage that Passive-Aggressives do to you. With luck, these techniques may even work on your teenagers.

**PAY ATTENTION NOW, OR PAY MORE LATER:** The best approach of all is prevention through attention. Notice Passive-Aggressives. Don't talk to them only when you want them to do something. Stop by on a regular basis, and listen more than you talk.

**CATCH THEM BEING GOOD, AND REWARD THEM:** Prevention involves structuring the situation so that Passive-Aggressives get more rewards for doing the job than for not doing it. If you are not in a supervisory position, you may think you have no control over Eileen's rewards, but that isn't necessarily true. You don't control her paycheck or her annual review, but those aren't the only contingencies in operation.

Remember that to Histrionics, the most important things in the world are attention and approval. For Passive-Aggressives like Eileen, there is an added component. She wants to get all that attention and approval while exerting as little effort as possible. To be effective, you need to accept this and go from there. Catch her being good, and reward her with the attention and approval she craves. When she does something right, praise her for it.

**FOCUS ON BEHAVIOR, NOT ATTITUDE:** You may be able to get Eileen to do her job, but you won't be able to get her to do it without snorting and eye rolling. Don't waste your time trying to improve her attitude or work ethic.

Remove morality from the equation. Your goal is not to make Eileen into a better person; it is to make it more likely that she will do specific tasks correctly and in a timely way. Accept the fact that she wants to get by with as little effort as possible, and use that to your advantage. To the best of your abilities, arrange contingencies so that it's harder to do the task wrong than it is to do it right.

**SPECIFY THE DELIVERABLES:** Clear, explicit directions, while absolutely necessary in dealing with Passive-Aggressive people, will not work as well as you think they ought.

**TURN YOURSELF INTO A REWARD:** Something that will work is piling on the praise. Most Passive-Aggressive people feel underappreciated. They need more praise for doing things right than do most other people. Figure on giving at least twice what you yourself would need (four times, if you pride yourself on your toughness or emotional security).

**LET THEM VENT:** Passive-Aggressives carry a lot of anger and resentment about, of which they are only vaguely aware. For most angry people, letting them talk about how angry they are just makes them angrier. This is not true with Passive-Aggressives. Letting them get something off their chest actually decreases the amount of stored-up hostility. Of course, since they're not aware of their anger, you have to go about the venting process indirectly.

Ask what other workers might be upset about. Passive-Aggressives will be only too happy to tell you what they feel if it's disguised as someone else's opinion. If Passive-Aggressives have a chance to voice resentments, however indirectly, they will have less need to act on them.

**MANAGE CONTINGENCIES LIKE A JEWISH MOTHER:** In addition to having thousands of years of tradition behind it, the Jewish mother strategy has a sound psychological basis. It involves using both the reward and avoidance paradigms to turn unsuspecting children into doctors, lawyers, stand-up comedians, and successful businesspeople. You don't have to be Jewish to be susceptible. Here are some basic elements of the Jewish mother strategy and suggestions about how you might use it at work.

*Use Food.* One of the best ways to make people perceive you as a reward is to feed them. A few little noshes can serve many purposes at the same time. They are not just positive reinforcement, but love manifest—nurturing in its material form. They are also a gentle form of guilt induction. How can you let down someone who feeds you so well? If there is not a deli nearby, you can use anything they sell at Starbucks. Food can also be used to set up an unmistakable contingency: no work, no eat.

*Tell Everybody.* Kibitz about the progress of whatever project you are working on every chance you get. Talk, send e-mails, and write notes in the newsletter. Mention everybody's stellar efforts, except for those who aren't making stellar efforts.

*Nudjie.* To nudjie is to nag in a loving but persistent way. A time-honored technique is tenacious overconcern. For a Passive-Aggressive like Elaine, always check on what and how she's doing. If it's not what you want, worry about her health. If she makes faces, ask if she's constipated and give her a bran muffin. If she messes up on a project, tell her your nephew did the same thing until he was diagnosed as having attention deficit hyperactivity disorder (ADHD) and put on medication. Give her the name of the doctor. Remember, nothing is too small to diagnose. Ask detailed questions, and make it clear that you will not stop until they are answered.

If done correctly, nudjieing is about as annoying as waterboarding, but far less messy.

Remember, it is avoidance that has the power. If you are constantly reminding Passive-Aggressives of what they need to do, they may do it just to get rid of you. That is the point, isn't it?

Nudjieing may be manipulative, but it is not heartless. When Passive-Aggressives have done what you want, praise them and maybe give them a little nosh to build up their strength.

Nobody wants to be a nag, because we all hate to be nagged. To me, this means that nagging works! The technical name for it is *negative reinforcement,* a term that is mistakenly applied to punishment. Negative reinforcers are stimuli that are rewarding when they are turned off. If you don't believe me when I tell you how well they work, ask your mom. Chances are that her nudjieing rather than your dad's lectures was what developed that work ethic you're so proud of today.

Passive-aggressive people cause more trouble than they need to. Their dynamics are simple, and they respond well to praise and attention. The problem is you can get so angry at how they act that you may not be able to think clearly about what is likely to be most effective.

## THE PATTERN TO STEP OUT OF: DRAMA

The basic structure of all drama is the struggle between a protagonist and an antagonist. This is the pattern you need to avoid.

Passive-Aggressives have a hard time believing that they would ever do anything wrong or bad. If you suggest otherwise, you will be the antagonist, and the very least that will happen is that they won't hear anything you have to say. Up until now, I've been telling you to give them lots of attention and pile on the praise. But what if you have to say something important and it is negative? Should you just keep your mouth shut?

No, but you need to step into their world and be careful that what you say does not needlessly contradict their view of themselves. Fortunately, that's not as difficult as you might think.

Histrionics tend to be conventional in their ideas about what a good person should be. In their world, that's who they are. Not just Histrionics but most of the people you deal with at work believe certain predictable things about themselves. If you want Histrionics to hear what you have to say, structure your comments so that they are consistent with these basic beliefs. If you don't, the drama will begin. Here are some basic beliefs most people hold about themselves:

### They Are Right

There is no point wasting time trying to convince Histrionics—or anyone else, for that matter—that they're wrong. Even if they are wrong, let them save face by suggesting any error was the result of misunderstanding. Decide what you want, and ask for that. If it is just acknowledgment that you're right, forget it.

## They Work Hard

One's own efforts always feel like they are worth more than those of other people. Always remember to acknowledge how hard Histrionics are working, especially if you want them to do more.

## They Always Give More than They Receive

Histrionics see themselves as givers. If in any way, shape, or form you imply that they are selfish, or even that they are acting in their own self-interest, they will vehemently deny it and anything else you say.

## They Are at Least Slightly Above Average in Intelligence

Histrionics will readily acknowledge that there are people who are brighter than they are—say, rocket scientists. If, however, you ask them where they fall in the overall continuum, they will usually place themselves above the mean. Even if you are dealing with someone who is intellectually challenged, remember that there is no way they can feel the lack of something they have never experienced in the first place.

## They Are Basically Honest

Histrionics are the only people on earth who never lie! If they say something that is not exactly true, it is because they didn't understand or they forgot a few details.

## They Are Good Drivers

This belief is especially prevalent in male Histrionics. Challenge it at your peril. Just watch out for them if you're on the road. They probably aren't paying attention to you.

### PASSIVE-AGGRESSIVES AND GOSSIP

Gossip and Passive-Aggressive Histrionics are made for each other. Passive-Aggressives get to say all sorts of nasty things about people, and nobody gets mad at them, because they didn't say it; somebody else did. Well, they *did* say it, but they were just sharing some information with you as a favor, because you ought to know. But don't tell anybody.

> Ann sidles up to Theresa in the break room. "What did you do to get Randy so pissed off?"

"I didn't do anything," Theresa says. "I talked to him yesterday at the project meeting. He didn't seem any more pissed off than usual."

"Well, I heard that this morning he was up in Delon's office saying he couldn't work with you and he wanted you off the project."

"You heard him say that?" Theresa asks.

"I didn't hear it; Jamie did. I wasn't supposed to tell you, but I thought you'd want to know. Randy was saying that your nitpicking was slowing things down, that the project would have been out the door two weeks ago, if you hadn't—"

"Yeah, it would have been out the door with all Randy's sloppy calculations. His numbers were way off. Delon knows about it. He saw all the spreadsheets. Did he say anything to Randy about that?"

"Jamie didn't tell me, but you know how Delon is sometimes."

"You mean, a wuss?"

The dynamics of gossip are as vague, contorted, and confusing as the inside of a Histrionic's mind. In what other situation can you come up to someone, insult them, and then expect them to thank you for sharing?

Not only that, you might give them more ammunition to use against someone else. How long do you think it will be before the word is out that Theresa thinks Delon is a wuss? Rumors can get started anywhere in an organization, but if it weren't for Passive-Aggressives, they would never spread so far so quickly.

Histrionics don't spread rumors intending to create grudges and factions; they just want a little drama. For them, gossiping about coworkers is a major source of entertainment. It's more fun than the company softball team, and you don't have to be a jock to play.

Gossip is also a major source of conflict and morale problems, particularly when it moves from being a vehicle for dissemination of general information to one for disseminating people's negative opinions of other people. Once that gets started, it's hard to stop. At the center of it all are sweet, innocent Passive-Aggressives like Ann, who are only trying to help.

Gossip usually takes you by surprise. Instead of thinking about what is going on, you are likely to respond with reactive fast thinking. Like Theresa, you hear something about yourself that isn't true. It makes you angry, and then and there you try to set the record straight, not stopping to think that by doing so, you are adding to the script of the Histrionic drama that is going on around you and are now a member of the cast.

What should you do instead? As in any situation involving emotional vampires, shift over to slow thinking.

Here are some suggestions.

**ANALYZE THE SITUATION BEFORE YOU RESPOND:** When you hear a rumor from a helpful person like Ann, always ask yourself: *Why is she telling me this?* As I've said before, this one little question will protect you from so much of the harm vampires can do. It is the doorway into mature, slow thinking.

Is the person trying to help you or just to stir things up? You may not know right away, so don't say anything until you do.

**ASSUME THE MIKE IS ON:** This is a good assumption to make about anything you say about anyone at work. Especially if you are saying it to someone who is telling you something that was told to her in confidence. With Passive Aggressives, there is no such thing as off the record.

**CONTROL YOUR RESPONSE:** Moment to moment, what keeps people gossiping is the listener's response. Watch people in the break room and see all the encouragement rumormongers get from nods, smiles, open mouths, people leaning conspiratorially closer, as well as adding embellishments. Gossip is a performance. If there is no audience response, the show is over.

Controlling your response takes a real effort of will. People like Ann who share negative stories about you are generally not doing it out of friendship. They want a reaction. They'd like you to get mad and maybe retaliate, which will give them more to talk about. There is nothing about this pattern that will benefit you in any way.

**DO THE UNEXPECTED: ANSWER BAD WITH GOOD:** Whenever gossips say something negative about someone, say something positive. Remember what happened when Dorothy threw water on the Wicked Witch of the West? This unexpected response will have a similar effect on people who are spreading toxic rumors. They may not evaporate, but their pretenses will.

Think about what would have happened if Theresa had said this to Ann. "Randy has been under a lot of stress, like all of us on this project, but he's competent and always professional. I'm sure if there is any dispute, we can work it out."

**SPREAD POSITIVE GOSSIP:** Take the last technique even further. Say good things about people. If the idea of positive gossip seems like an oxymoron, that's all the more reason to try it. It couldn't hurt, and it may help.

**BE DISCRETE:** If you have something negative to say to someone, talk directly and in private.

When you do this, don't tell the person that what he or she did was bad. Instead, tell the person your reaction, and ask if that was the intention—for example, "When you made the comment about my report, I felt put down. Was that what you meant to do?"

Always tell people what you would like them to do instead. Don't set up a situation in which they have to admit they were wrong in order for you to get what you want.

If you work in an office where gossip and backbiting make it difficult to come in most mornings, realize that it takes two to tango. If enough people follow the above advice, the most toxic rumors will simply die on the grapevine. Let it start with you.

## PASSIVE-AGGRESSIVES AND ILLNESS

Histrionics get sick. They are not faking, and they do not do it on purpose. If you've ever had to deal with a sickly Histrionic, you may find this hard to believe, but believe it you must. They really are sick. How they get sick is the question that keeps doctors guessing. Perhaps Histrionic internal turmoil causes their immune system to overload. Or maybe it's stress. Every illness known to humanity is exacerbated by stress. To make things even more complicated, the most common disorders that plague Histrionics tend to wax and wane in an unpredictable manner. Maybe we have it all backward and the medical disorders cause Histrionic Personality. All of these theories have been advanced, and I suppose that presenting them here is just a fancy way of saying we don't know.

What we do know is that Histrionic illnesses tend to occur at the most inopportune times.

> Marnie is out sick again, and Stan, her boss, doesn't know what to do. He feels sorry for her. He knows she has fibromyalgia, chronic fatigue syndrome, and several other things he can't remember the names of, but she always seems to be gone when the office is busiest. Marnie doesn't overuse her sick time, but she does manage to take every last day. The team is complaining about having to do her work.
>
> Stan knows he ought to do something, but what?

Stan is in a bind. He's caught on the horns of one of those dilemmas. He has to balance Marnie's needs with those of the team. Then, there are laws to consider, and politics. Every disorder that Histrionics fall prey to has its own constituency as well as hundreds of websites arguing that these illnesses are real and serious. That is true, but like everything else having to do with Histrionics, it's not the only truth. Histrionic illnesses also tend to get their sufferers out of doing things they don't want to do.

To decide what to do, Stan needs a way of thinking about Histrionic illness that goes beyond real and fake. Luckily, he has Freud to fall back on. Freud described Histrionic symptoms as having what he called primary and secondary gain.

The primary gain of a symptom was to bind up repressed internal conflicts into something more acceptable. Freud saw symptoms as metaphors for what was going on in his patients' unconscious minds.

Histrionic illnesses do have a tantalizingly poetic component. As therapists, we see back pain in people who are acting spineless and gastrointestinal symptoms in people who can't stomach specific situations. Analyzing symptoms can be very interesting, but sharing your insights with Histrionics is fraught with pitfalls that can make a bad situation worse. Leave it to the pros. Don't try it at home. Or at work.

Instead, focus on secondary gain, which is Freud's name for an avoidance contingency that operates whether people are aware of it or not. Sickness gets Histrionics out of doing things that they don't want to do.

Anything that leads to a positive result happens more often. What Stan can do is restructure the contingencies at work to decrease secondary gain by increasing the cost of staying home. This must be done subtly; a little goes a long way. The idea is not to punish sick people, but to slightly alter the balance of forces on mornings when they're deciding whether or not they're too sick to work.

On such days, you might go in because you'd feel guilty if you didn't. Histrionics repress guilt or rationalize it away, so it takes a little higher response cost to tip the balance. Here are some things a manager such as Stan might do that would shift the contingencies in a more positive direction both for Marnie and for the rest of the team.

**REQUIRE A DOCTOR'S NOTE:** If people are sick with more than an occasional virus, they should be getting appropriate treatment. Absences of more than a day or two, or that happen more than every few months, should be prescribed by a doctor rather than being used as self-medication.

If your policy and procedures manual has rules about doctors' notes, follow them to the letter for everyone. No selective enforcement.

**REDISTRIBUTE THE TEAM'S TASKS BY PRIORITY:** Everybody has tasks that must be done right away and some that can wait. The can-waits are generally less interesting than the right-aways. If someone is out, his or her right-aways need to be redistributed. When that person stays out for a while, or is gone a bit too frequently, it's only fair that he or she come back to a deskload of everybody's can-waits. You can exercise some discretion about this one, depending upon your assessment of the reasons for absence.

**NEVER ASK SICK HISTRIONICS HOW THEY'RE FEELING:** Talking about how sick you are is rewarding, especially to people who live for attention. Retelling the gory details makes a questionable illness seem more authentic, thereby quashing any nascent guilt feelings that might arise. When a Passive-Aggressive Histrionic returns to work, say welcome back, then outline the tasks to be done.

I have previously suggested that it's a good idea to let Passive-Aggressives vent. In the case of physical symptoms, this can be counterproductive, as the symptoms may be a Histrionic device for binding up negative feelings about the job or coworkers. Venting about negative feelings can help get rid of them. Venting about physical symptoms often makes them more dramatic.

Passive-Aggressive Histrionics can create problems, but they can only give you a headache if you let them. So much of emotional vampires' power to harm comes from your own expectations. If you believe children of the night ought to act like grown-ups, you'll be disappointed every time. They are what they are. With Histrionics, the most important thing to remember is, if you are outraged by outrageous people, you will be the one who suffers.

# Histrionic Cultures

**11**

In Histrionic cultures, perception is more important than reality. Businesses with such cultures always remind me of the cargo cult that developed in remote areas of the South Pacific after World War II. The war abruptly brought modern civilization to native tribespeople in New Guinea in the form of wondrous manufactured goods delivered from heaven by great metal birds. The tribespeople knew a good thing when they saw one, and they began to adopt some of the rituals the foreigners used to entreat the gods for cargo. They built decoy planes of sticks and leaves to attract the real ones down from the sky. Wearing carved headphones, they waved palm fronds in the air in dances that resembled semaphore. With great creativity, they copied the trappings of civilization and totally missed the essence.

In Histrionic cultures, management seems to be made of sticks and leaves. There is a lot of talking the talk but very little walking the walk. Histrionic cultures are most prevalent in smaller companies with few business-school-trained managers or in local divisions of larger companies, but they can show up anywhere, depending on the personalities of the people in charge.

Here are some typical characteristics.

## EVERYBODY IS NICE

Histrionic cultures are full of nice, professional-looking people. What isn't nice doesn't show, at least initially. As among popular kids in high school, there is a certain uniformity of look and behavior. Taste and understatement do not seem to be priorities, but you will see very few tattoos and piercings. Almost all the decoration that you do see is cheerful, inspirational, and very literal. Often pictures are emblazoned with words that tell you what they are supposed to mean. Soaring eagles are a favored motif.

## MOTIVATIONAL RALLIES

Histrionics believe in the magic of motivation and positive attitude with quasi-religious fervor. Team-building exercises are also popular. To Histrionic managers, motivation has little to do with external contingencies. It is more an internal spark that can be fanned by rhetoric into flames of performance. Fire imagery is often quite popular. What are missing are self-awareness and a frank discussion of problems. If you're motivated enough, there are no problems.

## BAD NEWS IS SUPPRESSED, AND DIFFICULTIES ARE SWEPT UNDER THE RUG

In Histrionic cultures, the greatest fear is that negative information will leak out and demotivate people. Demotivating data is treated in the same way the Centers for Disease Control treat samples of dangerous viruses.

## ANTI-INTELLECTUALISM

Histrionic cultures are based more on gut feelings than on thoughts. Common sense is considered more important than book sense. Other than cost and sales totals, very little is defined or measured. Successful careers are built on cost cutting and increasing sales. Anything else is considered too theoretical.

## SEXUAL ENTANGLEMENTS

At first, this may seem surprising among such nice, conventional people. Then, you realize that Histrionics tend to be unaware of unacceptable impulses like sexuality and aggression. Couple that with unrealistic views about the day-to-day difficulties of adult relationships, and you tend to find people stumbling into sexual entanglements believing that they have finally discovered their soul mate. As usual, the Histrionic world is like high school.

## DISGUISED BARBARITY

Again, it may seem surprising that Histrionic cultures are some of the most dangerous in which to work. Some regularly practice human sacrifice. People who ask too many embarrassing questions anger the gods, and they must be removed before the demotivation spreads. Human sacrifices are seldom fired directly. Most often they are tortured into leaving. Histrionic aggression is always passive

If you are in a culture that looks like the cargo cult, respect the traditions, keep your head down, and do your best to blend in. If you see emperors or chieftains walking around naked, for heaven's sake, don't say anything.

# Narcissists

**12**

OF ALL THE EMOTIONAL VAMPIRES you'll have to deal with at work, Narcissists may be the most difficult because of the confused and mixed feelings they elicit. They are undoubtedly the most hated of vampires, but they are also the most loved. Well, maybe the emotion is not so much loved as revered or perhaps admired from a distance. The closer you are to Narcissists, the more intense your feelings are apt to be. That is the danger. As with all the other vampires, rather than relying on your emotional reactions, either positive or negative, your best bet for protecting yourself is attempting to understand the way Narcissists think and the needs that drive them. Wherever you work, you *will* encounter them.

Narcissistic emotional vampires have a disorder that is both psychological and cosmological. They believe the universe revolves around them. Unlike Antisocials, who are addicted to excitement, or Histrionics, who crave attention, Narcissists just want to live out their fantasies of being the smartest, richest, most talented, and all-around best people in the world.

Some Narcissists turn out to be little more than legends in their own minds, but a surprising number are adept enough to turn some of their grandiose fantasies into reality. There may be narcissism without greatness, but there is no greatness without narcissism. One thing is certain, however: in the eyes of other people, Narcissists are never so great as they consider themselves to be.

Considering themselves is what Narcissists do best. The trait they most conspicuously lack is concern for the needs, thoughts, and feelings of other people.

These vampires have tendencies in the direction of what used to be called Narcissistic Personality Disorder. The name derives from Narcissus, a Greek youth who fell in love with his own reflection. To outsiders, it looks as if Narcissists are in love with themselves because they think they're better than other people. The actual relationship is a bit more complex.

More than loving themselves, Narcissists are absorbed with themselves. They feel their own desires so acutely that they can't pay attention to anything else. Imagine their disorder as a pair of binoculars. Narcissists look at their own needs through the magnifying side and the rest of the cosmos through the side that makes things small to the point of insignificance. It's not so much that Narcissists think they're better than other people as that they hardly think of other people at all—unless they need something.

Narcissistic need is tremendous. Just as sharks must continually swim to keep from drowning, Narcissists must constantly be reassured that they are special or they will sink like stones to the depths of depression. It may look as if they are trying to demonstrate their worth to other people, but their real audience is themselves.

Narcissists pursue the symbols of wealth, status, and power with a fervor that is almost spiritual. They can talk for hours about objects they own, the great things they've done or are going to do, and the famous people they hang out with. Often, they exaggerate shamelessly, even when they have plenty of real achievements they could brag about.

Nothing is ever enough for them. That's why Narcissists want you, or at least your adulation. They'll try so hard to impress you that it's easy to believe that you're actually important to them. This can be a fatal mistake; it's not *you* they want, only your worship. They'll suck that out and throw the rest away.

To Narcissists, the objects, the achievements, and the high regard of other people mean nothing in themselves. They are fuel, like water forced across gills so that oxygen can be extracted. The technical term is *Narcissistic supplies*. If Narcissists don't constantly demonstrate their specialness to themselves, they drown.

## WHAT IT'S LIKE TO BE NARCISSISTIC

To know how Narcissists experience life, imagine playing golf, tennis, or another competitive sport and having the best day of your career. You feel great, but the mental wall between confidence and fear is as thin as tissue paper. Everything is riding on the next shot—and then the one after that. For Narcissists, the game encompasses the whole world, and it is never over.

Imagine the pressure should the only meaningful goal in your life be proving that you are something more than human. Narcissists' greatest fear is of being ordinary. They can't feel connected to anything larger than themselves, because in their universe there *is* nothing larger. Beyond their frenetic attempts to prove the unprovable lies only a dark, unexplored void. You might be tempted to think of them as tragic figures if they weren't so petty and obnoxious.

Narcissists are often talented and intelligent. They are also among the most inconsiderate creatures on earth. You'd think that such smart people would recognize the importance of paying attention to other people. Dream on.

Narcissists are so wrapped up in their own dreams that there is no room for anything else. It is an ironic coincidence that sometimes the realization of Narcissistic dreams benefits all humanity. Narcissists invented art, science, sports, business, and everything else at which you can compete. They invented sainthood too, for that matter. Though we may hate to admit it, our lives are better because of Narcissists' attempts to prove themselves to be better than we are.

## THE NARCISSISTIC DILEMMA

More than any other vampire type, Narcissists evoke mixed feelings. We love their accomplishments, but we hate their conceit. We deplore the way they ignore our needs, yet unconsciously we respond to the infants inside them that need us so much. And we need them. Without Narcissists, who would lead us? Remember, there is plenty of narcissism without greatness, but no greatness without narcissism.

Or who, for that matter, would think themselves wise enough to say where leadership ends and narcissism begins? There's no doubt that too much narcissism is a dangerous thing. But how much is too much?

To live at all, we must have some instinct to put our own needs first. Narcissism may be the power behind all motivation. To live as human beings, we must balance that power with responsibility. Struggling with the Narcissistic dilemma is what being human is all is about. The great rabbi Hillel summed it up like this:

> If I am not for myself, who will be for me?
> If I am only for myself, what am I?
> If not now, when?

Emotional vampires are people who have for one reason or another abandoned the struggle with the Narcissistic dilemma. Antisocials ignore it because it's no fun. Histrionics pretend that they never act in their own self-interest, and Narcissists believe that what's good for them is all that exists. Vampires are forced to prey on other people for the answer that the rest of us must struggle to find within ourselves.

What's the answer? Another great rabbi summed that up:

Do unto others as you would have them do unto you.

Narcissists break the Golden Rule without so much as a thought. Does this make them evil or oblivious? Your answer will determine how much damage they do to you.

The easiest way to get drained is to take Narcissists' inconsideration personally, to get upset over what they must be thinking of you to treat you the way they do. *The most important thing to remember is that Narcissistic emotional vampires are not thinking of you at all.*

### NARCISSISM AND SELF-ESTEEM

Narcissism is not the same thing as high self-esteem. Self-esteem is a concept that has meaning primarily to people who don't have it. Narcissists don't need a concept to explain why they are special any more than sharks need a concept to explain water.

You might argue that their constant need for Narcissistic supplies to buoy them up is evidence that the whole purpose of their life is to compensate for low self-esteem. This may lead you into the mistaken belief that all it takes to fix Narcissists is to teach them how to feel good about who they are inside, so they can just relax and let themselves be regular people. To a Narcissist, being regular is the same as annihilation.

### NARCISSISTS AT WORK

At work you will come across the two main types of Narcissists: Superstars and Legends in Their Own Minds. The difference between the two is in achievement and willingness to work. Superstars are prepared to do whatever it takes to accomplish their grandiose goals, whether that involves hard work, taking advantage of others, or both. Legends feel that their talent and intelligence exempts them from having to do things they don't want to do, even if those things are required for success.

At work, you'll find Superstars upstairs in the corner office and on the board. The Legends will be coworkers and subordinates who are so talented that you wonder why they haven't achieved more than they have, until you need them to get a job done. Legends are just as willing to take advantage, but hard work on anything they don't like doing often eludes them.

## THE NARCISSISTIC VAMPIRE CHECKLIST

True or False: Score one point for each *true* answer.

1. This person has achieved more than most people his or her age.  T  F

2. This person is firmly convinced that he or she is better, smarter, or more talented than other people.  T  F

3. This person loves competition, but is a poor loser.  T  F

4. This person has fantasies of doing something great or being famous, and often expects to be treated as if these fantasies had already come true.  T  F

5. This person has very little interest in what other people are thinking or feeling, unless he or she wants something from them.  T  F

6. This person is a name-dropper.  T  F

7. To this person, it is very important to be in the right places and associate with the right people.  T  F

8. This person takes advantage of other people to achieve his or her own goals.  T  F

9. This person usually manages to be in a category by himself or herself.  T  F

10. This person often feels put-upon when asked to take care of his or her responsibilities to family, friends, or coworkers.  T  F

11. This person regularly disregards rules or expects them to be changed because he or she is, in some way, special.   T F

12. This person becomes irritated when other people don't automatically do what he or she wants them to do, even when they have a good reason for not complying.   T F

13. This person reviews sports, art, and literature by telling you what he or she would have done instead.   T F

14. This person thinks most criticisms of him or her are motivated by jealousy.   T F

15. This person regards anything short of worship to be rejection.   T F

16. This person suffers from a congenital inability to recognize his or her own mistakes. On the rare occasions that this person does recognize a mistake, even the slightest error can precipitate a major depression.   T F

17. This person unapologetically checks his or her phone when other people are talking.   T F

18. This person often complains of being mistreated or misunderstood.   T F

19. People either love or hate this person.   T F

20. Despite an overly high opinion of himself or herself, this person is really quite intelligent and talented.   T F

Scoring: Five or more true answers qualifies the person as a Narcissistic emotional vampire, though not necessarily for a diagnosis of Narcissistic personality disorder. If the person scores higher than 10 and is not a member of the royal family, be careful that you aren't mistaken for one of the servants.

## WHAT THE QUESTIONS MEASURE

The specific behaviors covered on the checklist relate to several underlying personality characteristics that define a Narcissistic emotional vampire.

### Well-Advertised Talent and Intelligence

The first thing you'll hear about Narcissists is that they are extremely intelligent and talented. You'll probably hear this from them directly, since they are not the least bit shy in saying good things about themselves.

A surprising number of Narcissists know their numerical IQ scores and share them with new acquaintances. You may also hear about famous people whom these vampires have met and in some way impressed.

At seminars and meetings, Narcissists often have their hands in the air, but they never ask real questions. They make comments to demonstrate to everyone that they know at least as much as and probably more than the person at the front of the room. Either that, or they sit at the back of the room conspicuously playing with their phones.

The pattern of trying to dazzle you with their talent and intelligence persists with Narcissists long after they make their first impression. They'll keep on until you're no longer visibly awed, then they'll ignore you completely.

### Achievement

Most Narcissists have achievements to back up their high opinion of themselves. Unlike other vampire types, who are just as happy to pretend, Narcissists are quite willing to work hard to glorify themselves.

In their careers, these vampires are usually focused and goal-directed. Many are workaholics, but unlike Histrionic people pleasers who'll work themselves half to death for approval and love, Narcissists take on only those tasks that pay off in money, fame, or power.

### Grandiosity

Narcissists are absolutely shameless in their fantasies about how great they are and how much everybody admires them, or should.

If you press them, they'll admit that they consider themselves the best in the world at something. Actually, you won't have to press very hard.

### Entitlement

Narcissists believe they are so special that the rules don't apply to them. They expect the red carpet to be rolled out for them wherever they go, and if it isn't, they get quite surly.

They don't wait, they don't recycle, they don't pay retail, they don't stand in line, they don't clean up after themselves, they don't let other people get in front of them in traffic, and their income taxes rival great works of fiction. Illness or even death is no excuse for other people not immediately jumping up to meet their needs. They aren't the least bit ashamed of using other people and systems for their own personal gain. They may even boast about how they take advantage of just about everybody.

## Competitiveness

Narcissists love to compete, but only when they win. Usually, they'll do whatever it takes to win, whether it be practice or stacking the deck in their favor.

Narcissists are obsessively concerned with status and power. They'll fight to the death over a corner office, not because they want a nice view, but because they know what a corner office means in the organizational hierarchy. They know what everything means in every hierarchy. What they wear, what they drive, where they live, and who they're seen with are not random choices based on something so silly as what they like. Everything Narcissists do is a move in the great game of self-aggrandizement, which is their main reason for living.

## Conspicuous Boredom

Unless the subject of the conversation is how great they are, Narcissists will become visibly bored. One of the main reasons Narcissists wear expensive watches is so they can look at them when someone else is talking. If they aren't looking at their watches, they're playing with their phones, which are never turned off.

Besides boredom, Narcissists have only two other emotional states. They're either on top of the world or on the bottom of the garbage heap. The slightest frustration can burst their balloon and send them crashing to the depths.

## Lack of Empathy

To a Narcissistic vampire, other people are either prospective purveyors of Narcissistic supplies or invisible. More than any other vampire type, Narcissists are incapable of seeing their fellow humans as having wants, needs, talents, and desires of their own. Needless to say, this lack of empathy is the source of untold amounts of pain to the people who love them.

But for their lack of human warmth, there is a lot about these vampires to love. Many people destroy themselves by believing that it's their fault that Narcissists don't love them back. They will work hard and long, sometimes for their whole lives, without realizing that these vampires can't give what they don't have.

A particularly scary trait that Narcissists share with Antisocials is the ability to feign empathy when they want something. Narcissists are the best flatterers on the planet. They give great ego massages even as they're draining people dry. Needless to say, this talent helps them to excel at politics of all kinds. Even though Antisocials and Histrionics can be sexy, all the best seducers are Narcissists.

## Inability to Accept Criticism

Narcissists' greatest fear is of being ordinary. God forbid they should do something as mundane as making a mistake. Even the smallest criticisms feel like stakes through the heart. If you reprimand Narcissists, the least they'll do is explain in great detail why your opinion is wrong. If you're right, the situation will be much worse. They will melt before your eyes into pitiful, dependent infants who need enormous amounts of reassurance and praise just to draw their next breath. You can't win. There's no such thing as a Narcissistic vampire being objective about his or her faults.

## Ambivalence in Other People

Other people usually feel strongly about Narcissists. They either love them for their talents or hate their guts for their blatant selfishness. Or both. It's hard to say what does most damage—the selfishness, the hatred, or the love.

Narcissists always know what they want from you. They won't be the least bit reticent about asking for it or just taking it. To deal effectively with these self-absorbed children of the night, you must be equally certain about what you want from them. Always drive a hard bargain, and always make them pay *before* they get what they want from you. Remember this rule, and there's not much else you need to know.

Well, maybe one more thing: unless you want your heart broken, never make Narcissists choose between you and their first love, themselves.

# Narcissistic Legends in Their Own Minds

**W**HAT YOU NOTICE first about Narcissistic Legends is their talent and intelligence. If you don't notice, you're probably not paying attention, because most of what they say and do is designed to demonstrate how special they are (and, all too often, how ordinary you are). What Narcissistic Legends won't be able to show you is a résumé that is anywhere near as impressive as their talents.

Should you be so crass as to ask why they haven't accomplished more, they will be only too happy to explain. They'll tell you it's because the game is rigged, everyone is threatened by their competence, or the world is not ready for their brilliance. After a few minutes of this sort of rationalization, you may begin to suspect that there are other reasons for Narcissistic Legends' lack of success.

The game *is* rigged. To succeed, you need talent and intelligence, but you also have to work hard. Specifically, in order to be successful in any endeavor, you have to do what needs to be done, not just what you feel like doing.

His name is Neal, but in school they called him Neo, because he's The One. There is nothing he cannot do with a computer. He can sit writing code for hours, swaying to its rhythms as if he were conducting the Philharmonic. Code monkeys and even the engineers who work with him stand in awe of his brilliance. Everyone knows what he's capable of doing, but the big question is whether he's going to do it.

Neo didn't see the point in finishing his engineering degree, since he already knew everything they were trying to teach him. Also, he has what he calls a few little issues with authority. Read that as *nobody who knows less than I do is going to tell me what to do.* In Neo's world, everybody knows less than he does.

It irritates Neo that management expects him to perform all sorts of tasks that are beneath him, such as fixing people's computers and keeping the network up and running. If he does those things at all, it takes him forever to get to them. Instead, he prefers to "correct" programming on systems that are working, but not up to his standards of elegance. He wants to be in on software development, but company rules say he can't do that without credentials. The engineers recognize his talent and keep telling him to go back to school. He won't. His dream is to break free from corporate bondage and work for a start-up where he can really show what he can do.

Some of the engineers talk about going out on their own with a spin-off and maybe bringing Neo along. He is a genius, but can they work with him? Can anybody?

Some Narcissistic Legends are like those "smartest guys in the world" who live in their parents' basements because they can't hold down a job. Some, like Neo, may be actual geniuses. The trait they share, the one that prevents them from succeeding, is *entitlement*, which is what normal people find most repugnant in Narcissists. Entitlement is Narcissists' belief that they are so special that they shouldn't have to follow the same rules everyone else does.

Because of their attitude of entitlement, Narcissistic Legends have never developed strategies for making themselves do what they don't want to do. Such strategies are absolutely necessary for becoming a successful adult in our society.

As early teenagers, we all hope that we can get by with as little work as possible. For most of us, the contingencies teach us otherwise. We learn that, to get what we want, we have to exert some effort, and through generalization, most of us come to value the effort itself. We develop an internal contingency in which the feeling of doing what needs to be done becomes a powerful reward. Call it work ethic or a shift from external to internal reinforcers, this transition is critical to becoming a mature working person. As we have seen in previous chapters, many emotional vampires never get that far. Antisocials and Histrionics learn that deception and social skills get them external rewards. Narcissistic Legends, who are often too smart for their own good, learn that talent in one area can exempt them from effort in others.

Neo was a precocious 12-year-old. He was so good with computers that he had no incentive to learn about people, his homework, or anything else that didn't interest him or that he didn't feel like doing. Now, at 34, he is still acting like a precocious 12-year-old. His job keeps making demands for effort that he perceives as stupid, unreasonable, and completely beneath him. Unfortunately for Neo, the world is no longer giving him a pass because of his talent. He sees this as the world's problem rather than his.

> For Neo, the most comforting sound is the opening of a beer bottle at happy hour. It's not the alcohol he craves, but the ambiance. His drinking buddies are all really bright people who are continually screwed over by idiots. In that group, sarcasm is an art form as they relate the tribulations of their lives. Everybody lets off a little steam and feels better, at least for a while.

Neo's buddies are Rebels; they can empathize with him because they too are struggling with the necessity of doing things they don't want to do. If Neo took the test in Chapter 3, he'd come out looking like a Rebel too, but there are some big differences. To start with, Neo probably wouldn't take the test. To him it's just psychological crap. He has little interest in learning about himself. He already knows all he needs to know. There are plenty of Rebels who would agree about the psychological crap. But their reasons would be different from Neo's.

Crap for Neo is anything that might contradict his image of himself as the best in the world. Beneath Narcissistic bravado is a terrible fear of being ordinary. To Narcissistic Legends, anything they are not best at is not worth doing.

As they grow older and see less competent people passing them by, the image of themselves as the best and smartest begins to wear thin. This is especially true if they have families with ever-increasing financial needs. As their rationalizations fade, Legends do what everyone does with broken dreams: they hold them more tightly. They get depressed, not because of their own shortcomings, but because the world is unfair and depressing.

The other difference between Neo and his Rebel buddies is related to the fear of being ordinary. Most Rebels see themselves as regular guys. They are good at developing a sense of camaraderie with people they perceive as being like them. In bars, in cubicles, and on battlefields, they empathize with each other and have each other's backs. They take strength in the feeling of "us against the world." For Narcissists, there is no *us*. Only *me*.

## APPROACHES THAT DON'T WORK

So, what do you do if you manage a person like Neo, with a big talent and an ego that is even bigger? Should you just let him go, or can he be changed into a productive team member?

First let's look at a couple of approaches that won't work.

An upper-level manager suggested sending Neo to one of Cleve Gower's Motivational Boot Camp weekends that the company puts on at regular intervals. The manager had gone himself, and it had done wonders for his attitude.

The Boot Camp started at 6:00 a.m. with jogging and a Spartan breakfast; then Cleve outlined the purpose of the program.

"The question I want to ask is, *'Have you got game? Do you want to win? Do you have what it takes to win the most important battle—the one with yourself?'* The first step in winning is taking responsibility for yourself. From this moment on, there will be no excuses! We are going to take full responsibility for ourselves and what happens to us. There is no one to blame but yourself! You are in charge!

"Let me hear you say it: 'I AM IN CHARGE! NO EXCUSES!'"

As the group was reciting the mantra, Neo Googled Cleve Gower on his phone and found a few things about Cleve's less-than-stellar NBA career. Since all the people at the boot camp were from the company, it didn't take much effort for Neo to hack into the notification system so he could send texts to all the phones in the room. He started with a short 1998 article about when Cleve, at the bottom of his game, was traded to the Nuggets. Cleve told a reporter that he was glad to go because there might be someone in Denver who knew how to coach. He also said that in the drier climate his asthma wouldn't hold him back as much.

All over the room, phones vibrated. Here and there, people surreptitiously checked their messages and snickered. Some passed their phones to the people next to them. Throughout the gym where the boot camp was held, there were little pockets of laughter that soon settled down, but they started up again when the next text came.

At first, Cleve acted like he took no notice, but soon his irritation began to show. He reminded participants of the no-cell-phone rule.

It was already too late.

There was nothing wrong with Cleve's message. In fact, it was just what Neo needed to hear. The problem was the delivery. Narcissistic Legends are immune to lectures. Like Rebels everywhere, they can detect bullshit in one or two parts per billion.

Not all motivational speakers are as transparent as Cleve Gower. The best of them are quite solid, and they might even have done Neo some good. As a general rule, however, no matter how inspiring, motivational seminars cannot turn problem employees into productive team members. This is especially true when the problem employees are Narcissistic Legends.

Another approach to rehabilitating Neo seemed like a really good idea at the time.

A couple of engineers from Neo's company did start their own software development operation. They hired Neo and told him that all he had to do was write code: no paperwork, no meetings, no corporate crap, just doing what he did best.

At first, it worked—or so it seemed. Neo came up with some really brilliant applications, but they weren't quite user-friendly enough. Everyone went to work on the interface problem. Everyone except Neo. He lost interest and was onto something else. Whatever they did, the principals couldn't keep him on task. They tried all sorts of incentives, such as letting him pick his own tasks, but it seemed that the more they needed him, the less available Neo became.

There is an important psychological truth in this example that applies to all emotional vampires, but to Narcissistic Legends especially. If you treat someone's hang-up as if it were a handicap, the hang-up gets worse.

A handicap is a problem that a person cannot help, such as being unable to walk and having to be in a wheelchair. If you accommodate a handicap by, say, building ramps and adjusting the height of counters, everyone profits. The person's life gets better, and the company gets a productive worker.

A hang-up involves an avoidance paradigm. Most often it has to do with fear. If a person is phobic of elevators and you accommodate that fear by encouraging him to take the stairs, the fear is likely to get worse and spread to other things. What seems like a humanitarian gesture is actually the most harmful thing you can do. The more you accommodate a hang-up, the worse the hang-up becomes.

In Neo's case, his hang-up is not doing things he doesn't want to do. Like most Narcissistic Legends, he has an underlying fear of failure that he has accommodated all his life by avoiding anything he can't immediately do well. More accommodation of this or any hang-up will only make the problem worse. This general truth is what the principals in Neo's start-up inadvertently discovered.

The only way to diminish a fear is to face it. Running away only makes it bigger and stronger. This is undoubtedly the most useful thing I've learned in 40 years of doing psychotherapy. The second most useful thing I've learned is that just telling people what's wrong with them merely makes them angry, not better. In psychotherapy, as in comedy, timing is everything.

With that in mind, I'd like to clear up a misconception about what we in the trade call an "interpretation." If you were to tell Neo that he avoids doing what he doesn't want to do because he is afraid of failure, he will either laugh in your face or use his "fear of failure" as an excuse for more avoidance. Premature interpretations do more harm than good. The only time an interpretation helps is after a patient has an experiential insight. Then, the interpretation can help him or her make sense of the experience and apply it to the rest of his or her life. If Neo catches himself avoiding a task because he is afraid of failing, then an interpretation may help him to generalize the insight.

The skill involved in psychotherapy is knowing when and how to make interpretations. It's easy to figure out what's wrong with another person. That's what popular psychology is all about. What is subtle and difficult is communicating that information in a way that doesn't make the situation worse.

The purpose of my digression into the theory of psychotherapy is this: Here you are halfway through a popular psychology book. You have undoubtedly recognized several people you work with, and you may even be thinking of showing them the appropriate chapter in the hope that they will finally understand themselves and change. If you try, you will see firsthand exactly how futile and even destructive a premature interpretation can be.

The explanations of personality disorders I'm presenting here are for you, not the vampires you work with. The explanations may help you recognize problems and understand why certain approaches are more likely to work than others. Telling a vampire that he or she is a vampire will not work any better than telling someone that he or she is in denial.

What *will* work are approaches that involve knowing how emotional vampires usually think and act, then stepping into their world to communicate with them, and stepping out of the response pattern that their behavior typically elicits.

## AN APPROACH THAT DOES WORK

Now back to Narcissistic Legends like Neo. In his world, he is so special that he doesn't have to do anything he doesn't want to do. The typical approaches that we have seen, exhortation and accommodation, don't work. What does?

Actually, there is a time-honored approach for turning self-centered young whippersnappers into productive team members: boot camp. Cleve got the name right, but he didn't get the underlying concepts that make a boot camp work. The image most of us have is of a lot of shouting and grueling exercise that makes you feel a greater sense of accomplishment for having lived through it. That's what boot camps are for people who already value hard work. They get a stronger feeling of self-worth for setting themselves a challenge and meeting it.

Real boot camps are different. They are designed to take a bunch of self-absorbed adolescents and teach them to subordinate their needs to the needs of the group and feel good about doing it. It takes more than shouting and push-ups in the mud to accomplish that.

Here are some of the principles that make military boot camps work along with some suggestions about how they might be applied in the case of a Narcissistic Legend like Neo.

### No Bluff, No Bull

The most important reason that boot camps succeed is because they are real. You pass or wash out, and an important element of your future depends on which you do.

For a Narcissistic Legend like Neo to improve, it has to be a do-or-die situation. Either he passes the training or he's out the door. Before you try something like this these days, you'll have to get an OK to do so from human resources and possibly the company lawyer. If there are loopholes in the contingencies, a Narcissist will find them.

The no-bull part is that you shouldn't ship someone like Neo off to a special place for training that he might subvert or, more likely, where he would excel but would fall back into the same old pattern once he return. The battle with himself is here and now, and this is where it must be fought.

### Know Your Goal

The goal of a boot camp is to teach a person to gain group membership by subordinating his or her needs to those of the group. It doesn't matter what he or she is thinking while doing it.

For a Narcissistic Legend like Neo, the goal is to get him to do things that need to be done regardless of how he feels about doing them. His reasons must be his own.

Believers, do not be so naïve as to think you or anyone else can teach empathy to a Narcissist. At the depths of their souls, they do not get it.

That's what makes them Narcissists. In five minutes, they will learn what to say to fool you into thinking that they really understand that others have rights too. It is incredible to me how much money is wasted trying to teach cultural sensitivity as if it were an academic subject. Empathy is not based on what people know so much as on what they believe.

## Be Tough

You've seen drill instructors in the movies. Punch them in the stomach, and you'll hurt your hand. Talk back, and you will enter the house of pain. The DI is tougher and stronger than any young boot could hope to be.

Toughness and strength are relative. For a military boot camp, a large part of it is physical. In an organizational setting, I wouldn't recommend stomach punching as a way to demonstrate strength.

A drill instructor for a Legend needs to be as smart as he is, more successful, and even more ruthless. The ideal would be to pair a guy like Neo with a bigger, stronger Narcissist. This is not as ridiculous as it sounds. As we will see in the next chapter, Narcissistic Superstars make the best mentors. If you survive their training, you can survive anything, and you *will* learn. There is no try—only do.

If you are not Yoda or a Narcissist and you take on the task of mentoring a Legend, you will have to find the toughness within yourself. Being nice will not cut it.

Often, companies hire consultants or therapists to be their drill instructors. As I said: get a bigger narcissist. If you do that, the process cannot occur in the isolation of someone's office or training camp. Your drill instructor will have to be able to assign tasks at the office and communicate freely about how they are accomplished. Be sure to get the appropriate information releases before you start.

## Acknowledge Self-Interest as the Only Possible Motivation

This is absolutely critical if you are to deal successfully with any Narcissist. They do not believe in altruism. They think Mother Theresa did what she did not out of the goodness of her heart but because she wanted to be a saint. Are they right? Only Mother Theresa can know. As I mentioned, there is plenty of narcissism without greatness but no greatness without narcissism. Believe me or not, but in order to have any credibility with

Narcissists you have to step into their world enough to admit that everybody takes.

Military boot camps stress time-tested concepts such as duty and honor. They do not present them as altruism, but as a valuable personal possession much like the Asian concept of "face." Soldiers will give their lives for us, but they do so at least partly because they could not tolerate themselves if they had to and didn't. In the military, there is nothing dishonorable in this sort of motivation.

## Set the Ordeal

Boot camps are an ordeal in the anthropological sense. Ordeals serve to teach an initiate to conquer personal fear and pain and, by so doing, become a member of the group. Ordeals are often physical, but what they teach is psychological. They can consist of push-ups in the mud, hanging by hooks from your pectoral muscles, or adult circumcision. All of these have been used successfully over the ages, but most are against OSHA regulations.

The best ordeals make an initiate face and master his or her greatest fear and, by doing that, learn a lesson that cannot be taught in any other way. At work, choosing the appropriate ordeal will take some creativity.

*"Okay, Neo," his mentor said. "Here's the deal. I'm going to set you an assignment for the next six months. Either you do it or you're out the door. If you succeed, you get a promotion and a chance to choose your next assignment. Are you in?"*

*"Aren't you going to tell me what it is first?"*

*"No. First you need to hear the terms, so that there is no misunderstanding. Then I'll tell you what the assignment is. Do you understand?"*

*"Yeah, sure."*

*"Your mission, should you decide to accept it, is to run a computer repair clinic. Anyone who has computer problems can come to you, and you will fix them, and do so cheerfully, and without making the people who come to you feel like idiots."*

*"You've got to be out of your mind. Do you realize—"*

*"Yes, I realize, and I probably am out of my mind. But that's the deal. Take it or leave it."*

Many Narcissistic Legends would walk, but Neo didn't. He has a family to support. Truth be known, he agreed, thinking that he'd be able to get around the rules as he has in every other situation.

## Follow-Through

Once the ordeal is set, it must be monitored and followed through to the letter. In an ideal world, the mentor–drill instructor would throw Neo into the pool, and that would teach him how to swim. In Neo's case, "swimming" is learning cognitive skills to help him master the fear and anger he must conquer in order to survive his ordeal. Mentor–drill instructors, especially if they are bigger narcissists, may not be up to the teaching part of the task. The most important part of their job at this point is to see that the initiate doesn't sneak out of the pool. This requires consistent monitoring. If mentor–drill instructors are Narcissists themselves, the monitoring can be part of *their* ordeal.

Organizations have access to many classes and trainers that can teach Neo the specific skills he needs, now that he knows he needs them. We will review the most important of these skills and how they are taught in the next section, on Narcissistic anger.

The biggest mistake that I see made over and over in this situation is putting people in classes before they recognize that they need to learn the material. This turns a perfectly good class into something to joke about on late-night TV. Can you imagine what the military would be like if new recruits were sent to How to Be a Soldier, Sailor, or Marine classes that were like the class you took on how to write your résumé?

Neo made it. For six months he fixed computer problems for people whom he had previously described as not knowing which end of the plug goes into the wall. Not only did he fix computers well but, with help and support, he also was able to teach people how to use them more easily and efficiently. His coworkers, who used to hold him in awe but considered him a pain in the ass, now also liked him and thought of him as a part of the group.

I'd like to say that that as a result of this ordeal, this Grinch's small heart grew six sizes that day, but we're talking about a Narcissist here. Enough to say that Neo learned how to do things he didn't want to do and even to take some pride in doing them well. For a Narcissistic Legend, that is good enough.

## NARCISSISTIC ANGER

Narcissistic Legends think they shouldn't have to do what they don't want to, but they are generally not slackers. Legends will bust their butts in some areas and totally ignore others. The "other" they most often ignore is social skills. They see no need to control their emotions and have little concern about the effect their emotional outbursts have on other people. Narcissistic anger can be legendary.

Dr. Karen Richardson, the new hospitalist, is smart and competent, and she has a good sense of humor, but she's everybody's last pick for Ms. Popularity. When things are going her way, she's reasonable; when they're not, she throws tantrums—at *people*.

Dr. Richardson does not suffer fools gladly. She makes them suffer. Fools, in her opinion, are incompetent nurses who fail to notify her of changes in her patients' condition; who call her at inconvenient times to ask ridiculous questions that they should have learned in first-year nursing; who misunderstand perfectly clear instructions; who are not immediately at her beck and call, following her orders to the letter; or who, God forbid, question her medical judgment.

The fact is that sometimes her judgment needs questioning. Dr. Karen prides herself on her efficiency. She works hard and quickly—sometimes too quickly. She doesn't make big mistakes, but she does occasionally overlook some details and sometimes doesn't take enough time to write clear orders.

The nurses on her floors started out by trying to be diplomatic, but they were often rewarded for their efforts by insults, sarcasm, tirades, and complaints about their competence to hospital administration. The climate became actively hostile, and the nurses began filing complaints of their own.

Much to her surprise and chagrin, Dr. Karen lost the power struggle. She was called in to the medical director's office, written up, and told that her bullying would not be tolerated.

Dr. Karen is not a bully like the ones we saw in Chapter 5. The distinction may be irrelevant to the nurses she chews out, but the dynamics of her anger are different. Bullies like to see people cringe, and they go out of their way to create conflict, especially with people who are weaker than they are. Dr. Karen's anger arises from her belief that, because of their training, doctors are a breed apart. In her opinion, the MD at the end of her name confers the same divine rights as those accorded to monarchs in the Middle Ages. The lower orders should obey her instantly, and they have no right to question her judgment. They should treat her in just the way she had to treat her professors in medical school. Anything less would be an insult to the medical profession.

Unlike Antisocial Bullies, Narcissistic Legends like Karen Richardson react to reprimands from superiors not with deference, but with confusion. Bullies see their bosses as bigger bullies. Narcissists see reprimands as breaking the rules of the professional club they thought they were members of, be it Management or Medicine. Narcissists who have been criticized feel like abandoned children. I'm not suggesting that you take pity on them, but that you understand their dynamics. Narcissists usually have only two emotional states: on top of the world or at the bottom of the garbage pile. The only time they are open to new learning is when they feel tossed into the garbage.

Even then, Narcissists seldom learn to get over their narcissism, but they can be taught to be less obnoxious. Explosive Narcissistic Legends like Karen are sometimes sent to anger management classes, which they consider to be adding insult to injury. The classroom approach seldom works for a number of reasons, the main one being that for a class to work, a student has to want to learn what's being taught. Narcissists believe that their anger is different and more justified than that of other people. They are right about the "different" part.

For any kind of learning to take place, Narcissists need to be engaged individually and sold on the idea that controlling their temper is in their own best interest. This must be done before they will go into treatment willingly. Sometimes, when this sales job is done well by the right kind of person, it is all the treatment that Narcissists need.

Rita has been night ward clerk as long as anyone can remember. She's seen doctors, nurses, patients, and administrators come and go, and she is regarded at the hospital as a force of nature.

She sees Karen trembling as she logs into a patient's chart.

"Honey," she says, "I think you need a break."

Karen looks at Rita, clearly perplexed.

"Should I have said *Doctor* Honey?"

Despite herself, Karen offers a weak smile. It's lonely in the garbage pile.

"Honey," continues Rita, "I know you're having a crappy day. You can make it worse or better. It's up to you."

"I don't see how it could get much worse."

"That's right, you *don't* see. It could get way worse if you get this load of shit dumped on your head and don't learn a thing from it."

Karen turns away. "I don't have the slightest idea what you're talking about."

"I *know* you don't know. Come with me. Let's go get a cup of coffee. I'll tell you."

In the back of the break room in the middle of the night, Rita and Karen sit drinking coffee.

"Honey, you're a smart girl and a good doctor, except when you've got your head up your butt."

"Look, if you're trying to tell me to be nicer to the poor nurses, Dr. Barth took care of that."

"No, I'm not gonna waste my time telling you that you should be nicer to nurses; you know that already. You don't think you should, and even if you did, you don't know how."

"You mean just ignore their incompetence?"

Rita laughs. "That's just what I mean. If that's what you think, you *don't* know how."

"And you're going to teach me?"

"Only if you want to learn."

"So what is it you think I need to learn?"

"How to stop getting yourself all pissed off when something doesn't go your way."

"I'm getting myself pissed off? What about them? You can't tell me that not following orders is OK. Do you know what happened yesterday? I wrote orders for IV's every two hours—"

"You're doing it now."

"Doing what?"

"Pissing yourself off; probably giving yourself a headache too. This world is full of people who don't do what they're supposed to do. The more you yell, the less they do. If you want them to do more, you gotta calm down and use your head. Suck up to them like you want them to suck up to you. Say something nice for a change. It couldn't hurt; it might help."

"So, are you trying to tell me I can catch more flies with sugar than I can with vinegar?"

Rita laughs. "Honey, if you want flies, forget the sugar. Use bullshit."

Rita has had years of experience with socializing young Narcissistic doctors who are full of themselves. They're full of other things as well. The first step in making them human is teaching them how to control their tempers. Rita is as skilled at anger management therapy as most doctors. She may not be able to list the steps in a treatment plan, but she knows what works.

For teaching Narcissistic Legends the basic people skills that they've neglected, wise mentors often do a better job than therapists, especially with people who won't deign to see therapists. You've probably noticed that Rita is using some of the same boot camp techniques that worked on Neo. Here are the basic elements of her method. Whether she knows it or not, she's doing the same things a seasoned therapist would do in treating narcissistic anger.

No Bluff, No Bull: The situation is real; Karen's job is in jeopardy. Rita, who has seen such situations before, approaches at a teachable moment when she's feeling bad and wants to feel better. Because of her years of experience, Rita is taking the dominant role of teacher and telling Karen that she can learn something that will make her feel better. This is a sales pitch, but it isn't a bluff. Rita knows she can help Karen if she listens.

Will Karen listen? That all depends on what she hears. Rita knows how to catch flies. If you're attempting to socialize a Narcissistic Legend, you'd better know how as well.

Tell Them They're Smart: Acknowledging Narcissists' intelligence is absolutely necessary if you want them to hear anything else you have to say.

As with any emotional vampire, if you want to communicate effectively, you have to step into their world and avoid saying anything that contradicts their view of themselves. If you don't tell Narcissistic Legends that they're smart, they'll keep trying to demonstrate their intelligence until you do.

**USE HUMOR:** Most Narcissists have a well-developed, often mordant, sense of humor. If an irritable person is humorless, she is probably not a Narcissist; instead, she most likely is an Obsessive-Compulsive, who would require a different approach, which we will discuss in the next section.

Rita has a lot of street credibility, so she can get away with teasing that is supportive and challenging at the same time. If you are not in a position to tease a Legend, you may not be the one to try an approach like this. Find someone who can.

**TELL THEM THEY'RE RIGHT:** Don't waste time and effort arguing about who's right or wrong. Narcissists are always right, but being right doesn't get them what they want. This is the point you want to make—not that they are wrong, but that their strategy is ineffective.

**FORGET TRYING TO TEACH EMPATHY:** The biggest mistake you can make with Narcissists is trying to sell them empathy directly. They won't buy. The pattern they expect is to be told they ought to care more than they do. They've heard it before. It didn't work then, and it won't work now.

In the Narcissistic world, it doesn't matter what other people feel as much as it does in yours. Believers especially should take note of this.

Any approach to empathy should be indirect, based solely on self-interest. You can teach Narcissists that how other people feel is directly related to their getting what they want. They can learn to fake empathy quite realistically. That's the bullshit Rita was talking about.

Before you get too shocked at the idea of teaching people to be phony and manipulative, recognize that this is how we all, as toddlers, learned the authentic empathy that we now prize in ourselves as adults. Didn't somebody have to keep after you to say "please" and "thank you"?

**TELL THEM WHAT'S IN IT FOR THEM:** Narcissists believe in self-interest. If what you're saying will not benefit them, they're not interested.

Teaching Narcissists anything is a sales job, but luckily in this case Rita has an excellent product, the secret to happiness, as well as the way for Karen to keep her job.

**SPEAK OF ANGER AS SOMETHING THEY DO, RATHER THAN SOMETHING THAT HAPPENS TO THEM:** The one key insight upon which treatment for anger or any other emotional outburst is based is that emotions are something you *do* as opposed to being inevitable reactions to other people's misbehavior. Anger starts as a spark of irritation that will quickly go out if you don't fan the flame.

If people don't grasp this critical fact, no amount of teaching anger management techniques will work. If they do understand this insight, almost any technique will work.

**SUGGEST THAT ANGER BURNS OUT IF YOU DON'T FAN THE FLAME:** Fanning the flame means repeating an injustice over and over internally or out loud. With each retelling it gets more grievous and connects with more injustices past, present, and future. Through retelling, what may have started as a simple misunderstanding becomes an assault upon natural law.

One of the most effective ways to teach people about fanning the flame is to catch them when they are doing it and stop them. Rita did this with Karen. There are no visuals with their dialogue. Had there been, we probably would have seen Karen doing what most people do when they're fanning the flame: pointing a finger in the air or counting on her fingers. When people do this in my office, I ask them to sit on their hands, which completely disrupts the pattern. It is almost impossible to fan a flame without using your hands. In the confusion that follows disruption of a pattern, some real gut-level learning may occur.

Speaking out in anger also fans the flame by reinforcing the feeling and by the fact that it usually leads to retaliation. As people are learning control, the first approximation is getting them to keep their mouth shut when they feel angry. I call this the "duct-tape solution." Rita probably uses surgical tape.

**POINT OUT THAT WHAT ANGER FEELS LIKE IS NOT WHAT IT IS:** Anger feels right and powerful when it is happening. Often, angry people mistake this for feeling good.

At work, losing your temper is usually regarded as a weakness. If there is a conflict, the coolest head is most likely to prevail. Aside from being ineffective, anger—even righteous indignation, its most seductive form—actually feels terrible, not to mention being terrible for your health. Anger is compelling, but the drive is to turn it off by getting what you want. It is a potent negative reinforcer. When people are experiencing anger, they seldom focus on how it feels. They are paying too much attention to what anger is telling them to do, which is usually to give their headache back to the person who gave it to them.

If you stop and think about it, which is always a good idea, there are other ways to get rid of a headache. At the top of the list is not giving it to yourself in the first place.

This is the point where we left Rita and Karen. In a short conversation, Rita outlined all the crucial elements of anger management treatment. The rest is repetition and practice. Perhaps they will continue their talks, or maybe Rita can refer Karen to a therapist now that she's more likely to profit from the experience.

The last and most significant thing to take away from the dialogue between Rita and Karen is that Rita focused on the outbursts themselves, not on the feeling of entitlement that lies beneath them. Even seasoned therapists don't go after that directly. If you aren't in a position to rehabilitate an angry Narcissistic Legend, still, in your dealings with them, always remember: if you are outraged by outrageous people, you will be the one who suffers.

## ENTREPRENEURS

We revere entrepreneurs, many of whom are Narcissists. This shouldn't surprise you. Who but a Narcissist would have the chutzpah to start a business?

The rest of us would be nowhere without entrepreneurs. There is a catch, however. One of the reasons that so many promising new businesses fail is that the people who start them are Narcissistic Legends, who take it for granted that expertise in one area automatically confers expertise in all.

Don is a mechanical genius. Nobody knows more about linkages than he does. In his garage, he has developed several prototypes that are simple, cheap, durable, and absolutely elegant, as is the process he devised for their manufacture. He started $D^2$ (for Donald Davis), found his niche, and before long his company had grown from 10 employees to more than 100. Maybe you saw his picture on the cover of several regional business magazines.

It all seems like the perfect success story, except for one problem: Don.

Don can't let go of anything. It's not that he's a control freak; he's more like a big amiable puppy who's there all the time, bounding around, getting in everyone's way. The company is his life, and he wants to be in on everything.

It used to be Don and two other guys in his garage doing everything. Now there are departments for Procurement, Marketing, Manufacturing, Sales, Finance, and Human Resources, and Don still acts as if they're all working together in his garage. He goes everywhere, talks to everybody, and tells them what he thinks they should be doing.

Sometimes his ideas are excellent. It's just that there are so many of them, and he doesn't seem to recognize how disruptive a change in procedure can be if it's not coordinated up and down the line.

Don's constant tweaking drives his managers crazy. However they set things up today could change tomorrow if the boss has a better idea.

Don is proud of $D^2$'s flexibility and openness to innovation. He doesn't seem to realize that too much flexibility is indistinguishable from chaos.

Don creates chaos because he doesn't understand that managing a company requires a completely different set of skills from creating elegant linkages.

In any business, there are three entities that must be managed: tasks, money, and people. Managers with training and experience know that you have to manage all three, not just the one at which you excel. Don, being a consummate engineer, is phenomenal at managing tasks. Whatever it is, he can figure out how to do it better. In his mind, that's all there is to it.

As with most entrepreneurial Narcissistic Legends, he is oblivious to the parts of management that don't interest him, which in Don's case is managing people and money.

The department heads have tried to explain this much management theory to Don, but he doesn't understand. His feelings get hurt, and then he gets mad. Regardless of what his managers tell him, he keeps coming back to the idea that if you do tasks in the best way possible, the company should prosper. Don doesn't change, so everybody else has to.

How his managers react to Don's intransigence creates even more chaos. Every one of them has developed an individual style of dealing with Don. The Believers try to accommodate him, because it's his company and they don't want to fight with him or hurt his feelings. Rebels don't mind hurting Don's feelings. They argue with him or say they'll do things his way and then don't. Competitors play their cards close to their chests. They hold back information, and when things don't go well, they point the finger anywhere they can. Pretty soon, everybody is blaming everybody else, and $D^2$ is going down the tubes.

Don thinks the company has problems because his managers are a bunch of squabbling malcontents, which they are. He doesn't see that it's his style that keeps the conflict going.

$D^2$ is about to become one of the many promising start-ups that self-destruct after a few years. If you ask anybody who works there, they will tell you what the problem is. They just don't know what to do about it.

Whatever the managers might tell you, the real issue they're dealing with is getting a Narcissistic Legend to understand or care about something beyond his own area of interest. Here are some ideas that might help.

**HANG TOGETHER OR HANG SEPARATELY:** The very first thing the managers have to do is decide that it is in their individual best interests to act in concert. This should be obvious. Lack of coordination is the problem; only coordination can solve it. The situation is like the prisoner's dilemma, in that cooperation is the best course only if everybody else is cooperating.

To get things started, there has to be a nucleus. If the three most powerful managers are on board, there's hope. If they aren't convinced, nobody will be. Convincing people will take time and some heavy-duty meetings without Don.

The first test of unity is agreeing what to say when Don finds out about the meetings, which he will. Everyone needs to say, "We aren't ready to talk about that yet. When we are, you will be the first to know."

If you get leaks to Don, which you will, you have to go back to discussing self-interest in the group of managers. Who benefits if the company runs into the ground? If someone thinks he or she might, then that person will be an obstacle. If that person is one of the top three managers, obstruction may prove fatal.

**KNOW YOUR GOAL:** The goal here is not to stop Don from meddling, which won't happen, but to adopt decision-making rules that keep his meddling from being so disruptive. The simplest solution in an organization like $D^2$ is to adopt a policy that no changes will be put into effect until they are discussed at regular management team meetings and a group decision is made as to when and how to implement. In addition, the group should agree on a chain of command structure such that direction in each department comes from the department head alone. This will make it safe for employees to tell Don that they have to check with their manager before acting on his suggestions.

**SPEAK THE ENTREPRENEUR'S LANGUAGE:** Don is an engineer who hasn't learned the standard vocabulary of business, so his managers will have to speak his language. They need to develop a metaphor through which rudimentary organizational theory can be presented in mechanical or mathematical terms that Don can understand and use to communicate with them. If he can grasp what is going on in the organization, he can use his analytical skills to be part of the solution rather than the source of the problem.

The managers put together a presentation. The first slide is a diagram of Don's elegant manufacturing process, which is the very essence of mechanical cooperation. As the group watches, below each node, a set of dials and levers appears. They are labeled "specifications."

The presenter can then show that changes set manually in one node require manual changes in other areas and ask, "What's wrong with this system?"

Don knows the answer, since the beauty of his system is in the sensors at each node that can detect and respond to changes in the other nodes. He elaborates on how this process works.

In the next slide, the names of the nodes change one by one to "Procurement," "Marketing," "Manufacturing," "Sales," and "Finance and Human Resources"—the organizational structure is represented as a mechanical process. The same dials and levers beneath the nodes are used to demonstrate the effects of manual changes. The striking conclusion is that there is no sensor mechanism through which all the nodes can coordinate. Since there is no way that electronic sensors can be implanted in the managers' brains, verbal communication is required. The presentation demonstrates that the regular meetings and adhering to the chain of command serve similar functions to the sensors in the manufacturing process.

Don, of course, explains how the sensing processes differ, but by doing so he is actually discussing a topic that he was unable or unwilling to talk about before. It will require work to hammer out the details, but with a common language, the work can now be done.

SIGN THE CONSTITUTION: Once the details are implemented, they should be codified into policies and procedures that are the new ground rules for running the business. Everyone in management should literally sign on. This is yet another metaphor that will ensure that the rules are important and are to be taken seriously.

Obviously, every entrepreneurial organization is different, but if they are to be successful, they must go through a critical stage of development in which day-to-day authority shifts from the entrepreneur to a management team.

Since so many entrepreneurs fit the pattern of Narcissistic Legends, that shift will require teaching them something that they have heretofore considered unimportant. If entrepreneurs are to learn anything from the people who work for them, the lessons must be presented in a language that Narcissists understand.

# Narcissistic Superstars

**14**

ARCISSISTIC SUPERSTARS believe that they are the most important people on earth, and they've got the résumé to prove it.

Unlike Legends, Superstars are usually successful. They're willing to do whatever it takes to turn their grandiose dreams into reality. Which means they're always doing. Superstars' dreams are always beyond their grasp. Their abilities, coupled with their tremendous drive, may bring them success, but never satisfaction. They build empires, lead nations, run businesses, create great works of art, and amass huge sums of money for one purpose only: to prove how great they are. Superstars may boast incessantly about what they have and what they've done, but once they have it or have done it, it loses value in their eyes. They always need more. Whether it's money, honors, status symbols, or sexual conquests, Superstars always want something. And they get it. Every one of them has a trophy collection. Adding to it is the sole purpose of Narcissistic existence; there is no higher goal.

Superstars are capable of great deeds and incredible pettiness. Everything is about them all the time. If you accept this fact and do nothing to contradict it, Superstars cease to be a danger and become merely an annoyance. If you are offended by their arrogance, and have fantasies about teaching them a lesson, you'd better get away quickly, because they will destroy you.

Unfortunately, there are few places you can get away to, because wherever you go, there will likely be a Narcissistic Superstar in a position of authority over you. So, what's it to be? Do you fight them, run from them, or learn how to deal with them?

Don't get him wrong, Galen likes his job, loves some of it. But then there's Ron, the VP, his boss.

The good part is that most of the time Ron couldn't care less how Galen runs things as long as he doesn't spend too much money. Ron's forte is cost control, the management philosophy also espoused by Michelle, the CEO. Neither of them likes spending money on anything but dividends and bonuses.

The hard part of Galen's job is trying to communicate with someone who has little interest in what it takes to run the department. Ron and Galen are supposed to have regular meetings, but for whatever reason they seldom happen. What's more typical is Ron dropping by Galen's office for a briefing, usually about a half hour before an executive team meeting.

"So, how are things going?" Ron asks.

Galen opens his notepad. "Pretty good, but there are a couple of things that need your attention."

"I need a PowerPoint for the meeting," Ron says as he plays with his phone, "Put together something showing the top five projects we're working on, when they'll come online, and what kind of return we expect. You know, stuff like that. Make it sexy. Have you got any coffee in here? No?" He picks up his phone. "Tell Cathy, 'Bring coffee.' At Galen's."

If you're a parent, isn't there something about Ron that seems familiar? The similarities between his behavior and that of a three-year-old are striking. Ron acts the way we all did as toddlers, before we began to recognize that we were not the center of the universe.

The instrumental side of Ron's personality, the part that sets goals and accomplishes tasks, is a sophisticated adult. The emotional side is stuck at about three and a half. Remember this if you ever have to babysit a Superstar.

Another way to think about it is that Narcissistic Superstars, like all emotional vampires, live by instincts programmed into the oldest part of their brains. They literally act like animals. Survival of the fittest is the whole of the law, supported by the dominance hierarchies that we discussed in Chapter 5. The rules for animals are straightforward: the biggest and strongest—the alphas—are better. They get the best food and the best sex. In return for this, in many species, they are responsible for protecting the group.

In the oldest part of our own brains, we are still programmed to believe that some creatures are better than others. Until very recently, dominance hierarchies were an unquestioned part of human existence. In every culture, there were nobles and commoners, alphas and omegas. There still are, though in most places this hierarchy is no longer the official doctrine.

The problem with the human version of this system is that alphas firmly subscribe to the "being better" part of this compact, but, unlike animals, they can sometimes ignore the part about protecting the group. Noblesse oblige but narcissism doesn't. Narcissistic nobles see others as obligated to them.

Narcissistic nobles do not deign to follow the same rules as mere commoners. For all the deference our nobility is accorded, what do they give back? This has been the question at the center of all political disputes since the dawn of time.

Politics aside, if you work for a Narcissistic Superstar like Ron, you will need to know how to communicate with someone of higher rank who considers himself to have more intrinsic value than you do. Whether you think he's worth more or not, you are not going to change his opinion. You *will* have to bow.

This, however, is not the end of the story. Bowing does not have to mean abject servitude. In most societies in which there were nobles and commoners, the commoners have believed that the nobles were not very bright. This may be the result of inbreeding, but it is also true that people who are adults in some areas and three-year-olds in others have certain blind spots that can be exploited to get the message across. It is not an accident that viziers reason with kings in much the same way that parents reason with toddlers.

There are subtle ways to control people who believe they are in control. If you work for a Narcissistic Superstar, you'd do well to learn some of them. No, you shouldn't have to, but there will be unpleasant consequences if you don't.

## THE CARE AND FEEDING OF NARCISSISTIC SUPERSTAR BOSSES

Now that we know what they are, how do we keep Narcissistic Superstars like Ron from grinding us under the heels of their booties? As with other emotional vampires, you have to step into their reality and do nothing to contradict their idea that they are smarter than everyone else and should take the lead in everything. To step out of the expected pattern, you need to use some of the same techniques that clever ministers have used on absolute monarchs from time immemorial: come at Narcissists from their blind side, and lead while appearing to follow. Here's how.

**FIRST, SUCK UP:** There is absolutely no way around this. If you want to communicate effectively with Narcissists, you have to suck up. That being said, if you think of it as sucking up, you're probably not doing it particularly well.

Eskimos supposedly have a hundred words for snow, which allows them to make finer and finer discriminations about an element that is critical to their survival. How many terms do you have to describe the vast array of political interactions that occur between superiors and subordinates? If there is only one, they will all tend to look the same.

Rebels and Believers generally have very small descriptive vocabularies for office politics; "sucking up" is the most common term and the least graphic. Unfortunately for them, it is very difficult to think about something you cannot name.

The two groups have different reasons for their lack of political sophistication. Rebels have a hard time acknowledging that anyone can tell them what to do, and they feel some hostility toward anyone who tries. Believers consider political maneuvering to be a lapse in morality akin to lying, cheating, or stealing. Competitors have understood and use politics, but unless they are careful to check their moral compasses, they can also be used by them.

Whichever group you belong to, add this to your lexicon: what many people call "sucking up" means acknowledging someone's importance. Viewed in this manner, is there anyone you shouldn't suck up to? This is a major blind spot in the thinking of Narcissists. Don't let it be one in yours. People above you expect deference, and those that you consider beneath your notice can still hold grudges.

**DO UNTO BOSSES AS THEY WOULD HAVE YOU DO UNTO THEM:** The Golden Rule is fine, but this one is more effective. As we saw in Chapter 9, depending upon their personalities, emotional vampires in power have differing expectations about how you should defer to them. Histrionics expect to be treated as they treated their high school teachers. Narcissistic Superstars expect to be treated like Hapsburg emperors.

Please note that these expectations have more to do with style than content. High school teachers actually like it when students engage in lively discussions. Emperors expect you to speak only when spoken to, and then only in bullet points.

**BE AVAILABLE:** Narcissists want what they want when they want it, and that means you. Now! When they call, you need to come running.

This does not necessarily mean being available 24/7 unless it is specifically demanded. Most Narcissists will accept less, but you will have to set the limits and defend them. Bear in mind that Narcissists have the same capacity for waiting as three-year-olds. They need to be trained to defer gratification in much the same way as you would train a toddler. Let them know how long it will be before they get what they want.

First, you have to decide what availability is reasonable. At the very least, Narcissistic bosses need to be your top priority during the workday. If they call, you need to drop what you're doing and answer. If you are involved in a task that cannot be interrupted, let them know in advance.

If you are going to say no to availability at times that you consider unreasonable, the way to do so is by stating firmly when you *will* be available. Then you will have to defend that boundary against manipulative attempts to push the limits. Superstars are much more likely to wear you down with small boundary incursions than they are to flatly state that you need to be available on nights, weekends, and vacations. Like most vampires, they prefer the grooming process, moving you a little at a time, over an outright demand. That way, it looks as if you are part of the process. If Narcissists do state that 24/7 availability is a job requirement, you have to decide whether the job is worth it.

> Galen allows after-work calls only in emergencies. His procedure is clearly stated on the voice-mail greeting on his work mobile: "If this is an emergency, please leave a message as to the nature of the problem, and I will decide on the most appropriate response." His subordinates respect this and are grateful for Galen's quick response to infrequent real emergencies.

Ron, as usual, is another story. The message he leaves is simply, "Call me."

Galen doesn't. There are three more messages of the same type. Then they stop.

The next day at work, Ron approaches Galen in the hall. "Where were you last night? I was worried. I almost called the police."

"I'm here now."

"Yeah, but where were you last night?"

"You know my procedure."

"What's with this procedure crap? It was no big deal. I just wanted to know the name of the guy you talk to at Grayson."

"Bob Grimes."

"You don't have to be such an asshole about it."

Most people would not dare to deal with a Narcissistic boss in this way. They think they will get fired, but that's not usually what happens, especially to people in key positions or in larger businesses. Narcissists may be insensitive and supercilious assholes, but unlike Antisocial Bullies, they don't bother to create conflict for its own sake.

Superstars expect their subordinates to stand up for themselves, and they don't respect them unless they do. Galen has often heard Ron say, "If you had a problem with it, you should have said something." Galen took that advice to heart, and said something. This is the only way to defend a boundary with a Superstar.

Actually, Galen's response was even stronger for what he didn't say. He didn't accuse Ron of doing anything wrong, and he didn't attempt to defend his procedure. He just followed it.

When Narcissists don't get what they want when they want it, they grumble. So what? If you give in to three-year-olds' tantrums, you just teach them that tantrums get them what they want.

Galen's steadfastness forced Ron into choosing whether to give a direct order to be available 24/7 or to drop the issue. Of course, Ron will get in a few digs, but Galen recognizes that as a sign of victory rather than defeat. Narcissists are never completely happy about anything except getting what they want when they want it, and then the happiness doesn't last long. If you think your job is to make Superstars happy, you are doomed. In most cases being totally available when you say you will be is your best defense against unreasonable demands.

**MAKE THEM PAY UP FRONT:** Never extend credit or accept promises from Narcissists. As soon as they get what they want, they will be on to the next thing, forgetting whatever they said they would do for you. Sometimes they make promises they don't intend to keep, but just as often, they merely forget. Either way, you should keep a ledger in your mind and make sure you get what they dangle in front of you before you give them what they want. With other people, this mercenary approach might seem insulting. Narcissists will respect you for it. Everything in their world is quid pro quo. They will rarely be offended by people looking out for themselves.

> Ron has goals for Galen's department that coincide with CEO Michelle's goals for the division. As is typical for the company, the goals are usually financial rather than relating to products or services. When the goals are set, Galen negotiates the bonuses for himself and the team should their performance exceed expectations, which it often does. He knows that the only time Narcissists like Ron are willing to pay for something is before they get it, and even then they prefer to put it on the credit card.
>
> When the bonus is negotiated, Galen sends an e-mail to Ron outlining the terms, and he does not move a muscle until he gets verification. He has learned the hard way that this is the only way to proceed. Without a written contract, there is always quibbling about details.

One of the biggest financial mistakes you can make if you work for a Superstar is to expect to be rewarded with raises and bonuses for good work that has already been done. The best you'll get at annual review time is a paltry percentage increase, and that is assuming you can get your Superstar boss to actually do an annual review.

People who value keeping their promises have a hard time remembering that a verbal contract with a vampire is not worth the paper it's written on. Superstars *will* pay for what they want, but only if you negotiate in advance and have a signed contract.

**NEVER SHARE CONFIDENCES:** Narcissists love to talk about themselves. They may sound as if they're being open and honest, but what they're doing has little to do with intimacy. Often, they are just turning on the external speakers to whatever thoughts happen to be going through their minds at the time. Do not reciprocate with stories about yourself, unless you want to hear them again at the most inopportune moment. Narcissists are experts at getting information out of people, and they are utterly ruthless about using it for their own purposes.

> Ron and Galen are at lunch at the deli. Ron looks at the menu and shakes his head. "I want the ham and Swiss, but the doctor says I can't have the cheese. I've been seeing her about this con-stipation problem, and she finally figured out that I'm lactose intolerant."
>
> Without thinking, Galen says, "I know the feeling. I was having problems with irritable bowel until the doc made me cut down on coffee."
>
> At a meeting a few days later, Ron asks if Galen wants coffee, and remarks that he doesn't need to worry, the men's room is right next door.

Narcissists delight in keeping people off-balance. Ron also calls Galen "Mr. Procedure" based on the phone message incident. Galen knows better than to make an issue of any such comments. He also knows better than to give any more personal information that he doesn't want handed back to him in public.

**LEARN, BUT DO NOT PRESUME TO TEACH:** Powerful people, be they emperors, Narcissists, or high school teachers, have another side as well. They are knowledgeable and effective in the areas they consider important. They also like to show off what they know. What good is all that wisdom without someone to appreciate it?

If a Superstar like Ron is feeling philosophical, he might call you in for a lesson. One of the perquisites of greatness is being able to lecture about whatever you want, whenever you want to. Listening is mandatory. You might as well learn something while you're at it.

Narcissistic lectures can be quite instructive. Aside from the self-aggrandizement, there is very little bull. Superstars tell it like it is—or at least like they *think* it is. If you pay attention, you'll learn how powerful people talk and, from that, how they think. You live and work in their world. You might as well know how that world operates. Unlike Histrionics, Narcissists will actually tell you.

Seriously, Narcissists make excellent mentors. This may surprise you if you think of mentoring as involving instruction, discussion, and lots of earnest feedback. That's not the way it's done in the big leagues.

Zen sword masters would make their students do menial tasks like cleaning house, cutting wood, and drawing water. As the students worked, the masters would sneak up and attack them with sticks. Students either developed warrior consciousness or they got the crap beaten out of them.

This is what it's like to have a Superstar as a mentor. You learn by getting the crap beaten out of you until you achieve enlightenment.

Even if you don't want a Narcissist for a mentor, there are still important things you'll need to learn, such as how to speak his language, which is a must if you ever want him to listen to you.

The best way to explain anything to Narcissists is to present it as if you actually learned it from them. There is no better hook than using Narcissists' own words to present a new idea as a direct result of their own revealed wisdom. Transparent though this ploy may be, it still works because it is consistent with the narcissistic view that all good ideas are theirs. Narcissists can be taught, but the best lessons are in their own words, or perhaps in the words of a bigger Narcissist that they revere enough to quote.

An easy way to do this is to take a favorite saying and show how your idea is just another version of that. It gets them almost every time, especially if you present it on a PowerPoint slide.

**TELL THEM WHAT THEY WANT TO HEAR:** No, I'm not suggesting that you lie or withhold information. In dealing with Narcissistic bosses, you have to step into their world and spoon out information in a form that is easy to digest. They all have a minimum daily requirement of being told how smart they are. Once they're full of that, they may be able to handle more adult fare, but it has to be presented well and quickly. Remember, Narcissistic bosses have a three-year-old's attention span, so use bullet points, and always cut to the chase.

What Narcissists don't want to hear is what "peasants" like you think, unless they ask. Even then you should answer cautiously, one step at a time, making sure that you know whether they're asking for an honest opinion or an ego massage. You don't have to lie. Just make sure you know how much of the truth they want to hear.

Ron collars Galen after a meeting. "So, how did my presentation go?"

"It was to the point."

"I thought so too. But maybe there were too many points? What do you think?"

"Well, there were quite a few."

"But not too many?"

"Well, I don't know. I heard that Lloyd [another Narcissistic VP] was saying he didn't get where you were going with it."

Ron laughs. "Well, that's Lloyd."

"Yes, that is Lloyd."

What Narcissistic bosses want to hear in detail is anything and everything you know about what the other big-time Narcissists in the company are doing, saying, and thinking. It stands to reason, then, that if you have something complex to discuss, you should couch it in terms of what other Narcissists think about the subject.

Be very careful what you say to one Narcissist about another. When there are several around, you can bet they will be circling each other like sharks. If you don't watch out, you could get eaten.

You have two choices as to how you approach this: either you are clearly your boss's ally and partisan, or you act like a parent dealing with sibling rivalry, listening to everyone but trying not to take sides. This latter approach is harder, because you are connected with your own boss and would not be expected to betray him or her except by accident. As we shall see, Superstar sharks like Lloyd are experts at making such accidents happen.

If you are closely allied with a Superstar Boss like Ron in his game of thrones, you may share in his rewards, depending on how loyal he feels to you or what you have negotiated. You will definitely share his punishments if and when he messes up.

To take on the more difficult neutral role, you have to give everybody something, but whatever you give one should not be taken away from somebody else. Information is the coin of the realm. Make sure you tell everybody the same thing at the same time. If there is an official story, stick to it unless it is deceptive. Superstar sharks like Ron may believe that they can fool other Superstars, but that is seldom the case. It is in your best interest to push hard for the truth or a reasonable facsimile of it. This, as we will see, is particularly important in a crisis situation when there is big money at stake.

**SPEAK THEIR LANGUAGE:**  From listening to Ron's lectures, Galen learned that he thinks of business in two dimensions: time and money. Whatever information you have to convey must be reduced to the common denominator and presented as bullet points in fluent Narcissist.

The network is down again. All the divisions use it, but it is in Ron's division and Galen's department. When it fails, it's Galen's problem.

The servers are old and stretched beyond the limits of their capacity. But divisional profits are down too, and Ron, whose eyes are always on the bottom line, doesn't want to invest money that will show up as an even bigger drop in quarterly earnings. Galen knows that to avert even bigger disasters, it's up to him to convince Ron to rethink his short-run view and seriously consider investing in a new system and the person power to get it up and running. Galen also knows that there is more to it than just the money. With Superstars, there always is.

The network crashed at 6:28 am. Now it's 7:30. Galen is assessing, coordinating, and deploying—doing whatever it takes to get the servers back online. Enter Ron.

"So, when will this sucker be fixed?" Ron asks.

"That's up to you."

"Up to me? What's that supposed to mean?"

"How much do you want to spend?"

"Well, whatever it takes. The network has to get up and running. How long will it take?"

"For a Band-Aid fix, to get it going for now—five hours, if we pay overtime and bring in all our consultants."

"Consultants? What do we need them for?"

"To get the job done today." Galen answers, sensibly avoiding an explanation of precisely what consultants will do.

"OK, take care of it."

"That's not all," Galen says. "The big problem is that no matter what we do today, the network will crash again—and soon."

"How soon?"

"I don't have a crystal ball, but if we don't upgrade the servers, it will happen for sure within three months."

"Well, let's talk about it then."

"The problem will be way worse then. We have a chance to upgrade now for a lower cost in time and money."

"So, how much will this upgrade cost?"

"600k."

"Yeah, right. How much can we knock off that?"

"600k is the bare minimum."

"Well, not today. Not with the whole cost going to this division. Do what you need to do to get this system up and running."

Galen knows that Ron is not going to spring for an upgrade without further persuasion. It takes a lot of work to get an emotional vampire like Ron to slow down his short-term fast thinking and adopt a long-run perspective. Then there is the issue that the network that everyone uses is a cost center in Ron's division. That battle of titans was fought before Galen's time, and Ron is still bitter about it.

Right now, while he has Ron's attention, Galen is just laying the groundwork by making the parameters at his end clear. More will have to happen before Ron will take them seriously.

Galen knows that more *will* happen.

**WHEN THERE'S BLOOD IN THE WATER, WATCH OUT FOR SHARKS:** As Ron goes out for coffee, Galen gets a call from Lloyd.

"Hey, Dude, what's up?" Lloyd seems to believe that this is the way everybody under 50 talks. "What's the story on the network?"

"Ron's here. He says it will be up in five hours, max."

"That's what he says. What do *you* say? You're the guy who knows."

"Best estimate is still five hours. Plan for that, but we might be able to shave some time off if we try a few tricks. Maybe even an hour. The minute I know something for sure, I'll call you."

"You'd better."

"No problem."

"Hey, Galen, while I have you here, tell me, what's with Ron? How long does he think he can put off an upgrade? Everybody knows the system is obsolete. Is he trying to hold us for ransom, or what?

"You'll have to ask Ron."

While he's talking to Lloyd, there are three other calls holding. All the VPs are on the line. Galen takes them in order, telling them all the same thing.

When there are several Superstars in an organization, every question will be considered on at least two levels: what the organization needs and how that affects the relative power of each Superstar. Nothing will be simple and direct.

Galen knows enough to avoid the political intrigues that surround the situation. His part is clear. Galen knows what the company needs, and his department has the expertise to get the job done. He needs the resources and the go-ahead. If those are to come, it will be up to Ron to fight for them. Galen has some understanding of the political issues, which he will use later as he reports to Ron on what the other VPs have said. Business as usual.

Galen's main concern is that, lacking the specific knowledge of what's needed, Ron and the executive team will try to upgrade the system on the cheap.

**DO THE POWERPOINT:** If someone, especially a Superstar, above you has to do a presentation to get something that is important to you, always do the PowerPoint presentation yourself. When you think about it, this idea makes a lot of sense. I am continually surprised at how few people think of it.

PowerPoint presentations are the literature of management, and the good ones are works of art, both written and visual. Art must be a labor of love, or at least of necessity. The person up the line may not have as much invested in the project as you do, and he or she will definitely not have as much knowledge as you do, and will not think that he or she needs to. So always cut to the chase. Edit and polish. An extra word, or God-forbid an extra slide, might lose you your audience.

Creating a PowerPoint is a chore. When it's done half-heartedly, it shows. All the slides look alike. Nothing says half-assed like posters with all the bullet points showing at the same time. Even with razzle-dazzle graphs, it's still boring.

An effective PowerPoint presentation is like an argument that proceeds in an orderly fashion. At the very least, well-composed bullet points should be animated to appear separately, one at a time. This composing is what takes time, thought, and effort. Even if you have an art department to do the formatting and the graphs, the argument should be yours. Remember that people with power, especially emotional vampires, pay most attention to the unexpected. Surprise them and you're more likely to get what you want.

Galen makes the PowerPoint for Ron to present. He works with his graphics people, but the ideas are his, and the slide show practically runs itself.

It starts with a simplified diagram of the whole network, showing how it connects to each VP's division. Nothing gets people's attention like seeing their own names on the screen. The servers are in red, as are the actual costs to each division when each of them goes down.

As we saw in the previous chapter, putting complex information on a single diagrammatic slide is useful when you need to capture Narcissists' fickle attention. If you can't snag it in three seconds, you never will.

In Galen's PowerPoint there are also slides that answer questions that are likely to be raised. One of them is "Why Can't We Just Replace the Bad Ones?" Galen is adept enough to include some technical data, but not enough to make anyone's eyes glaze over. Mostly, he has reduced the argument to the common denominators understood by all Superstars: time and money.

The overall conclusion is that upgrading the whole network now will be far cheaper than doing the job piecemeal or waiting for the next, more serious failure.

Galen knows that the problem needs to be clearly stated, which he can do better than Ron could.

He also knows that there will be group support for upgrading the network, since the cost will come out of Ron's budget, but having to pay for the whole upgrade may cause him to resist.

One slide breaks down the system usage by division. Galen has set things up so that Ron can argue that since the system affects everyone, everyone should share the cost. This is an argument close to Ron's heart, one that he can make effectively, but only if the executive group has already accepted the idea that the upgrade is necessary. This is the kind of maneuvering that Superstars love, the battle of titans.

If you make PowerPoints for Superstars, always call them "drafts," "suggestions for slides," or something equally tentative. Superstars may revise them or use them as is, but the credit will go to them. In the world of Superstars, the good ideas are always theirs. If you want something for yourself, you'll have to negotiate for it.

As a result of several meetings and some high-level compromises, the company gets the upgrade, the executives get the glory, and Galen's people get what they needed to do their jobs. Michelle and Ron are always talking about win-win situations (of course, there is a slide about win-win situations in Galen's deck). This time it looks as if they actually have created one.

**DON'T COVER FOR THEM:** Narcissists break rules all the time, because they don't believe that rules apply to them. Don't let them maneuver you into standing between them and the consequences of their behavior.

At best, that is a thankless position. At worst, they may be setting you up to take their fall.

Always keep a professional distance. Narcissists sometimes self-destruct in spectacular ways. When they do, they often bring down those closest to them. Even though there are benefits to being in a Superstar's inner circle, there are big risks as well. You do have to work effectively with Narcissistic bosses, but you don't have to be their friends or accomplices.

> Ron comes into Galen's office, looking surprisingly sheepish. After calling for coffee, he pulls himself together, and seems to be back in command.
>
> "I've been thinking about Ashley. I know she's one of your top people, and I think it's time to move her up to something bigger, with more responsibility, maybe in one of our out-of-town divisions. Something good. Why don't you talk to her and see what she'd like? She's, uh, kind of upset now. I think she misunderstood a few little things. I think an opportunity would make her feel a lot better and, you know, calm her down."
>
> "Ron," Galen says, "You need to talk to a lawyer."

## SEX AND THE SUPERSTAR

Narcissistic Superstars are famous for making fools of themselves over sex. Right now, you can probably name a dozen or so who have shot themselves in the foot by philandering. Well, maybe it's not the foot.

Sex is just one of the many forms of adulation that Narcissistic Superstars expect from other people. Superstars are major-league seducers and world-class adulterers but absolute rookies when it comes to love. Often, they don't see sex as related to love. It's more like a sport. The problem is that the people they get the sex from don't always feel that way.

> As she sits in her attorney's office, Ashley unconsciously shreds the tissue she's been using to dry her tears. Throughout this sordid mess, her feelings have fluttered back and forth between anger at Ron for using her and anger at herself for being used. Ashley always thought she was too smart to get entangled in

an office romance, but here she is discussing a sexual harassment suit, thinking at the same time that she has only herself to
blame. How did she let this happen?

Everybody knows the dangers of office romances, yet they take place all
the time. How *do* intelligent people like Ashley let things like this happen?

We could blame the Superstars, and we should. They're usually exploiting a position of greater power to get sex. So sue them. Still, deciding who's
to blame doesn't answer the question, *how do these romances happen?*

You may find it hard to believe, but people often fall into office
romances by accident. I'm talking about the kind of accidents that just
seem to happen when people rely on fast thinking instead of slow.

As with everything else that is important for survival, animals come
programmed with instincts for sex. On *National Geographic* specials, you've
probably seen birds puffing up their plumage and performing the steps of
an elaborate courtship dance. Humans do the same thing, but without the
feathers.

Courtship behavior in humans, as in most other animal species, follows
predictable and easily recognizable patterns. The dance is hardwired into
our brains. No conscious thought is needed; it's all automatic. Kids in middle school know the steps, and they will readily tease their peers for engaging in them. In offices people may be doing the same dance, but somehow
the people involved can fool themselves into thinking it's just a meaningful
business relationship and has nothing to do with sex or anything like that—
until it's too late.

Over the years, I've helped many clients pick up the pieces after dev-
astating office romances. Most of them ask themselves the same forlorn
question: *How did this happen?*

Because I heard the question so often, earlier in my career I thought
that people might be eager to learn and recognize the steps in the courtship
dance so they can make slow, informed decisions about whether to participate. This has definitely not been the case.

Before I go further, I feel I should warn you. No other subject that
I have written or spoken about has stirred up so much negative comment
as my attempts to delineate the steps of the courtship dance at work. People
get angry at me for suggesting that the harmless friendship they so value is,
at its heart, sexual. Forewarned then, they have to make a difficult choice:

Do they stop, continue, or pretend that I don't know what I'm talking about? Most choose the last, often with considerable animosity toward me for bringing the issue up.

Here, in writing, are the steps in the dance of office courtship. Read on, if you dare.

**NOTICING:** The dance begins with seeing the other person as different or somehow special. It's not necessarily sexual attraction, but attraction it is.

> The first time Ashley actually talked to Ron was when he appeared at her cubicle to tell her what a good job she did during the upgrade. She manages a group of techies who consistently have performed beyond the call of duty. Since managing techies is like herding cats, she must be good at what she does.
>
> Not that Ron actually knew about Ashley's work. Galen always tells him about people who have done a really good job, so he can stop by and say a word or two.
>
> Anyway, when Ron stopped by Ashley's cube, he noticed her *Memento* poster, because it was also one of his favorite films. They talked movies for a few minutes, and then Ron was gone.
>
> Ashley had heard about Ron being arrogant and was surprised to discover he had a nice side as well.
>
> She was really surprised when he came back.

Each step in the dance is a question that, if answered positively, signals a willingness to continue the dance. In the early stages, mere politeness may be enough of a signal to keep things going.

**DISPLAY:** When you notice the person, you want that person to notice you back. Birds use fluffed-out feathers. At the office, it's more likely to be witty comments, perceptive questions, and intelligent conversations. Ashley and Ron would speak to each other when they met in the halls. Often their comments referred to films or books they both enjoyed.

**"ACCIDENTAL" MEETINGS:** Reasons begin to appear for contacting the other person or for going places where he or she is likely to be.

Ron seemed to be wandering near Ashley's cube. Much more often than he used to. Likewise, Ashley started finding more reasons to go to the twelfth floor. It's not likely that either of them noticed a difference in their migratory patterns; they just seemed to run into each other more often.

**PLANNED COMMUNICATION:** Suddenly, each person thinks of things the other would like to know. E-mails go back and forth. Then somehow, their jobs seem to require a closer working relationship. At first, shared projects are discussed in the office; later on, discussions happen on cell phones, at restaurants, or during lunchtime walks on beautiful spring days. At this point, conversations begin to drift back and forth from work to more personal topics. For most people, the listening and understanding they get at this stage is far more seductive than mere sex.

Ashley was scheduled to do her first presentation to the executive team. She mentioned to Ron that she was a little nervous. He gave her a few useful suggestions, and he even offered to rehearse the presentation with her.

After a brief run-through, Ron told her he thought she'd do a super job.

Remember that Narcissists usually mentor like Zen sword masters, none of whom ever used the word *super*.

At this stage of the game, Ron is acting out of character, like a kind, caring leader. In theory, he could be there to help develop skills in one of Galen's promising team members, but it is definitely not his practice to associate with people this far below him.

To Ashley, it seems like Ron cares about her, and it probably seems that way to him as well. From the outside, it may look like Ron is faking the actions of someone who really cares in a cynical ploy to use his power to get sex. If that were true, Narcissists wouldn't be nearly as effective at seduction as they are. Seduction of all sorts is what Narcissists do best, because they really believe in what they're doing. When Narcissists want something, they will do whatever it takes to get it. To seduce Ashley, Ron needs to fall in love with her, so that's what he does.

His feelings look real to Ashley, because they are real. The problem is that Narcissistic love lasts only until Narcissists get what they want. Then it evaporates in their passion for the next thing, whatever that may be. If this idea seems chilling to normal people, it should be. It is the secret of the tremendous power that Narcissists can exert on everyone. We believe in them because they believe in us—until they let us down.

So, how could Ashley, or anyone, know at this stage what lies in store? She needs to remember the one aspect of human behavior about which psychology is absolutely certain: the best predictor of what people will do is what they have done in the past.

Ashley knows that Ron is on his third wife, but the hypnotic power of the courtship dance when people are in the midst of it is in the belief that it is real and different from anything that ever happened before.

Narcissists are very good at *compartmentalization*. They can draw a mental curtain around one area of their life and pretend that it has nothing to do with anything else. It's easy for them, because what connects the areas in our lives are people's feelings, something that Superstars rarely notice.

**BANTER:** In the fourth grade, boys chase the girls they like and hit them. Grown-ups in offices use teasing, joking, and playful aggression as signals of interest. It's as if Katherine Hepburn and Spencer Tracy have suddenly appeared in the IT department.

This is a dangerous stage, if the attention is unwanted. Returning the fire, laughing at jokes, or anything short of running away screaming will be interpreted as signs of reciprocal interest. The line between politeness and encouragement is so thin that it may require a jury to determine whether it actually exists.

**TOUCHING:** Neck massage, anyone? This is the point at which things become overtly sexual. If you don't believe it, watch the foot-rub sequence at the beginning of *Pulp Fiction*. Both Ashley and Ron have seen the film several times. Maybe at this point they still don't believe it applies to them, or maybe they don't care.

**CONFIDING:** At this stage, people start to believe they can tell each other everything, and they do. By far the most common way accidental sexual contact begins is with a heartfelt hug to console someone who is going through a difficult time.

These are the steps in the courtship dance. Narcissists do them exceedingly well, so be warned. I am not suggesting that Ashley should have recognized them and by so doing shares the culpability for what happened. I'll leave that to Ron's lawyer.

My goal here is to answer the question that Ashley and so many other people who were seduced and abandoned by Narcissistic Superstars have asked themselves: *How could I let something like this happen?*

I know there are times that all the interactions I've written about can occur and mean nothing. I also know that there are some office romances that work out beautifully. I assure you, I'm not in the least cynical about love. I merely think that love is far too important to fly into on automatic pilot. Just because Narcissists do, it doesn't mean you have to.

Upper-level management everywhere is full of Narcissistic Superstars. It's their world; you only work in it. Whether you like it or not, to survive and flourish, you will have to understand and live by their rules while keeping your own moral center. This is not an easy task, but it is the one that we all must face.

# Narcissistic Cultures

Narcissistic organizational culture is about robust capitalism—or at least that's what the Narcissists say. You'll often hear a lot of self-congratulatory talk about competition in the marketplace bringing out the best in people, products, services, wealth creation, and everything else the system has to offer. This may well be true, but the competition that most absorbs Narcissists is not in the marketplace but within their own organizations. Narcissists take care of themselves first. If their needs coincide with those of the organization, they can be exemplary leaders; if not, they'll sell out quicker than you can say "golden parachute." In Narcissistic cultures, the one thing you can count on is that it's every Narcissist for him- or herself.

Narcissistic cultures are about internal politics. Everything else is incidental. Alliances form and dissolve as the Narcissists at the top vie for position. Nothing is straightforward; everyone has an angle, and if you work in a Narcissistic organization, you'd better have one, too. Information is the coin of the realm, but most of what you get will be counterfeit.

In Narcissistic cultures there are two sets of rules: the ones that are written, which are mostly window dressing, and the rules that important people actually play by. Nobody will tell you the real rules, much less write them down. To prove that you are important enough to be noticed by the big guys, you have to separate the real rules from the window dressing and live by them.

Since there are so many Narcissistic Superstars in high places, in most organizations proving your worth by figuring out the unwritten rules is the rule itself rather than the exception.

Wherever you work, your success will be largely determined by your ability to figure out and live by rules that no one will tell you. Competitors know this already. Rebels and Believers have yet to learn.

The difference between typical organizational cultures in which there are some Narcissists in positions of authority and Narcissistic cultures in which the Narcissists run the whole show is in the angle of the playing field. Once enough Narcissists have clawed their way to the top, the first thing they do when they arrive is change the rules so that it is harder for other people to compete with them.

Though they pride themselves on living by the merciless standards of the marketplace, where rewards are directly proportional to risk, Narcissists are quite adept at hedging their bets by consolidating power at the top and pushing accountability downward onto the shoulders of lesser beings. In Narcissistic cultures, it is not unusual to see huge bonuses going to executives of companies that are hemorrhaging money.

There is nothing wrong or damaging about competition or even internal competition. The dividing line between normal and pathological organizations is in the use of power to change the rules of the game to favor the powerful. This happens regularly in Narcissistic organizations

In Narcissistic cultures, you have to be a Narcissist to survive. This makes Narcissism more contagious than other personality disorders. Here are some of the more salient characteristics of Narcissistic organizational cultures. If your workplace scores three or more, watch your back.

## PROPAGANDA

Virtually everything that is written or spoken aloud is purposely misleading. Most communications are press releases created by insiders for consumption by outsiders. To know what is really going on, you have to read between the lines.

## ALL POLITICS, ALL THE TIME

The most important issues in a Narcissistic organization are those involved with internal politics. Whatever you hear must be processed through the filter of who is in, who is out, and who is allied with whom. There are no facts; only factions.

## ACCOUNTABILITY-FREE ZONES

The third thing Narcissists do when they ascend to an executive position is to redefine leadership as an intangible that cannot be measured or evaluated in any objective manner. The first is doing away with the competition, and the second is negotiating their golden parachute.

## CYA IS JOB ONE

Everyone who is anyone has an elaborate system for filing e-mails and documents so that at any moment he or she can defend all actions by shifting responsibility to someone else.

## CASTE SYSTEM

In Narcissistic organizations, there is a definite hierarchy, but the rungs on the ladder are very uneven. The gulf between being nobody and being somebody is too wide for most people to cross. The rules vary according to status, and at every level they are biased in favor of the people who already hold power. The lower classes are often regarded as servants; their main responsibility is making life easier for those above them.

In Narcissistic caste systems, customers' needs are generally regarded as an inconvenience rather than the lifeblood of the company. Making deals is vastly more important and better compensated than seeing that those deals are consummated with high-quality products and services. Marketing generally means aggressively pushing the product with the highest profit margin rather than developing new products that are designed to meet customers' needs.

In Narcissistic organizations, status and compensation are usually inversely related to proximity to individual customers. Even when the organization provides professional services, face time with the Narcissist whose name is on the bill is as rare as an audience with the Pope. Surgery is a possible exception, but even then the customers are anesthetized. In most Narcissistic organizations, junior staff does the work while the big guys are out on the golf course making deals with other Narcissists.

## DECISIONS ARE MADE AT THE HIGHEST LEVEL

The most critical decisions in a Narcissistic organization are in the setting of ground rules rather than in choosing specific courses of action.

Narcissists at the top consolidate their hold on power by imposing the tone. If a specific action leads to profits or glory, it is an executive triumph. Ignominious results are usually caused by rogue employees acting alone. In Narcissistic organizations, senior executives generally manage to absolve themselves from responsibility for oversight. They are too big to fail.

## BET HEDGING

For all their talk about rewards for risk, Narcissists often manage to structure things so that they take little personal risk for the rewards they reap. They love to gamble, but most often it's with other people's money.

## MACHISMO

In Narcissistic organizations, even the women are supposed to have cojones. Perhaps this is because what I am defining as Narcissism bears quite a bit of similarity to the special rights and privileges accorded to males since the dawn of time.

## AFFAIRS

Boys will be boys, even if they happen to be girls. In Narcissistic organizations, sex is often considered a perquisite of the powerful. Unlike the messy entanglements in Histrionic cultures, Narcissistic sex is mostly businesslike and unemotional, at least until the story breaks.

## CONSPICUOUS LARGESSE

Narcissistic organizations are not stingy when it comes to giving to charity if their names and logos are figured prominently on the list of donors.

If the organization in which you work has some or all of the above characteristics, your chance of changing anything is slight. If you are a Rebel or a Believer, you're not likely to advance. With luck, you can maintain a place in a corporate backwater, where your fate will be determined by machinations that are far above your pay grade.

If you are a Competitor, you may prosper.

If you are prospering in an environment like this, you might go back and read the whole section on Narcissism again. If you stay on and are not a victim of internecine conflict, the section describes what you are likely to become. Remember, Narcissism is contagious.

# Obsessive-Compulsives

16

AN YOU IMAGINE an emotional vampire who drains you by working hard, being conscientious, and seeing that everybody always does the right thing? You know what I mean if an Obsessive-Compulsive has ever caught you in a tiny mistake, lectured you for 20 minutes on how to do a 10-minute job, or dragged a meeting on forever by bringing up everything that could possibly go wrong.

Obsessive-Compulsives are the living embodiment of too much of a good thing. In their world, no mistake is insignificant, and no detail is small enough to ignore. These vampires have characteristics of Obsessive-Compulsive personality disorder, which is, in the minds of the public, hopelessly confused with Obsessive-Compulsive disorder, a brain dysfunction characterized by ritual repetitions, such as hand washing and door locking.

Obsessive-Compulsive *disorder* probably involves some disruption in brain chemistry and is often treated with medication. Obsessive-Compulsive *personality* is a pattern of overly rigid and detail-oriented thoughts and actions that typically doesn't respond to drugs. To make things more confusing, Obsessive-Compulsive *disorder* often occurs in people with Obsessive-Compulsive *personalities.*

Colloquially, people often speak of being "a little OCD" when they mean having a slight tendency toward the *there's a right way and a wrong way to do everything* characteristics of Obsessive-Compulsive personality. This is almost as annoying to people in the field as calling Histrionics who act as if they had two competing personalities "schizophrenic." As you can already see, dealing effectively with Obsessive-Compulsives means keeping your details straight. You might also see that most professionals are a bit Obsessive-Compulsive.

The engine that runs both the disorder and the personality is fear. Obsessive-Compulsives are deathly afraid of doing anything wrong. To them, the smallest crack in their perfect facade leaves them open and vulnerable to all the seeping horrors of the universe.

Obsessive-Compulsives see their existence as a battle against the forces of chaos. Their weapons are hard work, adherence to rules, scrupulous attention to detail, and the capacity to delay gratification into the next life if need be.

Without Obsessive-Compulsives to do the unpleasant and painstaking tasks that make the world go, nations would fall and businesses would grind to a halt. At least, that's what Obsessive-Compulsives think, and it may be true. We *do* need them. We trust in their honesty, we depend on their ability, and we rely on their tireless effort. You could almost believe that *we're* the ones who drain *them*. There is, however, more to the story.

Obsessive-Compulsives want to create a secure world by making every-body Obsessive-Compulsive. Only then can they be safe from themselves.

Here's their secret: inside every Obsessive-Compulsive is a sexual, aggressive Antisocial trying to claw its way out. Obsessive-Compulsives try to keep the cage door locked with logic, hard work, attention to detail, and anything else that might distract them from the expression of their own dangerous emotions.

It's not as if Obsessive-Compulsives would be serial killers if they let themselves go. The monster inside is little more than a rebellious teenager, so long walled off from the rest of the personality that it has taken on the aspect of an alien menace.

Histrionics can just make the unacceptable parts of themselves disap-pear. Obsessive-Compulsives have to bury them in piles of work or drive them off with a flaming sword.

As we have seen, emotions that are suppressed do not go away. Outside awareness, they do more damage than if people accept and learn how to live with them.

Obsessive-Compulsives are not aware of their own aggressiveness. They see themselves as righteously protecting an ungrateful world from evil. Other people often see them as petty, overly critical control freaks who are just being mean on purpose.

Obsessive-Compulsives are usually surprised and threatened by the way people react to what they see as attempts to be helpful. Instead of thanking Obsessive-Compulsives for pointing out the error of their ways, people respond as if attacked. They resist and rebel, which causes the frightened and totally perplexed Obsessive-Compulsives to be even more critical. So goes the dance that confirms Obsessive-Compulsives' view of the world and the world's view of Obsessive-Compulsives. It is this mutual pattern of misunderstanding that creates and perpetuates authority issues between parents and children, teachers and students, and bosses and employees.

The first step in unraveling this self-destructive pattern is understanding the world of Obsessive-Compulsives.

## WHAT IT'S LIKE TO BE OBSESSIVE-COMPULSIVE

Imagine your entire future riding on a single critical action—an examination, a presentation, a sports event, or perhaps a job interview. You can't stop thinking about it. You go over every detail to make sure it's perfect, punctuating your thoughts with jolts of adrenaline when you envision forgetting something or making a mistake. This is how Obsessive-Compulsives feel most of the time.

What's going on here is part of the fight-or-flight response called "hypervigilance." In threatening situations, the brain goes on the alert to anticipate possible dangers. Needless to say, hypervigilance is a lifesaver in combat or in the primordial jungle.

In the present day, this protective mechanism leads to anticipating so many more dangers than actually materialize that the protection itself becomes a danger. Imagine what it would be like to live in perpetual fear of minuscule dangers, doing your best to plan for them and point them out to other people, only to have those people resent you for attempting to protect them. Welcome to the world of the Obsessive-Compulsive.

Hypervigilance is one part of the picture. For the other part, picture yourself walking into your office with your mind already filled to overflowing, then checking your e-mail and finding a hundred new messages marked "urgent," then looking up to see lines of people in the hall bringing in more work. Next, imagine looking around the office and noticing that everybody else is talking, laughing, and generally goofing off.

This is Obsessive-Compulsive consciousness—always working to fend off dangers that may not exist, terrified of mistakes, overwhelmed by trivial tasks, and resentful that nobody else seems to be paying attention. Can you imagine how terribly lonely you'd feel being the only competent person on the planet?

## HOW MUCH IS TOO MUCH?

There is no success without compulsion. Since you're reading a book on improving your interpersonal skills instead of watching TV, you probably know this. Being a little Obsessive-Compulsive leads to an accomplished and virtuous life. Being too Obsessive-Compulsive leads to defeating yourself and draining other people.

How much is too much? That's an excellent question, one that Obsessive-Compulsives are totally unable to answer. As we saw in the case of Narcissistic Legends, one of the critical elements of socialization is learning how to make yourself do things you don't want to do because they need to be done. Obsessive-Compulsives are dutiful to a fault. Given the choice, they often seem to prefer doing things they don't want to do. Obviously, that has to stop somewhere, but where? There must be a point at which a person works too hard or is too good.

Unfortunately, the answer can't be expressed as some sort of optimum good-to-evil or work-to-play ratio. The difference between normal conscientiousness and Obsessive-Compulsive behavior lies not in how much work people do, but in the strategy they use to keep themselves working when they'd rather play. Obsessive-Compulsives use psychological violence—jolts of fear, pangs of guilt, and sharp, icy threats of punishment. And that's just on themselves.

## THE OBSESSIVE-COMPULSIVE EMOTIONAL VAMPIRE CHECKLIST

True or False: Score one point for each *true* answer.

1. This person is a workaholic. T F

2. This person finds it difficult to relax, and seems to look down on people to whom relaxation comes easily. T F

3. This person believes there's a right way and a wrong way to do everything, and usually finds something wrong with other people's way of doing anything. T F

4. When this person does find something wrong, he or she sees pointing it out as helpful rather than critical. T F

5. This person is generally regarded as a control freak. T F

6. This person takes an inordinately long time to make up his or her mind, even about small matters.     T  F

7. This person seldom gives a simple yes or no answer.     T  F

8. This person's attention to detail may be annoying, but it has saved people from making dangerous or costly mistakes.     T  F

9. This person has a very clear moral code.     T  F

10. This person saves everything.     T  F

11. This person runs his or her life according to the adage "if you want something done right, do it yourself."     T  F

12. This person can spend almost as much time organizing a task as doing it.     T  F

13. This person never admits to being wrong.     T  F

14. In meetings, this person will often suggest delaying action until more information can be obtained.     T  F

15. This person balances his or her checkbook to the penny, and is surprised when other people don't.     T  F

16. This person is a micromanager.     T  F

17. This person does not see himself or herself as controlling, only right.     T  F

18. When asked to give input on something written, this person will always correct the grammar and spelling, and sometimes make no comment on the overall idea.     T  F

19. This person prides him- or herself on being unemotional.     T  F

20. This person becomes irritated or upset if asked to deviate from his or her routine.     T  F

21. This person often feels overwhelmed by all the work he or she has to do, but still seems to waste a lot of time on low-priority tasks.     T  F

22. Though this person never says it directly, it's clear that he or she takes pride in working harder than everybody else.     T  F

23. This person is a perfectionist.　　　　　　　　　　　　T　F

24. This person has a hard time finishing tasks.　　　　　　T　F

25. This person will go through any amount of personal difficulty
to make good on a promise, and expects you to do the same.　　T　F

Scoring: Five or more true answers qualifies the person as an Obsessive-Compulsive emotional vampire, though not necessarily for a diagnosis of Obsessive-Compulsive personality disorder. If the person scores higher than 10, whatever you do will never be enough.

## WHAT THE QUESTIONS MEASURE

The specific behaviors covered on the checklist relate to several underlying personality characteristics that define an Obsessive-Compulsive emotional vampire.

### Love of Work

Forget about simple carnality. The great passion in the lives of Obsessive-Compulsives is work. It is their pride, their joy, their obsession, their drug, the alpha and omega of their existence. It is their gift and the cross they have to bear. When Obsessive-Compulsives are working, they feel good about themselves and safe. If you want to feel safe, you'd better be working too.

### Reliability

You can trust Obsessive-Compulsives. They keep their promises, and they're honest to a fault. Their word is as good as a legal contract, and often as labyrinthine and confusing. In their world, the law is all letter and no spirit.

### Rigidity

Black-white, right-wrong, good-bad—Obsessive-Compulsives invented the dichotomy, which, like the straight line, does not exist in nature.

Obsessive-Compulsives also invented the straight line. Though these vampires love complexity, they have a hard time with ambiguity, especially moral ambiguity. They struggle all their lives to impose order on a capricious universe.

## Preoccupation with Details

Obsessive-Compulsives are famous for not seeing forests because of all the trees. They dash frantically from one detail to the next, never quite grasping that all the little details fit together into a big picture that they seldom get to see.

## Perfectionism

Perfectionism is a vice that masquerades as a virtue. It can lead to excellence, but it usually doesn't. Doing everything correctly has a tendency to become the top priority, eclipsing the importance of the task, or the feelings of other people. The wake of Obsessive-Compulsives is an orderly row of insignificant tasks done to perfection, and significant people feeling frustrated because they don't measure up.

## Emotional Constriction

Most Obsessive-Compulsives suffer from emotional constipation. Freud thought this was caused by strict toilet training. He called them *anal-retentives,* because not going potty on demand was how they gained control of their overly demanding universe.

For anal-retentives, holding back is a creative act. Emotional control is their major art form. They take pride in it the way any artist would. Obsessive-Compulsives all seem to come from the same planet as *Star Trek*'s Mr. Spock, a place where irritation at illogical thinking is the only feeling allowed.

## Indecisiveness

Obsessive-Compulsives try to keep their options open long after the windows of opportunity have shut. Their basic life strategy is minimizing loss rather than maximizing gain. This strategy is reflected in every conscious decision they make, or rather fail to make.

One of the most common manifestations of Obsessive-Compulsive indecisiveness is the amount of stuff that they accumulate, because they can never bring themselves to throw anything away. Often such people require more space to store useless items than they do to live or work in. The extreme of this behavior is hoarding, which is likely a manifestation of the brain dysfunction, rather than the personality. Obsessive-Compulsives keep useless things for a reason: they think they might have a use for them. Hoarders are just terrified of throwing anything away.

## Unacknowledged Hostility

Obsessive-Compulsives secretly resent people who are not as hardworking and upstanding as they are. That turns out to be almost everyone. The resentment is hidden only from them; everybody else knows about it all too well.

### THE OBSESSIVE-COMPULSIVE DILEMMA

Say what you will about Obsessive-Compulsives being difficult and draining. You have to admit that they put their money where their mouth is. Without their hard work and stern example, we would all be in as much danger as they seem to think we are.

# Obsessive-Compulsive Perfectionists and Puritans

**O**BSESSIVE-COMPULSIVES at work fall into two categories, Perfectionists and Puritans, depending on whether their primary obsession is getting everyone to do tasks perfectly or living perfect lives. Unfortunately, the techniques Obsessive-Compulsives use to accomplish these self-appointed missions usually have the opposite effect. Their lack of success only seems to make them work harder. They just keep on doing the same thing, but louder, longer, and in greater detail. It never dawns on them that their own actions may be causing the imperfections that so disturb them.

> Wearily, Shannon opens this morning's e-mail from Gary, her Perfectionist boss. Another set of instructions! This time for how to turn in your expense sheet, being sure that receipts are *clipped, not stapled* to the upper *left* corner of the form. Some poor fool must have stapled his receipts, causing Gary to send out another one of his stupid control-freak e-mails delineating the exact, step-by-step procedures for performing everyday tasks.
>
> *Before long,* Shannon thinks, *he's going to send out an e-mail telling us exactly how to use the bathroom.*

That's how it started. Pretty soon, Shannon found herself typing and laughing to herself. The result was her famous "Wipe front to back using one sheet" memo.

Everybody in the office considered it hilarious—except Gary, who wrote her a strong letter of warning about using work time for frivolous pursuits.

Obsessive-Compulsive Perfectionists rarely have a sense of humor about themselves. This is unfortunate, since their rigidity and preoccupation with detail invites parody, especially from creative Rebels like Shannon, who is certainly smart enough to know better.

Gary is also smart enough to know better. Perfectionists have read books and articles that say micromanagement is not productive, but they do it anyway. They think of it as due diligence. They can't seem to stop themselves from spelling out everything in excruciating detail lest their charges forget something or make a mistake. This is the *Compulsive* part of Obsessive-Compulsive—feeling a strong need to do something, even when you know, or at least ought to know, that it's not a good idea.

So we have two smart people—Gary the Perfectionist, and Shannon the Rebel—making really bad choices when it comes to dealing with each other. What's their problem? The answer, in a word, is fear. Gary is afraid of mistakes, and Shannon is afraid of losing her individual identity by blindly following someone else's rules. Perfectionists and Rebels are a match made in hell. Every day in offices all over the world, they torment each other with their irrational fears.

One of the few things we know in psychology with anything close to mathematical certainty is that the relationship between fear and productive behavior is curvilinear. A little fear improves performance, but too much fear inhibits it. The hard part for most of us is figuring out how much is too much. For Perfectionists, this is not just hard; it's almost impossible.

We already know that fear relates to the fight-or-flight response, an array of instantaneous physiological and psychological changes that are hardwired into our brains to protect us from physical danger. The component of the response that causes most of the problems for Obsessive-Compulsives is hypervigilance.

When we sense danger, we are programmed to scan for possible threats. This made good sense in the past, when dangers were simple, direct, and mostly physical. In today's complicated world, vigilance can quickly get out of hand because there is so much more that can go wrong on so many more levels.

Vigilant Obsessive-Compulsives turn up the gain on their antennas so high that they begin to register false positives. They overestimate present dangers, and they try to imagine all future dangers in the vain hope that somehow anticipating problems will keep them from happening. The common name for this practice is *worry*. It usually causes more problems than it prevents.

Obsessive-Compulsives will be quick to point out that *sometimes* their worrying does indeed prevent problems. This is definitely true, but it almost makes things worse, because any behavior that is rewarded unpredictably will keep repeating long past the point of diminishing returns. The same law of behavior that makes slot machines profitable keeps Obsessive-Compulsives worrying when there is nothing to worry about.

To make matters worse, our brains can't distinguish reality from fantasy, so that every danger that Obsessive-Compulsives imagine elicits an increase in the fight-or-flight response, which increases vigilance, which in turn increases fear.

Worrying creates yet another kind of problem. When we turn inward and use our imagination to search for danger, the process is more likely to spin out of control. This is why worry is more intense when we awaken in the middle of the night. Without external stimulation, the disasters we imagine have no boundaries.

Given the dangers of the response that protects us from danger, it's a wonder that we all are not reduced to quivering lumps of terror. What saves us is the ability to use our higher brain centers to manually override our automatic fear response. We look outward, rationally assess the danger, and in most cases decide that it is too insignificant to worry about. In Obsessive-Compulsive Perfectionists, this ability to gain perspective is what's broken. To them, *insignificant danger* is an oxymoron.

Obsessive-Compulsive Perfectionists like Gary try to alleviate their anxiety by doing every task, large or small, perfectly. This is, of course, impossible. It also has no beginning and no end.

Gary sits down to check his e-mail. He notices that his coffee cup has dripped and created a brown ring on his desk. He gets up and goes across the hall to the men's room to get a damp towel to wipe up the ring. There are no towels. On his way to the men's room, he noticed the janitor's cart down the hall. He goes to find the janitor and asks him to put towels in the dispenser. In addition, Gary points out a few problems with restroom hygiene that the janitor ought to correct.

On the way back to his office, he reminds a team member who has held an impromptu meeting in her cubicle that the extra chairs need to be returned to the common area. There is also a stack of papers in the hallway that needs to be moved, because it is prohibited by the fire code.

Finally, Gary goes back to his cubicle with his damp towel, now almost dry. Before he sits down, he notices a layer of dust behind his printer. Since he has a towel in his hand, he slides the printer out of the way and wipes up the dust. There's a lot of it there. By the time he has wiped it all up, his towel is dirty and dry, so he goes back to the men's room to get another.

On the way, one of his team members stops him and asks a question about the departmental budget. Gary doesn't know the specific answer. His teammate says it isn't a big deal, and Gary can get back to him later. But Gary wants to take care of it now while he's thinking of it, so they both go back to Gary's cubicle and he pulls up the spreadsheet on his computer. While doing that, he notices the coffee ring on his desk.

An hour later, Gary still hasn't gotten to his e-mail. He glances at the basket of expense reports and sees that the one on top has the receipts stapled to it. He looks in his drawer for his staple remover, and he can't find it. There are a few outdated phone slips in the drawer, which he pulls out and puts in the recycling bin. Then he gets up to go borrow a staple remover.

At six-thirty, Gary is working late again, writing the e-mail to his team about not stapling receipts.

This endlessly recursive pattern is why Perfectionistic Obsessive-Compulsives always seem to be working more, getting less done, and feeling overwhelmed by how much more there is to do. When the gain on your antenna is turned up too high, there is no such thing as efficiency. There is no such thing as setting priorities either, because every task seems dependent on every other. There is always something that must be done before something else can be started, and there is never enough information to make a final decision about anything.

Even though Perfectionists organize tasks for themselves and their departments into exceedingly complicated interlocking networks, from the outside their systems seem to be indistinguishable from chaos. Their desks may be neat and dust-free, but their goals and objectives are in a perpetual state of flux. A change in one area changes everything, and no venture stays the same from beginning to end. Any little error can bring a whole project to a grinding halt.

Gary does not see his own lack of perspective as the reason he can never seem to get anything done on time. To him, the problem is lazy janitors, careless staplers, and people who don't take their jobs as seriously as he does. He feels he must watch them all more closely to make sure they are not messing up or goofing off. Gary feels considerable resentment about having to do this, and his resentment is apparent to everyone.

Gary's approach to supervision follows the same recursive pattern as everything else he does. The more closely he looks, the more mistakes he sees that need to be corrected, the more overwhelmed and resentful he feels, and the harder he thinks he needs to crack down.

As Gary becomes more critical and controlling, the performance of his team deteriorates. Feeling hurt and worrying about criticism from Gary makes the Believers on his team overly cautious, so they make more mistakes. Competitors find ways to avoid him. Rebels may engage in Passive-Aggressive retaliation for constantly being told what to do. Whatever the cause, the poorer performance increases Gary's need for control, and performance deteriorates further. This is the sad lot of Perfectionistic Obsessive-Compulsive managers. The harder they work, the more there is for them to do.

To the people who are constantly being corrected, there is nothing sad about Obsessive-Compulsive managers.

Shannon worked two weeks on a report. She did an excellent job, even if she says so herself. She sent the report to Gary for review. A week and a half later, she gets it back without a single positive comment. He has corrected one typo, reordered the bullet points, and changed the wording in a couple of paragraphs.

> Shannon feels hurt and angry. *Why is Gary such a damn control freak? Does he think he has the only brain on the planet? Who does he think he is, my father?* Inside her head, the rant goes on and on.

Needless to say, Shannon may well be correct, but getting herself worked up in this way will only make the problem worse by making her more of a target. The situation with Gary reminds her so much of her teenage struggles (and perhaps ongoing ones) to separate herself from her father's domination that she confuses one with the other. Her fear of losing her identity activates the *fight* part of the fight-or-flight response just as it did when she was a teenager.

This sort of struggle is more intense in creative people. Creativity by definition means seeing things differently. Actually, we only call it creativity when it comes up with a useful product. The rest of the time we think of it as *being weird*. Creative people usually have authority issues with people who try to make them more normal.

Perfectionistic Obsessive-Compulsives can turn almost anyone into a rebellious teenager. Creative people like Shannon often use their talents to defend themselves against micromanaging bosses like Gary, whom they see as control freaks. Believers may protest as well. They see Obsessive-Compulsives as being picky and overly negative.

Whatever the reason, direct rebellion against a control freak rarely improves anything. Humorous e-mails or well-meaning petitions to higher authorities are often the first shot in a battle that never ends.

The big question is, *what to do instead?* How do you deal with a boss like Gary who is a Perfectionistic Obsessive-Compulsive control freak? The answer, as usual with emotional vampires, is to step into their world and step out of the expected pattern. You cannot fight control freaks; you must tame them with gentleness and subtlety.

## HOW TO BECOME A CONTROL-FREAK WHISPERER

Now that you know more than you probably wanted to know about how Perfectionistic Obsessive-Compulsives think, you can use that knowledge to create a strategy for dealing with them. Think of it as becoming a control-freak whisperer, using quiet reassurance to keep a micromanaging boss from feeling the need to control every aspect of your job.

The basic element of whispering technique was first described by Aesop, one of the world's great pre-Freudian therapists:

> The North wind and the Sun were arguing about who was stronger. They decided to put it to the test by seeing which one could take a traveler's cloak. First the wind blew his hardest, which only caused the traveler to wrap up in his cloak more tightly. Then, the sun began to shine. Soon the traveler got so warm that he took off his cloak himself.

The way to shine on Obsessive-Compulsives is to show them in word and deed that you take your tasks as seriously as they do. For them to believe in your dedication enough to relax and let go, you have to believe in it too. If Obsessive-Compulsives feel the faintest breath of impertinence, they will wrap you tightly in their cloak of overcontrol.

## Whisperer Training Phase One: Avoiding Threatening Gestures

The first phase of learning to be a control-freak whisperer involves controlling yourself so they won't think they have to. Here's how to get started.

SEE THEIR FEAR RATHER THAN YOUR IRRITATION: The most important thing to remember in dealing with overly controlling Perfectionistic Obsessive-Compulsives is that their micromanaging arises from fear of mistakes rather than sadism or love of control. Though their critical behavior may make you feel attacked, that is not its purpose. It's not about you. If you take it personally and get irritated, they will have one more thing to fear. The more frightened they are, the more controlling they will need to be.

DON'T CALL THEM CONTROL FREAKS: If you want to be a control-freak whisperer, you must stop calling them control freaks, either out loud or in the privacy of your mind. Obsessive-Compulsives pay attention to tiny details. They will see your irritation as clearly as if you'd posted it on a billboard outside their office window. Your attitude will serve as evidence that they should watch you even more closely. If you think of them as people who are terrified that something will go wrong, you will be much more likely to make the right choices.

Even if you bring it up in the kindest way possible, discussing the issue of control directly will backfire. Obsessive-Compulsives, even if they joke about it, never see themselves as *overly* controlling. They are only protecting an ungrateful world from the inevitable mistakes that result from not paying enough attention to detail. Forget trying to talk them out of it. Even seasoned therapists have trouble convincing the control obsessed that their behavior might be causing more problems than it's solving.

**DON'T LET YOUR INNER TEENAGER MAKE YOUR CAREER DECISIONS:** Maintaining the equanimity you need to be a whisperer is sometimes quite difficult because of your psychological issues. Nothing gets on most people's nerves like being told what to do. The reason for this is what Freud called "transference." It means reacting to people in the present as if they were characters from your past with whom you have unfinished business.

Most of us have unfinished business with our parents from when we were teenagers, trying to assert ourselves in spite of their ridiculous rules and constant meddling. Perfectionists can turn us into teenagers again through transference. Rebels bridle at being told what to do; Believers express hurt at being criticized and never praised; and Competitors sneak out after curfew. Or, like real teenagers, many of us do all three.

Needless to say, such immature responses are not productive when we are adults at work. We all know this, but it is very hard to hang on to maturity when Perfectionists are acting just as your parents did when you were 14.

Controlling Obsessive-Compulsives bring out your inner teenager. That does not mean that you should let your 14-year-old self make your career decisions. You need to recognize what is going on and step out of the pattern by doing a manual override of your emotional response. Feel it, but don't act on it. Instead of slamming the door to your room, ask yourself what you want to happen, and adjust your actions accordingly. This is what it means to act like a grown-up.

Gary's reprimand woke Shannon up. She realized that she liked her job and that she had a future in the company, which she could jeopardize by making jokes about Gary. After a long sleepless night, she decided that she needed to see things from

Gary's point of view. Her future would depend on his evaluation, so she would do whatever it took to get a good grade. It felt like going back to school rather than working in a grown-up job.

That feeling meant she was doing it right.

## Whisperer Training Phase Two:
## Becoming a Positive Stimulus

Once you get a handle on your own emotional responses, you're ready for the next phase of whisperer training, which is getting your Obsessive-Compulsive boss to see you in a positive light. To do that, you have to step into his or her world and look like you belong there.

The Obsessive-Compulsive's world is college. Unlike Histrionics, Obsessive-Compulsives were nerds in high school. They began to bloom in college classrooms where attention to detail was rewarded. In their minds, they are still there. They continually mistake the real world for a college classroom. To earn their confidence, that's where you have to go. The more you act like they did in college classes, the more they will trust you. Here are some suggestions.

**TAKE NOTES:** In college, Obsessive-Compulsives wrote down virtually everything their professors said because it might be on the test. No Obsessive-Compulsive would ever trust him- or herself to remember anything that isn't written down. If there is one single gesture you can make to show a Perfectionistic boss that you take your job seriously, it is taking notes whenever someone of importance is lecturing or giving instructions. If you don't, Perfectionists will be certain that you'll forget, and they will have to remind you. A simple notebook will do more for your credibility than any amount of good results.

Beyond looking like a good student, there is another reason for taking notes. Your lecture notes will help you come away with clear specifications of the end product required. This will be critical for the next phase of whisperer training.

**READ THE ASSIGNMENTS:** Nothing shows sloppy scholarship more blatantly than asking a question that is covered in the FAQs.

Obsessive-Compulsives love to write instructions, and they expect you to read them. Their instructions are sometimes superfluous and often confusing, but you should never ask for clarification without quoting the relevant passages chapter and verse.

Another reason to read the assignments is that you might actually learn something. Perfectionistic Obsessive-Compulsives have always done their homework and generally know what they're talking about.

By the way, if you have an overly controlling boss who doesn't give detailed instructions, or tries to tell you how to do things that he or she can't do, it is likely that you are dealing, not with an Obsessive-Compulsive, but with a Histrionic playing the part of diligent manager. If your boss acts like this, pay less attention to the instructions here and review the ones in Chapter 9.

**Generate Text:** Obsessive-Compulsives are not into brevity. In college, their papers may not have been the most incisive, but they were the longest. Nothing is more comforting to Obsessive-Compulsives than exhaustive detail. Never miss an opportunity to turn in a written assignment.

**Always Cite References:** What made Obsessive-Compulsives' papers so long were the collections of quotations and references that are the essence of scholarly research.

Obsessive-Compulsive bosses are threatened by anything that's not tried and true. If you have the audacity to come up with new ideas and expect your boss to listen, you must show that you have listened to people who know more than you do. Those people may be respected academics and authors or, better yet, the senior management of your own organization. Always review their ideas before mentioning your own.

### Whisperer Training Phase Three: Controlling the Controller

Learning to act like a diligent but not overly creative student will increase your credibility to the point that you can attempt to reason with an Obsessive-Compulsive boss. Bear in mind that all the techniques I'm suggesting are indirect. Think of them as a kind of psychological aikido: you must learn to use the Obsessive-Compulsive bosses' own momentum to gently redirect them toward more positive managerial behavior. Subtlety is everything.

**KNOW YOUR GOAL:**   As with all the emotional vampire bosses we have studied so far, Obsessive-Compulsives' personalities get in the way of effective management. In the case of Obsessive-Compulsives, the main impediment is their tendency to focus on small details that need to be fixed rather than the big picture. They can get caught in recursive loops that make even the simplest projects go on forever.

To avoid these endless loops, you need to influence your Perfectionistic boss to set firm priorities and stick with them from the beginning of a job until the end. To do this, you will need to exploit the Obsessive-Compulsive tendency to live by the letter of the law. Do this by carefully writing those letters yourself. Negotiating clear contracts is the main way that whisperers exert subtle control.

The other goal you may be able to achieve through negotiating a clear contract is getting your boss to be more accurate in assessing the quality of your work. To succeed, you will have to be as diligent and detail oriented as your Obsessive-Compulsive boss. The time to gain control is before a project begins.

**SPECIFY DELIVERABLES IN EXHAUSTIVE DETAIL:**  This is the key to managing Perfectionists. Every task has a product (whatever it is that needs to be done) and a process (the actual behaviors by which the end product is achieved). Obsessive-Compulsives tend to get so caught up in the process that they lose sight of the product. This is the doorway into recursion that you need to nail shut.

If at the beginning of the project you negotiate to deliver a very specific, measurable product at a very specific time, you will be on much firmer ground when, later on, your boss tries to control the process.

> Gary assigned Shannon to write a marketing report comparing their new product with the competition. Through what seemed like endless negotiation, Shannon was able to narrow the field down to the three top sellers in the present market and to specify the variables to be analyzed in terms of price and performance. Her goals for the project ran to three pages, which Gary changed several times, mostly trying to add variables for analysis.
>
> Throughout the negotiation, Shannon had to keep reminding Gary that the overall objective was to discover the niche that

their product would fill, not to analyze all the technical specs for everything everyone else is selling.

Finally, they agreed. Setting the goals took almost as long as doing the project.

Obsessive-Compulsives keep their word, but their anxiety sometimes makes them forget what they said. It will be to your advantage to have their words in writing in the form of airtight goals and objectives, which you need to compose yourself, based on the notes you took while listening to all those lectures. Never let your Perfectionistic boss write your goals for you. They will be less like goals and more like to-do lists of specific tasks that do not address the overall purpose. Needless to say, whatever goals you write will have to be revised and reworded. Take all the time you need to come up with a firm agreement about the product. You will be glad you did.

**Produce Regular, Written Progress Reports:** The most disruptive Obsessive-Compulsive management behaviors are caused by anxiety. Allay that anxiety by generating about three times more written progress reports than you think anyone would need. If your boss is not absolutely certain that you are paying attention to details, he or she will feel the need to step in and pay attention for you. Remember that nothing soothes Obsessive-Compulsives like excessive detail.

**Resist Attempts to Control the Process:** Here's where to draw your line in the sand. If your boss tries to control the process, ask if this means that the end product has changed. If the end product is not affected, why change the process? This is the place you can stand firm. Needless to say, you have to have some history of delivering the goods for a strategy like this to work.

Throughout the project, Gary kept suggesting more competing products and other variables for analysis. Shannon agreed that those analyses might be useful for another report that asked different questions than those they had agreed upon for this one. She even wrote goals for a future report, which she considered a small price to pay for not changing this one.

**KEEP UP THE GOOD WORK:** The secret of being a successful control-freak whisperer is consistency. If you follow this procedure several times and actually do what you say you are going to do when you say you are going to do it, your boss will become less worried about your performance, and she or he may go off to micromanage somebody less responsible.

**IF YOU WANT PRAISE, ASK FOR IT DIRECTLY:** For most people, the hardest part of dealing with Perfectionists is the perception that, like the parents of teenagers, they always criticize and never praise. This may be a perception rather than a fact. Many studies have shown that in order to be seen as equal, positive comments have to outnumber negative by 4 to 1. Be that as it may, our reality is made of our perceptions rather than objective facts, so, regardless of the actual count, we still have to deal with the feeling of being criticized all the time and never praised.

If you want your Obsessive-Compulsive boss to tell you you're doing a good job, you have to ask if you're doing a good job. Suggest that a fair measure would be counting the number of goals you've accomplished rather than the number of typos in your last report. Do pay attention to typos, because your boss will. Listen quietly to criticisms without becoming defensive, then sum up the conversation by asking for a global assessment of your performance.

---

As usual, Shannon worked hard and delivered a marketing report as specified two days ahead of schedule. Four days later, Gary handed it back with two typos circled in red. This time, Shannon's feelings were hurt, but she was not distracted. She fixed the typos and reprinted the report.

Shannon has learned a few lessons about letting her inner teenager make her career decisions. This time she decides to deal with her emotions in a more mature way.

"Gary," she says, "When you gave back the report with those corrections, it felt like you were saying it wasn't very good. Was that your intention?"

Like all Obsessive-Compulsives who are asked questions like this, Gary seems dumbfounded. "No, no," he says. "The report was really good. If it weren't, I would have had you rewrite the whole thing."

For a minute, Shannon's inner teenager feels damned by faint praise. Then the adult in her takes over, and she recognizes that she has just been awarded Gary's equivalent of the Nobel Prize in Literature.

"So, you thought it was good?" she asks.

"Yes, of course," Gary says.

That's about as good as it gets, so when you ask for praise and get an answer like this, recognize it for what it is.

## THE PURITAN ETHIC

Puritans want to make you a better person through fear of eternal punishment. In the old days, they did this by reminding heretics that the fires of hell await them. These days, heresy has been replaced by being politically incorrect. If you don't mend your ways, they will be only too happy to supply the eternal punishment.

Surya marches into Kinesha's office, obviously on a mission.

"What's up, Surya?" Kinesha asks.

"It's this memo," Surya says, holding up a sheet of bright red paper and laying it down on Kinesha's desk with a thump.

Kinesha recognizes the memo; she sent it out yesterday with the bonus checks to thank people in the department for their hard work over the year and to wish them a happy holiday season. She pulls it closer and reads it again.

"I don't see what the problem is," Kinesha says, as she hands the memo back to Surya.

"That *is* the problem. You don't *see* that this memo, with its direct references to a Christian observance, could be offensive to some people who don't choose to celebrate the same holidays as the dominant culture."

"But there's nothing in here about Christmas," Kinesha says. "I purposely didn't mention any specific holiday. I thought the memo could refer to Christmas, Hanukkah, or Kwanzaa."

"What about Rahim, who's a Muslim? Muslims don't have a so-called holiday season at this time of year. Or did you ever think about Kelly, who's a Jehovah's Witness? She doesn't believe in celebrating *any* holidays."

"I didn't know that Rahim and Kelly were upset. They didn't say anything—"

Surya folds her arms and glares. "Frankly, Kinesha, I expected a little more cultural sensitivity from you, of all people. Being African American, you must know what it's like to have people ignore your heritage."

Puritans invented political correctness. Only Obsessive-Compulsives could believe that they are helping people by publicly attacking them when their choice of words might be offensive to people too downtrodden to speak for themselves. An earlier Puritan invention was burning people at the stake to cleanse their souls, a punishment that was worse than the crime.

Like their creations, Puritans are a mass of contradictions. They'll make your life hell attempting to get you to heaven. They see no logical flaw in making people suffer to end suffering, or in publicly ridiculing some people to spare the feelings of others. Puritans try to bully everyone into being as fair and kind as they are. No matter how much they secretly enjoy making you suffer, Puritans always see their actions as totally selfless. If they are annoying or punitive, it's for your own good or for the good of humanity.

Before we consign these heartless emotional vampires to the pit, we ought to make an effort to understand them. It's possible that a little knowledge might help us make them less annoying.

Puritans think that the world is unkind to moral people, so they feel justified in returning the favor. Actually, the world is more ambiguous than unkind, but Puritans seldom appreciate this subtle distinction. The problem lies in the typical Obsessive-Compulsive confusion of process and product.

People with rigid black-and-white moral codes spend their lives following somewhat arbitrary rules because they expect concrete rewards for keeping the rules and punishment for breaking them. Puritans don't understand that virtue is its own reward. They keep expecting some higher power to step in to praise the saints and punish the sinners. Puritans firmly believe in the idea of heaven and hell for this purpose, but for many of them, the afterlife isn't soon enough to settle the score. They feel they have to step in and do God's work, at least when it comes to punishing sinners.

What Puritans are really looking for are a few earthly rewards. The problem is that here in the real world, rewards go to people who know how to get them, not necessarily to people who deserve them. Puritans scrupulously follow a process that they expect will lead to glory and riches, but all it gets them is stars in their crown.

Following rules *can* reward people with a feeling of connection with something larger than themselves—namely, the rest of humanity. Unfortunately, Puritans, in their quest for bottom-line settling up of moral accounts, often miss out on the greatest reward life has to offer. No wonder they're resentful.

## DEALING WITH PURITANS WITHOUT GETTING BURNED

There are two basic ways to deal with Puritans: you can humor them and laugh behind their backs, or you can show them how to get the earthly rewards they really want. The first is easier and far more commonly practiced.

If you want to try the second, you need to point out, gently, that it's Puritans' reliance on punishment and censorship that's causing the problems. Gentleness is necessary because Puritans model their external strategies on what they do to themselves inside their own heads. If you're too emphatic, they'll point out proudly that such tactics have made *them* what they are. This may leave you in a rather embarrassing position.

As we have seen, punishment, whether internal or external, is a terrible strategy for improving other people's behavior. To escape their internal punisher, Puritans avoid looking too closely at their own motivation. In their own minds, they are selfless givers who want to end suffering rather than cause it. They are never angry—only righteously indignant. They seldom ask for anything directly. They expect it will be bestowed upon them for their virtue and hard work. When the rewards don't come, they become resentful and lash out, never for themselves, but for the good of others.

Just as Perfectionists' tactics tend to increase imperfections, Puritans' strategies for dealing with iniquity generally bring out the worst in the people they are trying to save. This happens within the Puritans as well, but trying to explain *that* to them might just get you burned at the stake. Hypocrisy is something they are quick to notice in others but never in themselves.

The way to approach Puritans at work is to recognize their frustration and, beneath it, their longing for earthly rewards. As does everyone else, they want love, respect, and recognition for their efforts. But they are so lost in their obsessive concern with details of right and wrong that they somehow miss the big picture that is obvious to everyone else: love goes to people who are nice; respect goes to people who give respect; and recognition goes to people who know how to seize an opportunity.

If you work with a Puritan and don't want continual conflict, you have to see the longing that lies beneath what looks like a mean spirit. Take Surya in our example. In addition to justice for the downtrodden, she probably wants influential people such as Kinesha to respect her, listen to her ideas, and see her as a good employee, worthy of responsible work and possibly promotions. Surya is making just the opposite impression.

What can Kinesha tell her? About the memo, nothing. Kinesha should thank her and let the issue drop as quickly as possible. If Kinesha gives in and revises her wording or makes an apology, she will only be encouraging Surya's indirect attacks. If Kinesha gets angry, she will find herself in a moral battle with someone who may eagerly embrace martyrdom. People like Surya generally work hard and can be excellent team members, but only if their unexpressed personal needs are being met.

Kinesha needs to see the incident as an indication that Surya feels unappreciated, and that she might also be a bellwether for other dissatisfied Believers in the organization who work hard and play by the rules, but are frustrated because it doesn't seem to get them anywhere. Puritans are Believers with fangs.

If you are in a management position and are being attacked for your lack of political correctness, I'm not suggesting that you merely blow it off. Seek counsel about your sensitivity from a neutral person whom you trust. If you have actually offended someone, apologize directly to that person.

That being done, you need to focus on the underlying frustration. Believers, especially the more Obsessive-Compulsive ones, live by the letter of the law. In most organizational settings, what's written is confusing and sometimes downright deceptive. Embarrassing realities are seldom spoken aloud. People must figure them out for themselves. Competitors are good at this. Believers and Rebels are not. They think that if they do a good job, as defined by what is written, they will succeed. This is rarely true, since success involves discerning and following the unwritten rules.

Nobody tells Believers what they really need to do to get ahead, because the truth is often a little embarrassing. Surya and her hardworking cohorts spend their days plugging away at the tasks *they* believe should make a difference and getting more and more resentful when their efforts don't pay off.

To deal with the underlying problem, Kinesha needs to disabuse her team of the notion that hard work, in and of itself, will be rewarded and let them know how to really get ahead. Kinesha might start by explaining that doing a good job and succeeding are totally different concepts. Doing a good job means performing tasks well or competently managing the people below you in the organizational hierarchy. Success comes from managing the people above you. The skills involved are usually very different, so it's not a good idea to mistake one for the other.

Unbeknownst to Believers, especially the more Obsessive-Compulsive, the following activities are all part of doing a good job, but they will probably not have anything to do with whether you advance in the corporate hierarchy.

**WORKING DIRECTLY WITH CUSTOMERS:** In most businesses, customer service is an important corporate goal, but it is not accomplished by important corporate people. Selling is a possible exception. If you want to get ahead and you have to deal with customers, it is much better to be close to the people who buy your product than to the people who use it.

**SERVING ON WORK GROUPS AT YOUR LEVEL OR BELOW:** Task forces and committees solve problems, organize work, and get things done. They don't yield much in the way of glory to their participants.

**TRAINING:** Training is an absolute necessity, but the organizational world believes the old adage: *if you can, do; if you can't, teach*.

**COMING UP WITH COSTLY WAYS TO IMPROVE QUALITY OR MORALE:** If you're the owner or the CEO, you can take long-term financial risks and be praised for it. If you're anybody else, such ideas will be interpreted as evidence that you don't understand what business is all about.

The following activities may have little to do with doing a good job, but they *will* lead to organizational advancement.

**BRINGING IN NEW BUSINESS:** It doesn't have to be much business or even good business. In the corporate world, it is always the rainmakers who are on top of the heap. Compared with bringing in new business, putting out a high-quality product is small potatoes.

**CUTTING COSTS:** Cost cutting is a divinely ordained task of management. If you want to succeed, do it often and conspicuously. At meetings, always be the one who asks if it can be done more cheaply. There's one important exception: never talk about cost cutting and executive salaries in the same breath.

**DOING ANYTHING WITH PEOPLE OF HIGHER RANK:** This is especially true if you are the person in front of the room running a PowerPoint with killer graphics. If not, be the person on the task force who asks if it can be done more cheaply.

**TAKING MANAGEMENT'S SIDE ON CONTROVERSIAL ISSUES:** Doing a good job often involves cooperation and compromise. Getting ahead involves looking after your own interests or those of the people above you. This is sad but true. Promotions are not awarded by popular vote.

**GENERATING TEXT:** Almost anything that goes out with your name on it (other than e-mails criticizing management) will enhance your reputation. Reports, policies, procedures manuals, goal statements, mission statements, quality improvement plans, and pieces about corporate values are all good choices, the glossier the better. Avoid documents explaining government regulations, because they will cause people to mistake you for the government.

**SOCIALIZING:** The biggest rewards always go to the people who are out schmoozing, not the ones sitting in their offices producing product.

In the organizational world, the real secrets of success are often censored because Puritans such as Surya might be outraged if they knew them. Outrage is likely, but it's what Puritans do after the fuming and fussing dies down that's really important. If given the choice, most Puritans would prefer not to be martyrs for their principles. What they really want are the same things everybody else does. If you tell it to them like it is instead of patronizing them, they may learn and respond.

At first, they'll be offended that organizational reality is not what it should be. They'll undoubtedly want to lecture you on morality, but if you stick to your guns and don't apologize for telling the truth, they may come to respect you. Then they may even listen.

Have a little faith in Obsessive-Compulsives. Remember, we need them as much as they need us.

# Obsessive-Compulsive Cultures

OBSESSIVE-COMPULSIVE CULTURES are better known as *bureaucracies*. If you think that means a bunch of lazy civil servants sitting around doing nothing, think again. Bureaucracies are full of people who love to work. They just aren't very good at determining what work is most productive, so they all try to do everything. The entire organization follows the recursive Obsessive-Compulsive pattern. Everyone feels overwhelmed all the time. When coworkers meet in the hallways, the standard answer to "How are you?" is "Busy."

Unless you have too much to do, you're considered a slacker. Work is what Obsessive-Compulsives value; efficiency almost seems like goofing off. Actually it's easier for them to overwork themselves than to set priorities.

Obsessive-Compulsives are hardworking, detail oriented, and extremely vigilant. The organizations they create are ideal for the meticulous performance of boring and repetitive tasks. Unfortunately, everything they do seems to turn into boring and repetitive tasks. Meetings are frequent and long, with agendas that generally are a rehashing of the same old issues. Petty conflicts abound. The smaller the stakes, the bigger the battle.

In an organization created by people who excel at noticing tiny errors, nobody is satisfied with anything anybody else does. A hallmark of Obsessive-Compulsive cultures are the hand-lettered signs taped above office machines and break room equipment listing detailed instructions on how not to use them.

In Obsessive-Compulsive cultures, the focus is on process rather than product. The great concern is doing tasks correctly. There are manuals for everything. Every bookshelf is lined with binders. Cubicles are piled with work, and closets overflow.

Knowing the proclivities of Obsessive-Compulsives for a place for everything and everything in its place, you might expect neat desks with equipment lined up ruler-straight. There will be some of those, but only because that person's accumulated clutter is stored somewhere else. The hardest task for Obsessive-Compulsives is deciding what they don't need to do or don't need to keep.

Despite all the frenetic activity, the final output of Obsessive-Compulsive organizations is relatively small and often behind schedule. A lot of work gets done, but an inordinate amount of time seems to be spent waiting for approval before it goes out the door. What does go out is usually accurate, but boring, repetitive, and overly complicated.

Obsessive-Compulsives work hard and pay meticulous attention to detail, but the organizations they run are usually far from efficient. Here are some typical characteristics.

## BALKANIZATION

In Obsessive-Compulsive organizations, individual departments turn into autonomous ethnic areas with their own cultures and rituals. Each one believes that its way of doing things is the correct one that should be followed by all the others. There is continuous competition for resources. The power shifts according to the size of the budget and the number of direct reports.

Managers tend to put the interests of their own unit above those of the organization as a whole, not because they are greedy, but because they believe they are right. Also, they do so because there is little agreement on what the interests of the organization as a whole might be. Meetings are incessant, but there is little real communication or cooperation and no agreement on overall goals.

As you have probably guessed, many governmental organizations follow this Obsessive-Compulsive pattern and become governments in and of themselves.

## RESISTANCE TO CHANGE

Bureaucracies are the graveyards of new ideas. Innovative programs evolve into the same old thing because everyone believes that his or her way is the correct way to do things. In such cultures, very few people have the power to implement change, but almost anyone can stop a process cold by saying that more time is needed for study.

### PETTY FEUDS

Obsessive-Compulsives never believe that anyone else is doing things properly. No issue is too small to breed controversy.

### HOUNDING

In Obsessive-Compulsive organizations, people are rarely fired. People who get on their boss's wrong side are generally hounded into exiling themselves by thousands of small but nominally justifiable insults and humiliations.

### KVETCHING

Obsessive-Compulsives love to complain. Their complaints are almost always about how much extra work they have to do because of someone else's ineptitude.

### LAWFULNESS

Despite all the petty feuding, Obsessive-Compulsives tend to play by the rules. What those rules are is generally a matter of contention. Most individuals in such organizations have a high degree of personal integrity and an even higher degree of rectitude. Nevertheless, unlike organizations created by other kinds of emotional vampires, in Obsessive-Compulsive cultures there is an overall sense of fair play. This is a strength that can eventually lead to working out differences. It is also a weakness, as it makes the entire organization vulnerable to exploitation if another less scrupulous type of vampire ascends to power.

### HOW TO GET SOMETHING DONE IN AN OBSESSIVE-COMPULSIVE CULTURE

To implement even the smallest change in an Obsessive-Compulsive organization, you have to build a coalition. To do that, you must recognize that everyone in the organization has a very clear sense of right and wrong, but their ideas of which is which differ on various, often minuscule points that are to them absolutely critical.

To form a coalition, you have to structure things so that everyone is right, everyone appears magnanimous, and everybody secretly feels as if they are winning out over the competition. The name for this skill is *diplomacy*. Here are some suggestions on how to be an organizational diplomat.

**PUBLICLY PRAISE EACH AUTONOMOUS REGION:** This is an example of stepping into their world and stepping out of the pattern. The people in every center of power in an Obsessive-Compulsive organization believe that they are the repositories of truth about everything. They all want understanding and respect, but what they expect is criticism. Look for opportunities to surprise them with praise and your credibility will increase, and with it, your following.

The praise that you hand out cannot be lip service. They are used to that. To be effective, you need to do your homework to figure out what people are actually good at and praise them accordingly.

If by chance you are an Obsessive-Compulsive, do not succumb to the temptation to see yourself as a lone voice in the wilderness crying out for justice. Unless you have general support, you might as well stay in the wilderness, because at work, no one will be listening.

**MEET INDIVIDUALLY WITH EVERY GROUP:** Once your credibility is high enough, you need to form personal alliances. You do this in individual meetings in which you listen rather than talk. In those meetings, you need to listen for what the individual autonomous regions want for themselves and what they feel they are competing for with other departments.

**COPY EVERYONE ON EVERYTHING:** Let everyone know what you are learning every step of the way. Make everyone look good. Always ask for advice and input. Remember, with Obsessive-Compulsives, the more words, the better. Think which side of the bread the butter is on rather than bullet points.

**MENTION ALL THE INPUT YOU GET, AND SHOW WHAT YOU DO WITH IT:** You want people to think that everything you come up with is really their idea. Give credit to them, not yourself. You are only the guy that listened. Never leave anyone's ideas out of any document.

**WRITE IN CODE:** Obsessive-Compulsives usually think that it is bad form to act in your own self-interest, yet like everyone else, they must. They generally talk about self-interest in code that sounds as if they are advocating a universal value rather than their own interests. Think pro-life and pro-choice.

In any proposal you generate, communicate to each group about what they are getting using the appropriate code words. If all the power centers feel they are getting something, they may support you even while they are complaining that the other guys get a better deal.

# Paranoids

**19**

ANOTHER CONFUSING NAME. To most people, *paranoid* means delu-sions of persecution. The word really describes an exquisitely simple way of perceiving a complex world. Paranoids can't tolerate ambiguity. In their minds, nothing is accidental or random; everything means something, and everything relates to everything else. This sort of thinking can lead to genius or to psychosis, depending on how it's used.

There's no question that Paranoids see things that other people can't. But do the things they see actually exist? *That's* the question.

These emotional vampires have tendencies toward Paranoid person-ality disorder, which, like the Paranoids themselves, is often misunder-stood even by the people who treat it. The word *paranoia,* which means "thinking beside oneself," has been used to describe virtually all forms of craziness, especially those involving false beliefs. The problem with the concept, as any Paranoid will tell you, is that it's not all that simple to determine which beliefs are false and which are true.

Paranoia is easier to understand if you look at the patterns of thinking that lead to false beliefs, rather than at the beliefs themselves. Paranoids are blessed and cursed with the ability to perceive very tiny cues. Unlike Obses-sive-Compulsives, who become unfocused and overwhelmed by life's small details, Paranoids drive themselves crazy by trying to organize details into a coherent and unambiguous whole.

Paranoid vampires' perceptive ability and compulsion to organize may have their roots at the neurological level. Wherever they come from, these behaviors can create great ideas and tremendous problems in relating to human beings. When Paranoids look at other people, they see too much for their own good. And everybody else's.

Paranoids long for a simple world in which people can be trusted to say what they mean and mean what they say. Instead, Paranoids see the human condition in all its ambiguous detail. People exist on many different levels at the same time. No human thought is singular and no feeling pure. Many of the conflicts that people experience are observable in slight hesitations, small changes in expression, and slips of the tongue. Most people ignore these tiny cues, but Paranoids try to sort them into either-or categories—love or hate, yes or no, truth or falsehood. Sometimes, in their search for simple answers, Paranoids can see through all forms of subterfuge to the heart of a matter. Just as easily, they can rip that heart out and tear it to pieces—especially when it belongs to someone close to them whose only crime is being human.

Paranoids try to remove the ambiguity from their lives by organizing everything around a small number of black-and-white principles. Truth, loyalty, courage, honor, and the like are not abstractions in the minds of Paranoids. They are living, breathing presences that these vampires live by, and will kill or die for, if called upon to do so. At least that's the way the Paranoids themselves imagine it. The reality is, of course, more complex. Paranoids are just as likely as anybody else to justify their self-serving actions according to high-sounding principles. More likely, actually. The most dangerous thing about Paranoids is their utter certainty of their own virtue.

Paranoids are capable of extreme purity of thought. They can be excellent scientists, theorists, and religious leaders. Many discoveries of the organizing principles that bind the universe together are the products of Paranoid thinking. So is every crackpot conspiracy theory you've ever heard of.

The certainty that makes Paranoids dangerous also makes them attractive. They are born leaders. Less self-assured people happily follow them or promote them into positions of authority. When Paranoids are in charge, they tend to create cults. Their goal is to achieve a blissful organization in which everyone follows the same simple and rigid rules as they do. When people go along, Paranoids are ideal leaders—happy, loving, and giving. If by some chance other people want to think for themselves, Paranoids take it as a personal insult. They feel disappointed and hurt when people try to leave their little paradises. When Paranoids get hurt, they hurt others.

Of all the vampire types, Paranoids are the most determined and conscious hypnotists. They invented cults and the brainwashing that keeps them running. Whenever Paranoids put together any sort of organization—be it a cult, a family, a business, a political party, or a religious movement—they use their persuasive power to create unambiguous alternative realities in which all rewards are dependent on belief and loyalty. Obsessive-Compulsives tell you to work hard if you want to get into heaven. Paranoids say all you have to do is believe in them. If you stop believing, there will be hell to pay.

What Paranoids never see is their own role in creating the ambiguity that so terrifies them. Their distrust invites duplicity. Their suspiciousness keeps people from telling them the whole truth. Their incessant doubts drive away the people who say they'll always be there. Paranoids can feel like they're at the center of a vast conspiracy to rob them of the certainty they so fervently desire. Naturally, they become even more guarded and suspicious.

## THE PARANOID EMOTIONAL VAMPIRE CHECKLIST

True or False: Score one point for each *true* answer.

1. This person is overly suspicious.  T  F

2. This person may have followers, but has very few close
   friends.  T  F

3. This person can make a big deal out of nothing.  T  F

4. This person tends to see many situations as struggles
   between good and evil.  T  F

5. This person never seems to let go of a hurt or mistreatment.  T  F

6. This person seldom takes what he or she is told at face value.  T  F

7. This person regularly uses the cold shoulder, refusing to
   acknowledge or speak to coworkers whom he or she feels
   have slighted or disrespected him or her.  T  F

8. This person is able to detect the tiniest deceptions, and
   sometimes sees them when they are not there .  T  F

9. This person demands absolute loyalty in thought and deed.  T  F

10. This person sees disagreement as disrespect.  T  F

11. This person sees connections among things that most
    people would consider unrelated.  T  F

12. This person sees little mistakes, such as lack of punctuality or
    forgetting instructions, as indications of disloyalty or disrespect.  T  F

13. This person tells people what others might say only behind
    their backs.  T  F

14. This person may have a good sense of humor but cannot seem to laugh at himself or herself.　　T　F

15. What will make this person angry seems completely unpredictable.　　T　F

16. This person sees himself or herself as a victim of multiple discriminations.　　T　F

17. This person believes that trust is something to be earned.　　T　F

18. This person has been known to take ill-considered actions "on principle."　　T　F

19. This person often talks about suing people to redress wrongs.　　T　F

20. This person questions people to determine their loyalty and fidelity.　　T　F

21. This person collects little details that seem to prove his or her pet theories.　　T　F

22. This person believes in the literal interpretation of the Bible or some other religious text.　　T　F

23. This person is quite partisan, with utter contempt for the other side, seeing them as evil, stupid, or both.　　T　F

24. This person openly advocates cruel and unusual punishment for certain classes of people. A typical comment might begin, "They should take all the bigots and …"　　T　F

25. Though I won't always admit it, this person is sometimes embarrassingly correct in his or her assessment of me.　　T　F

Scoring: Five or more true answers qualifies the person as a Paranoid emotional vampire, though not necessarily for a diagnosis of Paranoid personality disorder. With 12 or more true answers, the slightest disagreement will put you on the enemies list.

## WHAT THE QUESTIONS MEASURE

The specific behaviors covered on the checklist relate to several underlying personality characteristics that define a Paranoid emotional vampire.

## Perceptiveness

Paranoid vampires see things that others can't. They may even see more than you want them to see. They're always looking below the surface for hidden meanings and deeper realities. Sometimes they discover great insights, but more often they find reasons to doubt the people whom they should be able to trust. In the world of Paranoids, the line between perceptiveness and suspicion is thin as a spider web and sharper than a razor blade.

## Intolerance of Ambiguity

Paranoids need answers, even when there are none. They love to explain how complex situations boil down to a few black-and-white concepts. For Paranoids, everything is simple and clear. The only reason everyone doesn't know what they do is that someone, somewhere, is conspiring to cover up the truth. Paranoids love nothing more than a good conspiracy theory.

Paranoids' oversimplification of the world can also lead to great courage and dedication. They are fierce defenders of themselves, their principles, and the few people and things they consider closest to them. Paranoids have been known to give their lives for what they believe in. They've also been known to take lives.

## Unpredictability

Paranoids can shower you with praise one minute and with ice water the next. Their moods are dependent on momentary perceptions of the honesty and faithfulness of the people around them. If Paranoids sense treachery, they attack so fast that you won't know what hit you. Or why.

They can back off just as quickly. Many of their attacks are tests of loyalty. If you submit, you pass, and they calm down immediately. If you don't, brace yourself to argue all night.

## Bombast

Paranoids long to be understood. Their idea of intimacy is to spend six or seven hours sharing their political or religious theories or explaining how your actions have hurt them or their organization.

## Jealousy

Paranoid vampires don't understand the concept of trust. They never seem to realize that trust is supposed to be in their own minds rather than in the actions of other people. Consequently, if you work closely with a Paranoid, you'll have to re-earn his or her trust every hour on the hour.

## Ideas of Reference

In their search for truth, Paranoids connect everything with everything else, then take it all personally. To poor, virtuous Paranoids, the universe may seem like a conspiracy designed to make them miserable.

If you work with a Paranoid, it won't be possible for you to say or do anything that does not relate to him or her.

## Vindictiveness

Paranoids believe that revenge is the cure for what ails them. They never seem to see that it is also the cause. It's not that Paranoids never forgive; they just do it at the same rate as glaciers melt.

Paranoid vampires live in a simple alternative universe in which everything is wonderful as long as everyone is faithful to them in word and deed. The certainty of their world can be very attractive from the outside, but once you go in, it's hard to get out, and even harder to pass the ever-increasing tests of loyalty. To be safe, first and foremost, know what you're getting into.

If you're already inside the world of a Paranoid, there are three things to remember:

1. Don't hide anything. A Paranoid will find it.

2. Be loyal, but never accept the burden of proving your loyalty. Once you pick it up, you'll never be able to put it down.

3. If you're offered Kool-Aid, think carefully before drinking it.

# Vampire Visionaries

**P**ARANOID EMOTIONAL VAMPIRES are visionaries because they see simple truths and complex interrelationships that others people can't. Whether those truths and connections actually exist is the big question that you will have to answer for yourself. Your answer should be an internal guide for you, but never a topic for discussion with a Paranoid.

## WORKING FOR A PATRIOT

Paranoids see external behaviors, sometimes very small ones, as indicators of internal attributes such as honesty, loyalty and morality. These internal states are the most important things in Paranoids' lives. If you manage a Paranoid, you will have to conspicuously show respect for his or her beliefs. If you work for a Paranoid, you will have to share those beliefs or suffer the consequences.

> Jeb Carver started his company from nothing; now, by the grace of God and good old American know-how, it is the regional leader in agricultural supplies.
>
> If you work for Jeb, you will have to believe in God and America as strongly as he does. Every day starts with the Pledge of Allegiance and a prayer. There are flags on every lapel, embroidered on caps and coveralls, and prominently displayed on all company vehicles. When the weekend comes around—Jeb doesn't care if it's Saturday or Sunday—all virtuous employees attend the house of worship of their choice.

Before I get too far into this section, I want to point out that there is nothing wrong with Jeb's values. The problem comes when competent and otherwise exemplary employees don't adhere to those values in the same way that Jeb does. I also want to point out, lest I offend someone, that Jeb's red-state values are much more common in businesses than more liberal leanings. On the West Coast and elsewhere, there are businesses run by Paranoid vegan bicyclists that follow similar patterns, but even in Portland, where I live, they are rare.

Maria is a first-rate accountant. She's worked for Jeb's company for two years now and has gotten nothing but sterling reviews. When her boss retired, it seemed like she was a shoo-in to replace him—that is, until she was passed over for a much-less-qualified candidate.

The word was that Jeb himself had turned her down.

Maria's brother is gay. He and his longtime partner made the news by going to another state to get married. In the photo that appeared in the local paper, Maria was at the ceremony, wishing her brother well.

Was her tacit support for same-sex marriage the reason she wasn't promoted? People seem to think so, but there's not enough evidence to prove it in court.

Yes, there are laws against discrimination of all sorts, but they are difficult and expensive to enforce, and Paranoids know all the tricks for getting around them. If not sharing a Paranoid owner or manager's values hinders your career progress, you can make a federal case of it, though I would not advise you to do so unless you have a really good lawyer.

I have seen enough cases like Maria's to say to anyone whose work life is controlled by a value-driven Paranoid, "If you do not share those values, look for a different job."

If adherence to any belief system not directly related to doing the job is an unwritten requirement for success and you are not part of that system, you cannot succeed. Unless you are a really good actor, your own beliefs will eventually show and detract from any positive work you do. If you *are* a good actor, the internal conflict will get you, and that can be far worse than being passed over for promotion.

Paranoids in power, whatever their politics, turn businesses into dysfunctional families in which they are old-time father figures, the absolute authorities on everything. Any mistake, transgression, or deviation in thought is taken as a personal affront to them. Punishments are based, not on the severity of the crime or its effect on the business, but on how angry it makes the Paranoid in charge.

Jeb keeps an eagle eye on expenses. When he noticed that the amount spent on miscellaneous items was steadily rising, he had the people in purchasing break it down so he could see just where the money was going. He concluded that the company was buying far more office supplies than could actually be used on the premises. It was obvious to Jeb that some employees were pilfering supplies and using them elsewhere.

This so incensed him that he had purchasing develop an individual requisition system to ration supplies so that employees would have no more at any given time than Jeb thought they would actually need.

Jeb was gratified to see that the pilfering decreased significantly. Problem solved.

The result he did not see or seem to care about was that people were running out of supplies in the midst of projects and having to go to purchasing to sign out more. The whole system was so ungainly and time consuming that some managers resorted to buying supplies out of their own pockets so their people wouldn't run out at a critical moment.

Some of Jeb's managers tried to explain that office supplies were a minuscule part of overall expenditures, and the systems he put in place were costing far more in work time and employee frustration than the entire supplies budget. Their argument gained no traction. Jeb said it was not the money and time, but the principle of the thing. He would not condone stealing at any level, no matter how small. If people can steal small things, pretty soon they start taking bigger things. If you don't nip a problem like this in the bud, it can destroy the whole company. His lecture on principles and loyalty went on for almost an hour.

The system stayed in place, forcing manages to develop their own creative workarounds so their departments didn't run out of supplies.

Paranoids like Jeb often lose sight of the overall purpose of a business. Like Jeb, they might create expensive control policies that inconvenience an entire company to prevent a few people from breaking the rules. It's always the principle of the thing.

Just as they do in a dysfunctional family, draconian policies in a business cause people to be sneaky and deceptive. When Paranoids discover deception, they crack down harder, which typically creates more deception. Paranoids always believe that people are trying to deceive them. Generally, this is not a delusion. Paranoids usually have something to be paranoid about. What they don't see is that it is their own tendency to overreact rather than moral turpitude that causes people to hide things from them.

Partisan Paranoids like Jeb are dangerous to people who don't share their beliefs, but they can be even more dangerous to people who do. Remember, Paranoids invented cults and brainwashing. Even if you share most of a Paranoid's beliefs, you may still be subjected to tests of loyalty.

> Jeb believes in his country, right or wrong. What he defines as his country, however, is the nation that he believes that the framers of the Constitution had in mind. Jefferson would not have put up with ridiculous federal regulations, so Jeb doesn't either. He doesn't specifically tell anyone to ignore them, but if you bring up an OSHA or environmental regulation, you will be treated as if you wrote the rules yourself and lectured on why they are immoral, unconstitutional, and just plain stupid.
>
> Do you break the rules or defend them? When it comes to following regulations, Jeb's managers must continually struggle with their consciences, because Jeb never has to struggle with his.

Visionary Paranoids' adherence to their belief systems can produce institutions such as religions, the military, and business and charitable organizations that benefit everyone. That same obedience also creates cults that can steal your soul. If you work for a Visionary Paranoid, you'll have to decide which is which.

The soul-stealing Paranoids are the avowed true believers who pick and choose among the rules in a given system, citing convoluted rationalizations for ignoring the ones that don't benefit them. The really dangerous Paranoids are those who believe that they don't have to obey laws that should not have been passed or follow commandments that God didn't really intend.

Often pathology is subtle. Every organization has an underlying belief system, whether posted on the walls or implicit in the choices its adherents make. Healthy, mature people create healthy organizations. Emotional vampires, as we have seen, create cultures in their own image. If your organization is run by a Paranoid, here are some questions to ask yourself about the belief system before you drink any Kool-Aid.

## Who Benefits?

As we saw in the first chapter, the basic difference between emotional vampires and regular people is lack of empathy. Vampires believe that their needs are more important than anyone else's. Anything they create will be self-serving, no matter what spiritual or philosophical justifications they offer.

Paranoids will always tell you that following them will benefit you, your country, or the world. In the most damaging and dangerous cults, the greatest benefit is always to the cult leaders.

It's easy to see the shortcomings of a cult when the Guru has a collection of Rolls-Royces, but bear in mind that the benefits that most move Paranoids are not material, but psychological. They hunger for followers who affirm their vision and accept their every word as law. Power, reverence, loyalty, and obedience are the rewards they seek.

What do cult members get in return? In businesses, there are financial rewards, of course, but for most members, the lure is seeing themselves as better people than they were before they joined.

There are cultlike structures that can be beneficial to all concerned. Military training is a good example. The contract is clear. A warrior is expected to offer his or her life for the benefit of the country. In return, he or she becomes a part of something larger with grand traditions of duty and honor. There are benefits to all concerned.

There is no question that military service builds character in many people, but it destroys others. Everything depends on who's leading the army.

## How Does the Organization See Nonmembers?

The most damaging cults teach people to look down on anyone who is not a member. In general, the more contempt a cult has for outsiders, the more psychological damage it does to its members. The damage is done by the pressure to adhere strictly to the belief system. If you don't, you become one of *them*.

## What Part of the Brain Does the Doctrine Come From?

Throughout this book, I have written about fast and slow thinking that involve lower versus higher brain centers. The lower centers come preprogrammed with instincts that are the basis of self-interest. The higher, more evolved, brain centers use thought, decision making, and weighing of evidence to come to conclusions about ethics, morality, and being a part of a larger world.

One way to tell the difference between organizations that are dangerous and those that are beneficial is by speculating about which part of the brain the group's doctrine seems to comes from.

At the lowest, instinctive level, our brains are programmed to organize the complexity of world into two-category systems. At the reptile level, there is only *me* and *not me*. One is safe; the other, dangerous. From this instinctive understanding comes the perception of right and wrong, truth and falsehood, and good and evil. We see these two-category systems as properties of the external world rather than artifacts of our own perception. The most damaging cults perpetuate the delusion that the world is black and white. Everyone who agrees with the cult is good; everyone who doesn't is evil.

All the great religious visionaries point us in the direction of our higher brain centers. The world they speak of has many shades of gray. Their words are aids to help you decide for yourself. Their doctrine is less concerned with *what* to think and more with *how* to think.

Beneficial organizations do their jobs and make money. They also promote, or at least do not stand in the way of, psychological health and maturity, which in Chapter 2 I attempted to characterize as having three components: the perception that you are in control of your own fate, a feeling of connection to something larger than yourself, and the pursuit of challenge.

Damaging cultlike organizations cause most of their problems, because Paranoids often confuse themselves with something larger than themselves. Their conception of the greatest power in the universe can be as petty and mean-spirited as they are.

The potential harm that a cult can do is directly related to how much its conception of the universe corresponds to the simple two-category system that is wired into our brains.

## What Is Truth

In the most damaging organizations, truth is revealed, not discovered. Belief is required; evidence is not. Everything that the cult leaders say is true, no matter how preposterous. Everything that people outside the cult propose is false, regardless of the reasoning behind it.

Before you laugh at this childish simplicity of thought, listen to the solons of Liberalism and Conservatism on talk radio.

## What Happens to You if You Doubt

In the most destructive cults, doubt and irreverence are sins. They could lead to thinking for yourself, which is the worst sin of all.

## Does the Group See Itself as a Persecuted Minority?

Throughout history, the greatest crimes against humanity have always been done by people who saw themselves as persecuted. The way this has been done since time immemorial is by portraying people who are different as actively trying to destroy *our* way of life. In this manner, instinctive prejudice is miraculously transformed into defense of all that is good and true. This transformation is Paranoia at its most malevolent. A psychological truth that we have encountered before, and will unfortunately encounter again and again, is that victims use their suffering as a license to victimize.

The greatest danger you face from Paranoid emotional vampires and the cults they create is not losing your job for being a nonbeliever. The real peril is within. Paranoids can rob you of your own identity by subtly persuading you to let them do your thinking for you until you find it very difficult to think for yourself.

# Paranoid
# Cultures

A s we have seen throughout this book, people with personality disorders have both positive and negative characteristics. With Paranoids the range of possibilities is tremendous. They can be religious and philosophical visionaries or business innovators who change the world for the better. They can also be mean-spirited bigots. Which they are in your estimation depends on whether you agree with them or not. Paranoids are the rarest of the emotional vampires you will encounter at work or anywhere else, but they are often the most dangerous. Their certainty and singleness of purpose make them natural leaders. People want to follow them.

Paranoid leaders create organizations that are structured more like cults than like businesses in that their purpose is as much to advance a system of belief as to produce products and services that make money.

Like all emotional vampires, Paranoids elicit and encourage fast thinking as a means of control. Your only protection is in using your own higher brain centers to override your emotional responses and carefully analyze what you see, what you feel, and what you are being told. What follows are some of the more salient characteristics of Paranoid cultures. If you are involved with an organization that looks like this, never let anyone discourage you from thinking for yourself.

## CENTRAL BELIEF SYSTEM

Paranoid organizations always have a belief system at their core. It can be explicit or implicit, but it is there, if you look for it. In constructive organizations, the system relates directly to the products or services provided. In more dangerous organizations, the goals seem to relate as much to advancing the belief system as to doing what the organization is purported to do. The farther the belief system deviates from the purpose of the organization, the more wary you need to be. For example, to sell insurance, it isn't necessary to be part of an ethnic or religious group or to hold any particular political convictions. If those seem to be required for advancement in your organization, be careful, and hang onto your soul.

### In Group and Out Group

Hierarchies in Paranoid cultures often relate more to purity of belief than to expertise at doing the job. There is an *us* and *them* mentality, but unlike most businesses, where *them* is the competition, in Paranoid cultures, the outsiders are just as likely to be people in the organization who are not as staunch in the central belief and are therefore not to be trusted.

### Regressive Accountability

In Paranoid cultures, accountability is inversely proportional to your position in the hierarchy. Cult leaders answer only to God, and sometimes not even to Him.

### Management of Information

In Paranoid organizations, nothing is as it seems. There is a party line about everything. Information is a closely guarded commodity that belongs solely to upper management. There is no transparency, and leaks are punished severely.

### Banishment of Dissidents

Paranoid bosses have less compunction about summarily firing employees than any other type of emotional vampires, less even than Antisocial Bullies. Firing usually has more to do with suspected disloyalty than with inability to do the job.

### High Aspirations

Based on the characteristics described so far, you might believe that Paranoid organizations would be full of weak-minded people who need to be told what to think.

Nothing could be further from the truth. Paranoid organizations attract the best of the best, people with high aspirations who want to accomplish something and make a difference. This, more than financial gain, is the reward that Paranoid organizations offer.

There's no doubt that Paranoid organizations do make a difference. Whether that difference is positive or negative depends solely on what you believe.

# Dangerously Dysfunctional Cultures

## 15 Signs that an Organization Is Run by Vampires for Vampires

A S WE HAVE SEEN, when emotional vampires run organizations, they create cultures that are reflections of their own dysfunctional personalities. They don't set out to do this; it just happens. To survive within those cultures, people have to follow the same unwritten rules the boss does. Before long, everyone is acting like a vampire whether they want to or not.

There is another, even more frightening part to this story: vampires flock together. The people who are most likely to thrive in a dysfunctional culture created by one type of vampire are other vampires. This makes sense in that bosses with personality disorders are likely to hire managers who will give them what they want, which to a vampire is indistinguishable from being able to do a good job. Since emotional vampires excel at looking like whatever you're looking for, they have an edge when it comes to getting hired. The result of this process of selection is a culture that combines elements of various personality disorders so that they are dysfunctional in many different ways. If your organization seems to fit several of the vampire cultures I have described, this is the reason. If it does, watch out!

It's one thing to be part of a healthy culture in which you have a few vampires here and there. Working in a culture created by vampires for vampires is a whole different story. The chances of being preyed upon or turning into a vampire yourself are extremely high. Even using all the techniques I have described in this book, it will be almost impossible to rise above the fray.

Vampire organizations may do great deeds and rake in piles of money, but they are destructive to the people who work for them and often to society as a whole.

## THE 15 DANGER SIGNS

How do you know if you're working in a culture created by vampires for vampires? Here are the 15 danger signs.

### Conspicuously Posted Vision or Value Statements Are Filled with Vague but Important-Sounding Words Such as *Excellence and Quality*

These words are seldom defined, and the concepts they allude to are never measured. The unwritten rule here is *what's real is what I say, not what I do.* Misdirection is emotional vampires' stock in trade, though different types use it differently. Histrionic managers, who invented the practice of decorating with words, firmly believe their own PR. They expect everyone else will too. Narcissists go along because they know that confusion can be a useful tool for maintaining control. Antisocials are often more direct about the deception involved. They may tell you that the words are for public consumption and the real rule is *do it as quickly and cheaply as possible.*

Believers are most vulnerable to this kind of misdirection. They get mixed up about whether to believe what they're told or what they see with their own eyes. They waste energy trying to make vampires say what they mean and mean what they say.

Competitors are not bothered by inconsistency. They quickly learn the buzzwords and use them appropriately. Rebels aren't bothered either because they don't read vision statements or anything else they consider corporate crap. None of these automatic responses are particularly productive because they all in one way or another cede control to the vampires.

To deal more effectively with this very common manifestation of vampire culture, you should first recognize it for what it is. Understand that the more direct instruction you get about what you should believe, the less likely it is to be true. To find out what is true, ask carefully crafted questions, such as, "What is excellence in this context? How do we know when we've achieved it?" The questions may not be answered, but asking them is your best bet at finding whatever clarity there is. As we have seen throughout this book, when dealing with vampires, questions are always more powerful than statements.

If you keep asking questions and never get a straight answer, that *is* your answer.

## Bringing Up a Problem Is Considered More as Evidence of a Personality Defect Rather than as an Actual Observation of Reality

In a vampire-run organization, what it looks like not only is more important than what it is, it *is* what it is. If you don't believe that, *you* are the problem. Pointing out discrepancies is useless and can be dangerous.

Vampires operate best in the dark. When they are in charge, a surprising amount of information is classified. Dysfunctional companies have more state secrets than the CIA.

Histrionics fear that the facts will be demotivating. Narcissists suspect they will be embarrassing. Antisocials are not particularly concerned about facts. They are confident that if you disagree, they can sweet-talk or bully you into seeing things their way.

If in your company, people get in trouble for stating the obvious, don't. Countless Rebels have been sent to corporate Siberia for making snide comments about things that vampires do not consider funny.

## If by Chance There Are Problems, the Usual Solution Is a Motivational Seminar

Histrionics have tremendous and perhaps undeserved influence. Their belief that attitude is everything, and their efforts to suppress anything that is demotivating, are pervasive throughout the organizational world, especially in places where facts are illegal, embarrassing, or inconvenient. Other vampire types love working for Histrionics because they turn a blind eye to everything they don't want to see.

In a dysfunctional family, there's an elephant—usually a drunken, abusive parent—in the parlor, but no one ever mentions him or her. To appear sane, you have to pretend that the elephant is invisible, and that drives you crazy. Vampire-run organizations are full of invisible elephants also. Usually they are things that might cause difficulties for people with enough clout to prevent their discussion. The emperor may be naked, but if you have a good attitude, you won't mention it. Vampires of all types thrive in this kind of darkness.

## Double Messages Are Delivered with a Straight Face

Quality and quantity are both job one. You *can* do it both cheaper and better, just don't ask how. If you're motivated enough you should know already. This is yet another Histrionic belief that serves all the other vampire types quite well.

In response to this kind of double message, Believers typically get confused about what to do and just work harder. Rebels may argue their side of the equation by presenting facts and figures to which nobody pays attention. Competitors respond to double messages by correctly reading between the lines and going with the side that has most effect on this quarter's bottom line.

Again, these automatic responses serve to firm the vampires' hold on power.

## Internal Competition Is Encouraged and Rewarded

The word *teamwork* may be batted around like a softball at a company picnic, but in a dysfunctional company, the star players are the only ones who get recognition and big bucks. Histrionics delude themselves into thinking that internal competition keeps everyone sharp. The other vampire types thrive in the chaos and distrust that internecine warfare provides.

A strategy that all the vampire types use to maintain their hold on power is *picking off the competition*. As soon as they achieve a level of power, their first task is to get rid of the people who are almost as qualified as they are and might compete with them for the next promotion. This practice is one of the clearest examples of how emotional vampires create dysfunctional cultures by putting their own needs above the needs of the organization. Each vampire type destroys its rivals in different ways. If you are competent, your greatest danger in a dysfunctional organization is having a vampire in power see you as a threat to his or her own climb up the corporate ladder.

## Management Approaches from the Latest Best Seller Are Regularly Misunderstood to Mean What We're Doing Already Is Right on the Mark

Inspirational business books such as *The Seven Habits of Highly Effective People, Good to Great,* and *Who Moved My Cheese?* all seem to boil down to one thing: *quit complaining and do more with less.* Histrionics always give themselves a grade of A plus. If you work for one, you should too.

## History Is Regularly Edited to Make Executive Decisions More Correct and Correct Decisions More Executive than They Actually Were

Narcissists with power generally award themselves huge salaries that require *some* justification. They have been known to take credit for the fact that the sun rises in the east.

## Directions Are Ambiguous and Often Vaguely Threatening

The *do it or else* style is favored by Antisocials and organized crime.

Before you respond to one of these vague threats, remember that virtually every corporate scandal began with someone saying, "Just get it done; I don't care how." That person is seldom the one who gets indicted.

## You Are Expected to Feel Lucky to Have a Job, and Know You Could Lose It if You Don't Toe the Line

Antisocials invented Theory X management in the early days of the industrial revolution when most work was physical and done by ruffians. The basic idea behind Theory X is that employees really don't want to work, so to get them to do their jobs, managers must continually kick butt and take names. This antiquated theory is alive and well today, but the ruffians wear suits instead of coveralls. Dysfunctional companies maintain control using the threat of punishment. Most will maintain that they also use positive rewards—like your paycheck. The precept is as simple and elegant as most Antisocial creations are: *do it, or we'll find someone who will.*

## People Are Discouraged from Putting Things in Writing

What *is* written, especially contracts and financial records, is purposely confusing. Antisocials know not to leave a paper trail. Vampires of all types can always use a little deniability.

## Decisions Are Made at the Highest Level Possible

Regardless of what is to be done, you have to check with your boss before doing it. She also has to check with her boss.

This is the kind of bureaucratic culture that Obsessive-Compulsives set up when they are in charge. No detail is too small to warrant central control.

Believers, who are good at filling out forms, tend to handle bureaucracies better than Rebels or Competitors do.

## Delegating Means Telling Somebody to Do Something, Not Giving Them the Power to Do It

According to Webster, you delegate *authority*, not *tasks*. In dysfunctional companies, you may have responsibility, but the authority lives in the office upstairs. This style is another creation of Obsessive-Compulsives, who believe that if you want something done right, you have to do it yourself.

## Resources Are Tightly Controlled

Your department may need upgraded software, but there's a spending freeze that's been going on since 2009. Obsessive-Compulsive bean counters invented this style, but the other vampire types recognize an opportunity to exploit when they see it.

Cost control is entry-level management, but in a dysfunctional company anything more sophisticated is considered too touchy-feely. Whatever you propose to do, the first question you will be asked is, "Can it be done more cheaply?"

## Rules Are Enforced Based on Who You Are Rather than on What You Do

In a dysfunctional company, there are clearly insiders and outsiders, and everyone knows who belongs in each group. *Accountability* has different meanings, depending on which group you're in.

This is the style that Paranoids favor. When they run the show, power is often invested in a particular racial, ethnic, familial, or religious group. Everybody knows that this arrangement is illegal, but there's never enough evidence to prove anything in court.

## The Company Fails the *Dilbert* Test

Emotional vampires do not have enough insight to laugh at themselves. In the dysfunctional organizations they create, you make fun of people below you rather than above. People who post unflattering cartoons about management risk joining the ranks of the disappeared.

### SURVIVING A VAMPIRE CULTURE

These are 15 examples of some of the kinds of organizations that are direct reflections of the personality disorders of the people in charge. Dealing with one emotional vampire as a boss is feasible. Trying to deal with an entrenched culture of vampires may be futile. Such cultures are almost impossible to change from anywhere but the top of the organizational chart.

Vampire cultures are basically inefficient, in that most of their resources are devoted to satisfying the irrational needs of the people in charge instead of taking care of business. Such organizations are even less efficient if you factor in human and societal cost, which to emotional vampires is less than nothing.

If you see your entire company in more than 7 of the 15 examples I have offered here, you might have to become an emotional vampire yourself to survive. There are better places to work. Finding one might be your best protection.

# Epilogue

EMOTIONAL VAMPIRES are everywhere. You have undoubtedly recognized some who work in your own organization. If you have, good for you! The first step in protecting yourself is seeing through vampires' illusions to what they actually are.

The next step is using your higher brain centers to think more slowly than they do. If you keep your wits about you, you can step into their world and step out of the expected pattern. By doing that, you can not only protect yourself but also exert more control over your job and your life than you may have thought possible. Demonstrating that is my ultimate purpose in writing this book.

Trust yourself and go safely back into the night.

# Index

# About the Author

**Albert J. Bernstein,** PhD, lives in Portland, Oregon, with his family. He has been practicing as a clinical psychologist, speaker and business consultant for more than 40 years.

He prides himself on teaching people how to think like psychologists without having to talk like them. His books on dealing with difficult and dangerous people have been translated into more than 20 languages.

Visit his website: albernstein.com